CONCEPTS OF

DATABASE MANAGEMENT

Third Edition

Philip J. Pratt
University of Sinclair

Joseph J. Adamski
University of Kalamazoo

ONE MAIN STREET, CAMBRIDGE, MA 02142

Australia • Canada • Denmark • Japan • Mexico • New Zealand • Philippines
Puerto Rico • Singapore • South Africa • Spain • United Kingdom • United States

Concepts of Database Management, Third Edition is published by Course Technology.

Senior Editor	Jennifer Normandin
Associate Vice President, Associate Publisher	Kristen Duerr
Production Editor	Ellina Beletsky
Development Editor	Amanda Brodkin
Associate Product Manager	Amanda Young
Marketing Manager	Susan Ogar
Text Designer	Books By Design
Cover Designer	Efrat Reis

Disclaimer
Course Technology reserves the right to revise this publication and make changes from time to time in its content without notice.

The Web addresses in this book are subject to change from time to time as necessary without notice.

For more information, contact Course Technology, One Main Street, Cambridge, MA 02142; or find us on the World Wide Web at *www.course.com*.

For permission to use material from this text or product, contact us by
- Web: www.thomsonrights.com
- Phone: 1-800-730-2214
- Fax: 1-800-730-2215

ISBN 0-619-00057-0

Printed in America
1 2 3 4 5 CODE 02 01 00 99

CONTENTS

PREFACE

The advent of database management systems for personal computers in the 1980s moved database management beyond the realm of database professionals and into the hands of everyday users from all segments of the population. A field once limited to highly trained users of large, mainframe, database-oriented application systems became an essential productivity tool for such diverse groups as home computer owners, owners of small businesses, and end-users in large organizations.

The major PC-based database software systems have continually added features to increase their ease of use, allowing users to enjoy the benefits of database tools relatively quickly. Truly effective use of such a product, however, requires more than just knowledge of the product itself, although that is obviously important. It requires a general knowledge of the database area, including such topics as database design, database administration, and application development using these systems. While the depth of understanding required is certainly not as great for the majority of users as it is for the data processing professional, a lack of any understanding in these areas precludes effective use of the product in all but the most limited applications.

About This Book

This book is intended for anyone who is interested in gaining some familiarity with database management. It is appropriate for students in introductory database classes in computer science or information systems programs. It is appropriate for students in database courses in related disciplines, such as business, at either the undergraduate or graduate level. Such students require a general understanding of the database environment. In addition, courses introducing students of any discipline to database management have become increasingly popular over the past few years and this book is ideal for such courses. It is also appropriate for individuals considering purchasing a PC-based database package and who want to make effective use of such a package.

This book assumes that you have some familiarity with computers. A single introductory course is all the background that is required. While you need not have any background in programming to use this text effectively, there are certain areas where a little programming background will enable you to explore topics in more depth.

While database management on mainframes is discussed in the book, the main focus is on PC-based database management.

Special Features
Detailed Coverage of the Relational Model

The text features detailed coverage of the important aspects of the relational model including comprehensive coverage of SQL. It also covers Query-by-Example and the relational algebra as well as advanced aspects of the model such as views, the use of indexes, the catalog, and the relational integrity rules.

Database Design

The important process of database design is given detailed treatment. A highly useful methodology for designing databases is presented and illustrated through a variety of examples. There is also a comprehensive design example, illustrating the application of the complete design process to a large and complex set of requirements. After mastering the design methodology presented in this text, you should be able to produce correct database designs for whatever set of requirements you encounter.

Functions Provided by a DBMS

With such a wide range of features included in current PC-based database management systems, it is important for you to know the functions that such systems should provide. These functions are presented and discussed in detail.

Database Administration (DBA)

While database administration (DBA) is absolutely essential in the mainframe environment, it is also important in a personal computer environment, especially if the database is to be shared among several users. Thus, this text includes a detailed discussion of the database administration function.

DBMS Selection

The process of selecting a DBMS is important given the myriad systems that are available. Unfortunately, this is not an easy task. To prepare students to be able to do an effective job in this area, the text includes a detailed discussion of the process together with a comprehensive checklist that greatly assists in making such a selection.

Advanced Topics

The text also covers distributed database management systems, client/server systems, data warehouses, object-oriented database management systems, and the impact of the Internet on database management systems. Each of these topics encompasses an enormous amount of complex information, so you'll simply be introduced to the topics.

Glossary

There is a glossary containing definitions to the important terms in the text.

Numerous Realistic Examples

The book contains numerous examples illustrating each of the concepts. Two running "case" examples—Henry's Bookstores and Premiere Products—are used throughout the book to illustrate concepts. The examples are realistic and representative of the kinds of problems that are encountered in the design, manipulation, and administration of databases.

Review Material

The book contains a wide variety of questions. At key points within the chapters, you are asked questions to reinforce your understanding of the material before proceeding. The answers to these questions are given immediately following the questions. At the end of each chapter, there are review questions that test your recall of the important points in the chapter and that occasionally test your ability to apply what you have learned. The answers to the odd-numbered review questions are given at the end of the text.

Instructor's Manual

The accompanying instructor's manual contains detailed teaching tips, answers to review questions in the text, test questions (and answers), and transparency masters.

ORGANIZATION OF THE TEXTBOOK

The textbook consists of nine chapters. The chapters deal with general database topics and are not geared to any specific database management system. A brief description of the organization of topics in the chapters and an overview of updates from the second edition follows.

Introduction

Chapter 1 provides a general introduction to the field of database management. This chapter has been expanded from its previous version to include a brief history of database management systems, including a discussion of database models such as hierarchical and network.

The Relational Model

The relational model is covered in detail in Chapters 2, 3, and 4. Chapter 2 covers the data definition and manipulation aspects of the model using QBE and the relational algebra. The text uses Access (rather than Paradox, which was used in the previous edition) to illustrate the QBE material. The relational algebra section has been expanded to include the entire relational algebra (all eight commands) rather than just the three commands covered in the previous edition.

Note: The extra material on the relational algebra is optional and can be omitted if desired.

Chapter 3 is devoted exclusively to SQL. The SQL material is now illustrated using Access.

Chapter 4 covers some advanced aspects of the model such as views, the use of indexes, the catalog, and the relational integrity rules.

Database Design

Chapters 5 and 6 are devoted to database design. Chapter 5 covers the normalization process, which enables you to identify and correct bad designs. This chapter has been expanded to include a discussion of fourth normal form.

Note: The material on fourth normal form is optional and can be omitted if desired.

Note: Chapters 5 and 6 can be covered immediately after Chapter 2 if desired.

In Chapter 6, a methodology for database design is presented and illustrated through a number of examples. This chapter has been expanded from the previous edition to include a discussion of Entity-Relationship diagrams. It also includes a detailed, comprehensive database design example.

Note: The comprehensive design example is optional.

Functions of a Database Management System

Chapter 7 discusses the features that should be provided by a full-functioned PC-based database management system. This chapter has been expanded from the previous edition to include timestamping and more information about two-phase locking.

Database Administration

Chapter 8 is devoted to the role of database administration. Included in this chapter is also a discussion of the process of selecting a DBMS.

Advanced Topics

This chapter provides an overview of several advanced topics: distributed databases, client/server systems, data warehouses, object-oriented databases, and the impact of the Internet and intranets on DBMSs.

GENERAL NOTES TO THE STUDENT

Embedded Questions

There are a number of places in the text where special questions have been embedded. Sometimes the purpose of these questions is to ensure that you understand some crucial material before you proceed. In other cases, the questions are designed to give you the chance to consider some special concept in advance of its actual presentation. In all cases, the answers to these questions are given immediately after the question. You could simply read the question and its answer. You will receive maximum benefit from the text, however, if you take the time to work out the answers to the questions and then check your answer against the one given in the text before you continue with your reading.

End-of-Chapter Material

The end-of-chapter material consists of a summary, a list of key terms, and review questions. The summary briefly describes the material covered in the chapter. The review questions require you to recall and apply the important material in the chapter. The answers to the odd-numbered exercises are given in the text.

ACKNOWLEDGMENTS

We would like to acknowledge the following individuals who all made contributions during the preparation of this book. We appreciate the following individuals who reviewed the text and made many helpful suggestions: Patty Santoianni, Sinclair Community College; Chris Davis, Baker College of Muskegon; Rahul Tikekar, Southern Oregon University; and Phil Chmielewski, Milwaukee Area Technical College. The efforts of the following individuals have been invaluable: Kristen Duerr, associate vice president, associate publisher; Jennifer Normandin, senior editor; Amanda Brodkin, development editor; Ellina Beletsky, production editor; Amanda Young, editorial assistant; Carol Keller of Books By Design, designer; and Patty Stephan, production director.

CHAPTER **1**

Introduction to Database Management

OBJECTIVES

- Provide a general introduction to the field of database management.

- Introduce basic terminology.

- Describe the advantages and disadvantages of database processing.

- Provide a brief history of database management.

- Describe the hierarchical and network data models.

Introduction

This chapter uses the example of Henry, who owns a chain of four bookstores, to illustrate the basic concepts behind database management.

When Henry took control of the bookstores several years ago, he inherited a computerized file-oriented system that organized the information he needed to run the bookstores. The file system consists of documents that are lists of facts that allow Henry to gather and organize basic data about publishers, authors, and books. Each book is identified by a unique code. In addition, Henry records the title, publisher, type of book, price, and whether the book is a paperback. He also records the author or authors of the books, along with the number of copies of the book in stock at each of the branches.

Henry uses this information in a variety of ways. For example, a customer might be interested in books written by a certain author or of a certain type. Henry wants to be able to tell the customer which books by the author or of that type he currently has in stock. If the customer wants a book that is not in stock at one branch, Henry needs to be able to determine if any of the other branches have it.

A programmer hired by the former bookstore owner developed Henry's computerized file-oriented system. The system is proving to be difficult and costly to use by Henry and his staff. For example, Henry must pay the programmer to change the system every time new data needs to be tracked or new information needs to be generated. Henry's staff also feels they shouldn't have to enter facts about a book, for instance the book title and price, for each branch that stocks the book; they want to enter these data only once. Consequently, Henry hired a local computer consultant to assess the system and recommend what action he should take to allow him to manage his data more effectively.

Henry's problem is common to many businesses and individuals. They need to store and retrieve data in an efficient and organized way. Furthermore, all of them are interested in more than one category of information. In database terminology, these categories are referred to as **entities**. Henry is interested in entities such as books, authors, publishers, and branches. A school is interested in students, faculty, and classes; a real estate agency is interested in clients, houses, and agents; and a used car dealer is interested in customers, vehicles, and manufacturers.

Besides wanting to store data that pertain to more than one entity, Henry is also interested in relationships between the entities. For example, he wants to be able to relate books to the authors who wrote them, to the publishers who published them, and to the branches that have them in stock. Likewise, a real estate agency wants to know not only about clients, houses, and agents, but also about the relationship between clients and houses (which clients have listed which houses and which clients have expressed interest in which houses), between agents and houses (which agent sold which house), and so on. In a file-oriented system, a programmer must create software to handle all the required relationships and then must modify the software to add new relationships and new data as the system matures.

The consultant told Henry that he should switch from the file-oriented system to a database system. A **database** is a structure that contains information about many kinds of entities and about the relationships between the entities. Like the file-oriented system, Henry's database will contain information about books, authors, branches, and publishers. However, it will also provide facts that relate authors to the books they wrote and branches to the books they currently have in stock. With the use of a database and using a few automated computer commands, Henry will be able to enter the title of a particular book and find out who wrote it, as well as which branches have it. Alternatively, he can start with an author and find all the books that he or she wrote, together with the publishers of these books. Using a database, Henry not only will be able to maintain his data better, he also will be able to use the data in the database to produce a variety of reports and to answer a variety of questions.

Henry's Basic Data

The consultant starts reviewing the data contained in Henry's file-oriented system. The system uses several files. A **file** is an organized collection of data about a single entity. One of Henry's files, called Branch, contains data about each branch bookstore Henry owns. The Branch file, shown in Figure 1.1, is represented in the form of a table. The rows in a table are called records, and the columns are called fields. A **record** pertains to a specific person, place, thing, or event. Each record consists of a number of **fields** that contain facts about that specific person, place, thing, or event. The Branch file contains four records, each with values for the fields of Branch Number, Branch Name, Branch Location, and Number of Employees.

FIGURE 1.1

Branch file

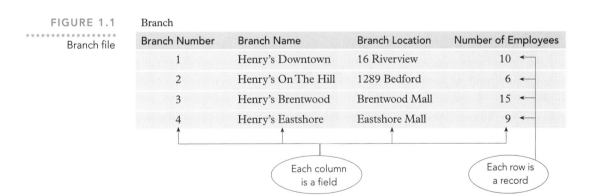

Branch

Branch Number	Branch Name	Branch Location	Number of Employees
1	Henry's Downtown	16 Riverview	10
2	Henry's On The Hill	1289 Bedford	6
3	Henry's Brentwood	Brentwood Mall	15
4	Henry's Eastshore	Eastshore Mall	9

Each column is a field

Each row is a record

Two additional files for Henry's system are shown in Figure 1.2. The files are called Publisher and Author.

FIGURE 1.2
·····················
Publisher and
Author files

Publisher

Publisher Code	Name	City
AH	Arkham House Publishing	Sauk City WI
AP	Arcade Publishing	New York
AW	Addison-Wesley	Reading MA
BB	Bantam Books	New York
BF	boyd & fraser	Boston
JT	Jeremy P. Tarcher	Los Angeles
MP	McPherson and Co.	Kingston
PB	Pocket Books	New York
RH	Random House	New York
RZ	Rizzoli	New York
SB	Schoken Books	New York
SI	Signet	New York
TH	Thames and Hudson	New York
WN	W.W. Norton and Co.	New York

Author

Author Number	Name
1	Archer, Jeffrey
2	Christie, Agatha
3	Clarke, Arthur C.
4	Francis, Dick
5	Cussler, Clive
6	King, Stephen
7	Pratt, Philip
8	Adamski, Joseph
10	Harmon, Willis
11	Rheingold, Howard
12	Owen, Barbara
13	Williams, Peter
14	Kafka, Franz
15	Novalis
16	Lovecraft, H. P.
17	Paz, Octavio
18	Camus, Albert
19	Castleman, Riva
20	Zinbardo, Philip
21	Gimferrer, Pere
22	Last, Mary
23	Leidig, Paul

The Book file is shown in Figure 1.3.

Book

Book Code	Title	Publisher Code	Type	Price	Paperback
0180	Shyness	BB	PSY	7.65	Y
0189	Kane and Abel	PB	FIC	5.55	Y
0200	The Stranger	BB	FIC	8.75	Y
0378	The Dunwich Horror and Others	PB	HOR	19.75	N
079X	Smokescreen	PB	MYS	4.55	Y
0808	Knockdown	PB	MYS	4.75	Y
1351	Cujo	SI	HOR	6.65	Y
1382	Marcel Duchamp	PB	ART	11.25	Y
138X	Death on the Nile	BB	MYS	3.95	Y
2226	Ghost from the Grand Banks	BB	SFI	19.95	N
2281	Prints of the 20th Century	PB	ART	13.25	Y
2766	The Prodigal Daughter	PB	FIC	5.45	Y
2908	Hymns to the Night	BB	POE	6.75	Y
3350	Higher Creativity	PB	PSY	9.75	Y
3743	First Among Equals	PB	FIC	3.95	Y
3906	Vortex	BB	SUS	5.45	Y
5163	The Organ	SI	MUS	16.95	Y
5790	Database Systems	BF	CS	54.95	N
6128	Evil Under the Sun	PB	MYS	4.45	Y
6328	Vixen 07	BB	SUS	5.55	Y
669X	A Guide to SQL	BF	CS	23.95	Y
6908	Using Microsoft Access	BF	CS	20.50	Y
7405	Night Probe	BB	SUS	5.65	Y
7443	Carrie	SI	HOR	6.75	Y
7559	Risk	PB	MYS	3.95	Y
8092	Magritte	SI	ART	21.95	N
8720	The Castle	BB	FIC	12.15	Y
9611	Amerika	BB	FIC	10.95	Y

To check your understanding of the relationship between publishers and books, answer the following questions: Who published *Knockdown*? Which books did Signet publish?

ANSWER

The Publisher Code in the row in the Book file for *Knockdown* is PB. Examining the Publisher file, you see that PB is the code assigned to Pocket Books.

To find the books published by Signet, look up its code in the Publisher file and see that it is SI. Next, look for all records in the Book file for which the publisher code is SI and find that Signet published *Cujo*, *The Organ*, *Carrie*, and *Magritte*.

The file called Book-Author, shown in Figure 1.4, is used to relate books and authors. The Sequence field indicates the order in which the authors of a particular book are listed on the cover. The file Book-Branch in the same figure is used to indicate the number of copies of a particular book that are currently on hand at a particular branch. The first row, for example, indicates that there are two copies of the book whose code is 0180 currently on hand at Branch 1.

QUESTION

To check your understanding of the relationship between authors and books, answer the following questions: Who wrote *The Organ*? (Be sure to list the authors in the correct order.) Which books did Jeffrey Archer write?

ANSWER

To determine who wrote *The Organ*, you first examine the Book file to find its book code (5163). Next, look for all rows in the Book-Author file in which the Book Code value is 5163. There are two such rows. In one of them, the Author Number is 12, and in the other it is 13. Then, look in the Author file to find the authors who have been assigned the numbers 12 and 13. The answer is Barbara Owen (12) and Peter Williams (13). The sequence number for author 12 is 2, however, and the sequence number for author 13 is 1. Thus, listing the authors in the proper order, the authors are Peter Williams and Barbara Owen.

To find the books written by Jeffrey Archer, you look up his number in the Author file and find that it is 1. Then, look for all rows in the Book-Author file for which the author number is 1. There are three such rows. The corresponding Book Code values are 0189, 2766, and 3743. Looking up these codes in the Book file, you find that Jeffrey Archer wrote *Kane and Abel*, *The Prodigal Daughter*, and *First Among Equals*.

QUESTION

A customer in Branch 1 wishes to purchase the book titled *Vortex*. Is it currently in stock in Branch 1?

ANSWER

Looking up the code for *Vortex* in the Book file, you find it is 3906. To find out how many copies are in stock in Branch 1, look for a row in the Book-Branch file with 3906 in the Book Code column and 1 in the Branch Number column. There is no such row, which means that Branch 1 doesn't have any copies of *Vortex*.

QUESTION

You would like to obtain a copy of *Vortex* for this customer. Which other branches currently have it in stock and how many copies do they have?

ANSWER

You already know that the code for *Vortex* is 3906. (If you didn't, you would simply look it up in the Book file.) To find out which branches have copies, look for rows in the Book-Branch table with 3906 in the Book Code column. There are two such rows. The first one indicates that Branch 2 has one copy. The second indicates that Branch 3 has two copies.

FIGURE 1.4

....

Book-Author and
Book-Branch files

Book-Author

Book Code	Author Number	Sequence
0180	20	1
0189	1	1
0200	18	1
0378	16	1
079X	4	1
0808	4	1
1351	6	1
1382	17	1
138X	2	1
2226	3	1
2281	19	1
2766	1	1
2908	15	1
3350	10	1
3350	11	2
3743	1	1
3906	5	1
5163	12	2
5163	13	1
5790	7	1
5790	8	2
6128	2	1
6328	5	1
669X	7	1
6908	7	1
6908	22	3
6908	23	2
7405	5	1
7443	6	1
7559	4	1
8092	21	1
8720	14	1
9611	14	1

Book-Branch

Book Code	Branch Number	On Hand
0180	1	2
0189	2	2
0200	1	1
0200	2	3
0378	3	2
079X	2	1
079X	3	2
079X	4	3
0808	2	1
1351	2	4
1351	3	2
1382	2	1
138X	2	3
2226	1	3
2226	3	2
2226	4	1
2281	4	3
2766	3	2
2908	1	3
2908	4	1
3350	1	2
3743	2	1
3906	2	1
3906	3	2
5163	1	1
5790	4	2
6128	2	4
6128	3	3
6328	2	2
669X	1	1
6908	2	2
7405	3	2
7443	4	1
7559	2	2
8092	3	1
8720	1	3
9611	1	2

The consultant found that Henry's system includes several programs to allow him to update the data in his files. Separate programs are required to allow for the addition, correction, and deletion of branches, books, publishers, and authors. The system also includes several programs to produce the reports Henry needs. Furthermore, the logic just discussed for relating books and publishers, authors and books, and books and branches has to be built into these programs.

Using A Database Management System

Henry's file-oriented system, in effect, includes many of the characteristics of a database. The system certainly maintains data on entities (branches, books, publishers, and authors). It also maintains relationships between these entities. However, it is only through the efforts of Henry's programs that the crucial relationships are maintained. Another way of stating this would be to say that Henry's programs *manage* the data, a very complex task.

Fortunately, you no longer need your own programs, because the computer is able to assist in managing the database. The tool it uses is called a database management system, or DBMS. A DBMS is a program or collection of programs whose function is to manage a database on behalf of the people who use it. It greatly simplifies the task of manipulating and using a database. The consultant told Henry that a DBMS could be used to replace his file-oriented system without the need to write a single program.

Henry agreed with the consultant's recommendation and they decided that a DBMS could fulfill his needs. They determined the structure of the database he needs—this is called database design. Henry's database design contains the information he needs about branches, books, publishers, and authors. Then Henry enters this design in the DBMS, creates several forms—screen objects used to maintain, view, and print records from a database—and begins to enter data.

The form he uses to process branch data is shown in Figure 1.5. Using this form, Henry can enter a new branch; view, change, or delete an existing branch; and print the information for a branch. Henry does not write a program to create this form; instead, the DBMS creates the form based on answers from him in response to its questions about the form's contents and appearance.

FIGURE 1.5
....
Branch form

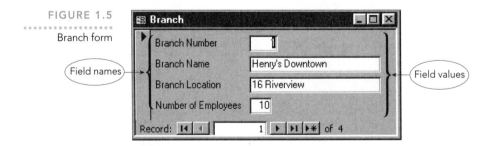

The DBMS creates the other forms Henry needs in this same way. A more complicated form for processing book data is shown in Figure 1.6. This form uses data about books, authors, and the relationship between books and authors.

8

FIGURE 1.6
•••••••••••••••••••
Book form

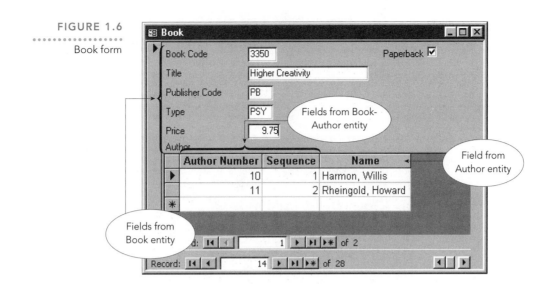

Henry is able to create the reports he needs in a similar way—the database asks him questions about the desired content and appearance of each report and creates them automatically based on Henry's answers. The book report, listing each book title, publisher name, price, and author, is shown in Figure 1.7.

FIGURE 1.7
•••••••••••••••••••
Book report

Books

Title	Publisher Name	Price	Author Name
A Guide to SQL	boyd & fraser	23.95	Pratt, Philip
Amerika	Bantam Books	10.95	Kafka, Franz
Carrie	Signet	6.75	King, Stephen
Cujo		6.65	King, Stephen
Database Systems	boyd & fraser	54.95	Pratt, Philip
			Adamski, Joseph
Death on the Nile	Bantam Books	3.95	Christie, Agatha
Evil Under the Sun	Pocket Books	4.45	Christie, Agatha
First Among Equals		3.95	Archer, Jeffrey
Ghost from the Grand Banks	Bantam Books	19.95	Clarke, Arthur C.
Higher Creativity	Pocket Books	9.75	Hamon, Willis
			Rheingold, Howard
Hymns to the Night	Bantam Books	6.75	Novalis
Kane and Abel	Pocket Books	5.55	Archer, Jeffrey
Knockdown		4.75	Francis, Dick
Magritte	Signet	21.95	Gimferrer, Pere
Marcel Duchamp	Pocket Books	11.25	Paz, Octavio
Night Probe	Bantam Books	5.65	Cussler, Clive
Prints of the 20th Century	Pocket Books	13.25	Castleman, Riva
Risk		3.95	Francis, Dick
Shyness	Bantam Books	7.65	Zinbardo, Philip
Smokescreen	Pocket Books	4.55	Francis, Dick
The Castle	Bantam Books	12.15	Kafka, Franz
The Dunwich Horror and Others	Pocket Books	19.75	Lovecraft, H.P.
The Organ	Signet	16.95	Williams, Peter
			Owen, Barbara
The Prodigal Daughter	Pocket Books	5.45	Archer, Jeffrey
The Stranger	Bantam Books	8.75	Camus, Albert
Using Microsoft Access	boyd & fraser	20.50	Pratt, Philip
			Leidig, Paul
			Last, Mary
Vixen 07	Bantam Books	5.55	Cussler, Clive
Vortex		5.45	Cussler, Clive

Finally, Henry creates a switchboard system—a set of special forms used to provide controlled access to the data, forms, reports, and other objects of a database. The switchboard system contains a main switchboard (Figure 1.8), which appears when Henry starts work with his database, and two other switchboards: "Maintain Data" and "Produce Reports."

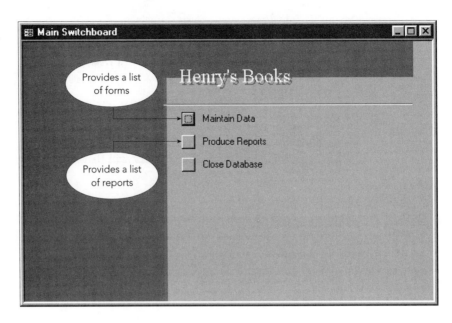

When Henry chooses the "Maintain Data" option on the main switchboard, the switchboard shown in Figure 1.9 appears. Depending on which data he wants to maintain in the database, he chooses the corresponding option on this switchboard.

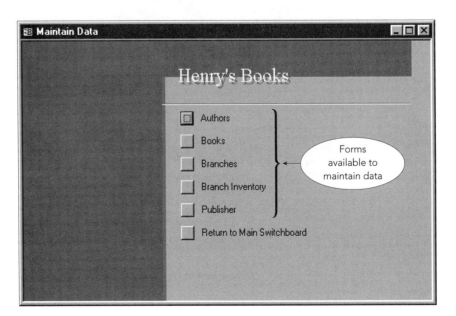

Henry's interests and needs are typical of those of today's PC users. Ever-increasing numbers of people around the world are finding that a database management system is the ideal tool for solving a wide variety of simple and complex problems. Later in this text, you will learn about Henry's use of more advanced features of a DBMS, such as replication—synchronizing copies of a database—and the impact of the Internet on database management.

The next section presents some background material on database management and some of the most commonly used terms. You then will examine some of the advantages and disadvantages of database management systems. The last two sections present a brief history of database management systems and the hierarchical and network database models.

Background

This section introduces some terminology and concepts that are very important in the database environment. Some of the terms will be familiar to you from the material in the preceding section.

Entities, Attributes, and Relationships

The most fundamental database terms are entity, attribute, and relationship. An entity is really just like a noun; it is a person, place, thing, or event.

An attribute is a property of an entity. The term is used here exactly as it is used in everyday English. For the entity Person, for example, the list of attributes might include such things as eye color and height. For Henry, the attributes of interest for the entity Book are such things as code, title, type of book, price, and so on.

Figure 1.10 shows two entities, Publisher and Book, and a number of attributes. The Publisher entity has three attributes: Publisher Code, Name, and City. The attributes are really just the columns or fields in the table. The Book entity has six attributes: Book Code, Title, Publisher Code, Type, Price, and Paperback. (The last attribute simply indicates whether the book is paperback.)

FIGURE 1.10

Entities and attributes

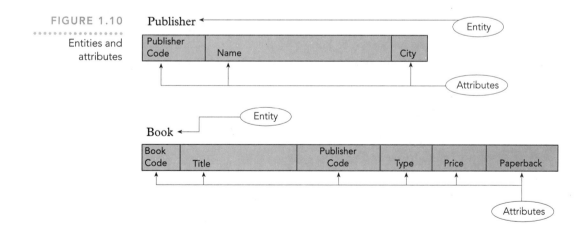

The final fundamental term is relationship. A relationship is an association between entities. There is an association between publishers and books, for example. A publisher is associated with all the books that it publishes, and a book is associated with its publisher. Equivalently, you would say that a publisher is *related to* all the books it published, and a book is *related to* its publisher.

This particular relationship is called a one-to-many relationship. *One* publisher is associated with *many* books, but each book is associated with only *one* publisher. (In this type of relationship, the word *many* is used differently than in everyday English; it may not always mean a large number. In this context, it would mean that a publisher can be associated with *any number* of books. That is, one publisher can be associated with zero, one, or more books.)

A one-to-many relationship often is represented visually in the manner shown in Figure 1.11. In such a diagram, entities and attributes are represented in precisely the same way as they are shown in Figure 1.10. The relationship is represented by an arrow. The *one* part of the relationship, in this case Publisher, is indicated by a single-headed arrow, and the *many* part of the relationship, in this case Book, is indicated by a double-headed arrow.

FIGURE 1.11
··························
One-to-many
relationship

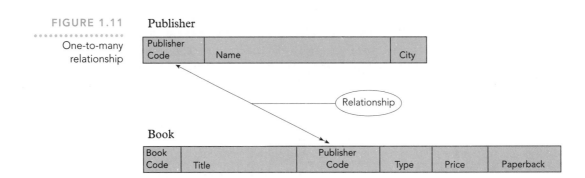

Files and Databases

You encountered the word *file* earlier in this chapter. If you have used a computer or done some programming yourself, you may be familiar with the word. Basically, a file used to store data, which is often called a data file, is the computer counterpart to an ordinary paper file you might keep in a filing cabinet. The crucial aspect of a data file is that it stores information on a single entity and the attributes of that entity. In Henry's old file-oriented system, an example of a single entity is a book. Each record in this data file keeps information on the crucial attributes of one book.

A database, however, is much more than a file. Unlike a typical data file, a database can store information about multiple entities. There is also another difference. A database holds information about the relationships among the various entities. Not only will Henry's database have information about both books and publishers, for example, it will also hold information relating publishers to the books they have produced, books to authors, branches to books, and so on. Formally, the definition of a database is as follows:

Definition: A database is a structure that can store information about multiple types of entities, the attributes of these entities, and the relationships among the entities.

Database Management System (DBMS)

Managing a database is inherently a complicated task. Fortunately, DBMS software packages can do the job of manipulating databases for us. A DBMS is a software product through which users interact with a database. The actual manipulation of the underlying database is handled by the DBMS. In some cases, users may interact with the DBMS directly, as shown in Figure 1.12a. In other cases, users may interact with programs, such as those created with Visual Basic or C++; these programs in turn interact with the DBMS (Figure 1.12b). In either case, it is only the DBMS that actually accesses the database.

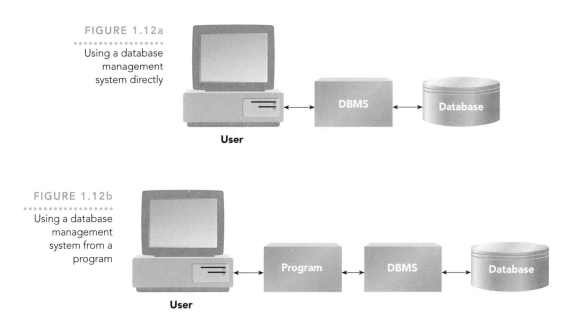

FIGURE 1.12a

Using a database management system directly

FIGURE 1.12b

Using a database management system from a program

Using a DBMS, for example, Henry can request the system to find publisher PB and the system either will locate this publisher and give him the data or tell him that no such publisher exists in the database. All the work involved in this task is performed by the DBMS. Henry does not have to go into his files and try to find the publisher. If publisher PB is in the database, Henry can then ask for the books this publisher has published, and again the system will perform all the work involved in locating these books. Likewise, when Henry adds data on a new book to the database, the DBMS performs all the tasks necessary to ensure that the book is related to the appropriate publisher.

Mainframe DBMSs have been in use since the 1960s. They have been enhanced continually over the years, gaining in selection of features and in performance. DBMSs that possess many of the features of their mainframe counterparts have been available on PCs since the mid-1980s. The leading products in this field, such as Access from Microsoft, also are improved on a continual basis. They make the power of database management available to large numbers of PC users. The focus of this text is on database management systems used on PCs.

Database Processing

When the term **database processing** is used, the data to be processed are stored in a database and the data in the database are being manipulated by a DBMS. You have seen how database processing benefits Henry with his individual system. A greater benefit is obtained by combining the activities of several users and allowing them to share a common database.

Let's first consider the nondatabase approach illustrated in Figure 1.13. Mary, Jeff, and Lucia are three separate users at the same college. Mary is in charge of enrolling students in courses, in producing class lists, and so on. She has her own system of programs and files that she uses to perform this activity on the computer. Her files contain information on classes, on faculty members who teach these classes, and on the students who are enrolled in the classes.

FIGURE 1.13
....
Nondatabase
approach

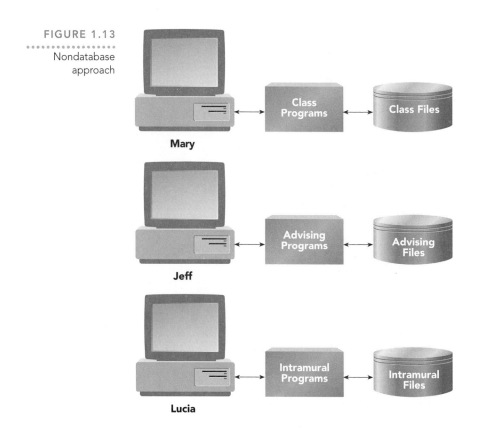

Jeff is in charge of the advising process, that is, advising students about their educational programs and their progress toward a degree. He has his own system of programs and files. His files, which are totally separate from Mary's, contain information on faculty members, on the students who are advised by them, and on the academic requirements that already have been fulfilled by these students.

Lucia is in charge of maintaining information on the intramural athletic programs. She, too, has her own system of programs and files. Her files contain information on the various sports that are available, the teams that participate in these sports, the students who belong to these teams, and the current records of the teams.

Two major problems arise with this nondatabase approach. The first problem is duplication of data. Mary, Jeff, and Lucia are each keeping information about students. Presumably, each of them will need the address of all the students. Thus, the address of each student is stored in at least three separate places in the computer. Not only does this waste space, but it causes a real headache when a student moves and his or her address must be changed multiple times.

The second problem is that it is extremely difficult to fulfill requirements that involve data from more than one system. For example, producing a report showing students and the courses that they're enrolled in and that they've completed would need data from Mary's and Jeff's systems. Mary, Jeff and Lucia may or may not have their files set up in the same way. The format of the files may not even be compatible from one system to another.

· ·

QUESTION Suppose you want to list the number, name, and address of a particular student. You also want to list the classes in which the student is currently enrolled, the name of the student's advisor, and the intramural sports in which the student is participating. Where would you find the necessary data?

ANSWER The student's number, name, and address can come from any one of the three systems. The classes in which the student is enrolled are found in Mary's system. The name of the student's advisor is found in Jeff's system. The sports in which the student participates are found in Lucia's system. Thus, this requirement involves data from all three systems.

· ·

By contrast, in a database approach, instead of having separate collections of files, Mary, Jeff, and Lucia share a common database managed by a DBMS (Figure 1.14).

FIGURE 1.14

· · · · · · · · · · · · · · · · · · · ·

Database approach (using a database management system)

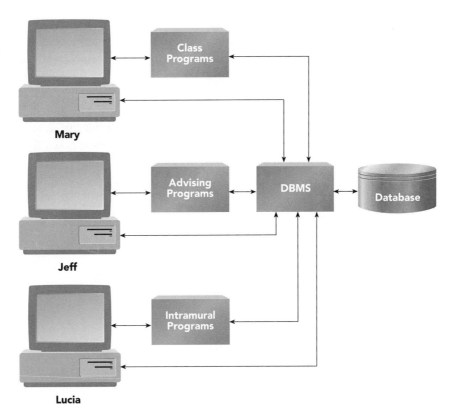

With the DBMS approach, each student appears only once in the system, so his or her address likewise appears only once. No space is wasted, and changing a student's address is a very simple procedure. Furthermore, because all the data are in a single database, it is possible to list the information on a student, the student's classes, the student's advisor, and the sports in which the student participates. In fact, with a good DBMS, it is a simple task.

■ Advantages of Database Processing

The database approach to processing, using a DBMS on a PC, offers nine clear advantages over alternate data management systems. They are listed in Figure 1.15 and are discussed in the following pages.

FIGURE 1.15

Advantages of Distributed Processing

Advantages of database processing

1. Getting more information from the same amount of data
2. Sharing of data
3. Balancing conflicting requirements
4. Controlling redundancy
5. Consistency
6. Integrity
7. Security
8. Increasing productivity
9. Data independence

1. *Getting more information from the same amount of data.* The primary goal of a computer system is to turn data—recorded facts—into information—the knowledge gained by processing these facts. In a nondatabase file-oriented environment, data often are partitioned into several disjointed systems, each system having its own collection of files. Any request for information that necessitates accessing data from more than one of these collections is extremely difficult. In many cases, for all practical purposes, it is considered impossible. Thus, the desired information is unavailable, not because it is not stored in the computer, but because of the way it has been broken down into the various collections of files. Instead, when all the data for the various systems are stored in a single database, the information becomes available. Given the power of a modern DBMS, not only is the information available, but the process of getting it can be a quick and easy one.

2. ***Sharing of data.*** The data of various users can be combined and shared among authorized users, allowing all users access to a greater pool of data. Several users can have access to the same piece of data—for example, a customer's address—and still use it in a variety of ways. When an address is changed, the new address immediately becomes available to all users. In addition, the existing data can be used in new ways (such as generating new types of reports) without having to create additional data files (as in the nondatabase approach).

3. ***Balancing conflicting requirements.*** For the database approach to function adequately within an organization, a person or group should be in charge of the database itself, especially if it is to serve a number of users. This person or group is often called **Database Administration** (**DBA**) or the Database Administrator. By keeping the overall needs of the organization in mind, DBA can structure the database in such a way that it benefits the entire organization, not just a single group. While this may mean that an individual user group is served less well than it would have been if it had its own isolated system, the organization as a whole is better off. Ultimately, when the organization benefits, so do the individual groups of users.

4. ***Controlling redundancy.*** With database processing, data that formerly were kept separate in a nondatabase file-oriented system are integrated into a single database, so multiple copies of the same data no longer exist. With the nondatabase approach, Mary, Jeff, and Lucia each have a copy of the address of each student. With the database approach, each student's address occurs only once, thus eliminating duplication, called **redundancy**.

   Eliminating redundancy not only saves space, but also makes the process of updating much simpler. With the database approach, changing the address of a student means making one single change. With the nondatabase approach, the same change of address means that three changes have to be made.

   Although eliminating redundancy is the ideal, it is not always possible. Sometimes, for reasons having to do with performance, you might choose to introduce a limited amount of redundancy into a database. But, even in these cases, you would be able to keep the redundancy under tight control, thus obtaining the same advantages. This is why it is better to say that you *control* redundancy rather than *eliminate* it.

5. ***Consistency.*** Suppose an individual student's address appears in more than one place. Student 176, for example, might be listed at 926 Meadowbrook at one spot within the data and 2856 Wisner at another. The data in the computer are then inconsistent. Because the potential for this sort of problem is a direct result of redundancy, and because the database approach reduces redundancy, there is much less potential for the occurrence of this sort of inconsistency with the database approach.

6. *Integrity.* An integrity constraint is a rule that must be followed by data in the database. Here is an example of an integrity constraint: The publisher code given for any book must be that of a publisher that is already in the database. In other words, users cannot type in an incorrect publisher's name. A database has integrity if the data in it satisfy all established integrity constraints. A good DBMS should provide an opportunity for users to build in these integrity constraints when they design the database. The DBMS then should ensure that these constraints are never violated. According to the integrity constraint about publishers, the DBMS should *not allow* you to store data about a given book if the publisher code that you enter is not the code of a publisher that already is in the database.

7. *Security.* Security is the prevention of access to the database by unauthorized users. A good DBMS has a number of features that help ensure the enforcement of security measures.

8. *Increasing productivity.* A DBMS frees the programmers who are writing database access programs from having to engage in mundane data manipulation activities, such as adding new data and deleting existing data, thus making the programmers more productive. A good DBMS comes with many features that allow users to gain access to data in the database without having to do any programming at all. This increases the productivity both of programmers, who may not need to write complex programs in order to perform certain tasks, and of nonprogrammers, who may be able to get the results they seek from the data in the database without waiting for a program to be written for them.

9. *Data independence.* The structure of a database often needs to be changed. For example, changing user requirements may necessitate the addition of an entity, an attribute, or a relationship, or a change may be required to improve performance. A good DBMS provides data independence, which is a property that allows the structure of a database to be changed without the programs that access the database having to change. Without data independence, a lot of unnecessary effort can be expended in changing programs to match the new structure of the database. The presence of many programs in the system may make this effort so prohibitive that a decision is made not to change the database. With data independence, the decision to change the database structure is more likely to be made.

■ Disadvantages of Database Processing

As you would expect, if there are advantages to doing something in a certain way, there are also disadvantages. Database processing is no exception. In terms of numbers alone, the advantages outweigh the disadvantages, but the latter are listed in Figure 1.16 and explained below.

Disadvantages of Database Processing

1. DBMS size
2. DBMS complexity
3. Greater impact of failure
4. More difficult recovery

1. ***DBMS size.*** In order to support all the complex functions that it provides to users, a DBMS must be a large program that occupies a large amount of disk space as well as a substantial amount of internal memory.

2. ***DBMS complexity.*** The complexity and breadth of the functions provided by a DBMS make it a complex product. Users of the DBMS must learn a great deal to understand the features of the system in order to take full advantage of it. In the design and implementation of a new system that uses a DBMS, many choices have to be made; it is possible to make incorrect choices, especially with an insufficient understanding of the system. Unfortunately, a few incorrect choices can spell disaster for the whole project. A sound database design is critical to the successful use of a DBMS.

3. ***Greater impact of a failure.*** In a nondatabase file-oriented system, each user has a completely separate system; the failure of any single user's system does not necessarily affect any other user. On the other hand, if several users are sharing the same database, a failure on the part of any one user that damages the database in some way may affect all the other users.

4. ***More difficult recovery.*** Because a database is inherently more complex than a simple file, the process of recovering it in the event of a catastrophe also is more complicated. This is particularly true if the database is being updated by a large number of users at the same time. It must first be restored to the condition it was in when it was last known to be correct; any updates made by users since that time must be redone. The greater the number of users involved in updating the database, the more complicated this task becomes.

▧ History of Database Management

It is difficult to pinpoint exactly when the field of database management began. However, there is good reason to place its beginnings with the APOLLO project of the early 1960s, which was launched in response to President John F. Kennedy's stated goal of landing a person on the moon by the end of the decade. At that time, no available systems were capable of handling the coordination of the vast amounts of data required for the project. North American Rockwell, the prime contractor for the project, asked IBM to develop such a system. In response, IBM developed the Generalized Update Access Method (GUAM), which went into production in 1964.

IBM realized that this product would be useful in other environments and made the product available to the general public in 1966 under the name Data Language/I (DL/I). This product is actually the data management component of the Information Management System (IMS), which was the dominant DBMS for many years. IBM has enhanced IMS over the years; and IMS still is used widely today by companies in their legacy systems, which are systems developed before PCs became widely used.

Also in the mid-1960s, Charles Bachman led a General Electric team that developed a DBMS named Integrated Data Store (I-D-S). I-D-S led to a whole class of database management systems—the CODASYL systems—that were popular and influential through the late 1980s.

In the late 1960s, CODASYL, the COnference on DAta SYstems Languages, the group responsible for the programming language COBOL, tackled the problem of providing a standard for DBMSs. CODASYL charged a task group, the DataBase Task Group (DBTG), with the job of developing specifications for DBMSs. The DBTG did this, and in 1971, CODASYL presented these specifications to the American National Standards Institute (ANSI) for adoption as a national standard. Although these specifications were not accepted as a standard by ANSI, a number of systems were developed following the CODASYL guidelines.

In 1970, Dr. E.F. Codd proposed a new and radically different approach to the management of data: the relational model. Throughout the 1970s, the relational model (which will be discussed later in this book) was the subject of intense research. In addition to purely theoretical research, prototype systems were developed, the most important being a system called System R, which was developed by IBM. It was not until the 1980s, however, that commercial relational DBMSs began to appear. Systems that are at least partly relational now exist in abundance on computers ranging from the smallest personal computer to the largest mainframe. While System R never became a commercial system, it led to IBM's commercial relational product, DB2.

Beginning in the late 1970s, considerable research was conducted with object-oriented approaches to the development of computer software. In the 1980s, this research led to the development of object-oriented programming languages and object-oriented database management systems (OODBMSs). One of the first OODBMSs, Gemstone from Servio Corporation, appeared in 1987 and is still widely used today.

◼ Hierarchical and Network Databases

Database management systems are characterized by the model of data they follow. There are four types of data models, each of which has two components: structure and operations. The structure refers to the way the system structures data or, at least, the way the users of the DBMS feel the data are structured. The operations are the facilities given to the users of the DBMS to manipulate data within the database. What is crucial in operations development is the way things feel to the user—it doesn't matter how the designers of the DBMS choose to implement these facilities behind the scenes.

The four DBMS data models are: the network model, the hierarchical model, the relational model, and the object-oriented model. The relational and object-oriented models are discussed later in this book. The following brief descriptions of the network and hierarchical models will be sufficient because their use is rapidly declining.

Network Model

A network model database is perceived by a user as a collection of record types and relationships between these record types. Such a structure is called a network, and it is from this that the model takes its name. Consider the database shown in Figure 1.17. The rectangles represent the record types in the database. There is one record type for each of the entities: publishers, books, book-authors, book-branches, authors, and branches. The arrows represent the relationships. In particular, they represent the one-to-many relationship, which was discussed earlier. For example, each publisher is related to many books, and each book is related to exactly one publisher.

FIGURE 1.17

Network database structure

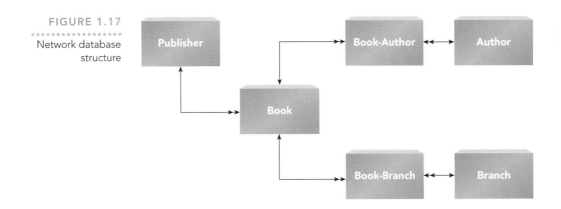

You manipulate a network model database by essentially following the arrows. This procedure is often referred to as database navigation. Arrows may be followed in either direction. Suppose you need to print a list of all books published by Signet. You first ask the DBMS to find Signet in the Publisher record. You then repeatedly ask to find the next book published by Signet until reaching the end of the list of Signet books. While you're on a given book, you can ask to find the number of the author related to the book. Here you follow the arrow from Book to Book-Author in the reverse direction. If you also want to print the author's name, you can ask the DBMS to find the author related to the current author number.

Note that you find the publisher to which a book is related by following the arrow, not by looking at a publisher code field in a Book record. There is no need for such a field, because the relationships are part of the physical structure of a network model database. In general, there is no need to have fields in network model records to implement the relationships.

I-D-S and other CODASYL systems are examples of DBMSs that conform to the network data model.

Hierarchical Model

A hierarchical model database is perceived by a user as a collection of hierarchies, or trees. Figure 1.18 shows a hierarchical database at a typical school, where each Department employs many Faculty, and each Faculty advises many Students. At the same time, each Student is advised by exactly one Faculty, and each Faculty is employed in exactly one Department.

FIGURE 1.18

Hierarchical database structure

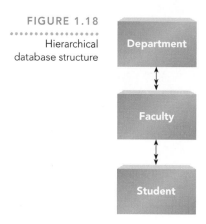

A hierarchy is really a network with an added restriction: no rectangle can have more than one "many" arrow entering the rectangle. (It doesn't matter how many "one" arrows leave a rectangle.) A hierarchy is thus a more restrictive structure than a network. Because two "many" arrows—one from Book and a second from Author—enter the Book-Author rectangle in the Figure 1.17 database, this database is not a hierarchy and cannot be implemented directly in a hierarchy model DBMS. IBM's GUAM, DL/I, and IMS are examples of DBMSs that conform to the hierarchical model.

SUMMARY

- An entity is a person, place, thing, or event. An attribute is a property of an entity. A relationship is an association between entities.

- A database is a structure that can store information about many different entities and about the relationships between these entities.

- A database management system is a software package whose function is to manipulate a database on behalf of users.

- Database processing offers a number of advantages, including the following:
  - getting more information from the same amount of data
  - sharing of data
  - balancing conflicting requirements
  - controlling redundancy
  - consistency
  - integrity
  - security
  - increasing productivity
  - data independence

- The disadvantages of a database include the following:
  - DBMS size
  - DBMS complexity
  - greater impact of a failure
  - more difficult recovery

- IBM completed its development of Generalized Update Access Method (GUAM), the first DBMS, in 1964 and released it publicly as Data Language/I (DL/I) in 1966. DL/I is the data management component of the Information Management System (IMS).

- A General Electric team led by Charles Bachman developed the Integrated Data Store (I-D-S) DBMS, the first of the CODASYL systems, in the mid-1960s.

- Dr. E.F. Codd originated the relational model for databases, publishing his groundbreaking paper in 1970. IBM's System R was an early prototype DBMS that followed this model.

- In 1987 Servio Corporation's Gemstone was one of the first object-oriented database management systems (OODBMSs), which are based on object-oriented concepts.

- A data model consists of structure and operations components. DBMSs are characterized by the data model they follow. The four data models are network, hierarchical, relational, and object-oriented.

- A network model database is a collection of record types and relationships between the record types.

- A hierarchical model database is a collection of hierarchies, or trees, where a hierarchy is a network with an additional restriction: each record type cannot be related on the "many" side in more than one one-to-many relationship.

KEY TERMS

American National Standards Institute (ANSI)
attribute
Conference on Data Systems Languages
    (CODASYL)
data file

data independence
Data Language/I (DL/I)
data model
database
Database Administration (DBA)

database design

database management system (DBMS)

database navigation

database processing

Database Task Group (DBTG)

entity

field

file

form

Generalized Update Access Method (GUAM)

hierarchy

hierarchical model

Information Management System (IMS)

Integrated Data Store (I-D-S)

integrity

integrity constraint

network

network model

object-oriented database management system (OODBMS)

object-oriented model

one-to-many

operations

record

redundancy

relational model

relationship

security

structure

switchboard

REVIEW QUESTIONS

1. What is a file? A record? A field?

2. What is an entity? An attribute?

3. When you speak of relationships, what exactly do you mean?

4. What is a one-to-many relationship? Give two examples of entities that have one-to-many relationships.

5. What is a database?

6. What is a DBMS?

7. How is it possible to get more information from the same amount of data by using a database approach as opposed to a file approach?

8. What is meant by the sharing of data?

9. What is DBA? What kinds of things does DBA do in a database environment?

10. What is redundancy? What are the problems associated with redundancy?

11. How does consistency result from controlling redundancy?

12. What is meant by integrity as it is used in this chapter?

13. What is meant by security? What does the DBMS have to do with security?

14. What is meant by data independence? Why is it desirable?

15. How can the size of a DBMS be a disadvantage?

16. How can the complexity of a DBMS be a disadvantage?

17. Why can a failure in a database environment be more serious than one in a nondatabase system?

18. Why can recovery be more difficult in a database environment?

19. Which DBMS is considered to be the first product offered to the public?

20. What is the chief difference between network and hierarchical model databases?

CHAPTER 2

The Relational Model 1: Introduction, QBE, and the Relational Algebra

OBJECTIVES

- Introduce Premiere Products, the company that is used as a basis for many of the examples throughout the text.

- Describe the relational model.

- Present QBE (Query-by-Example).

- Discuss the use of criteria in QBE.

- Examine the creation of calculated columns in QBE.

- Describe the manner in which statistics are calculated in QBE.

- Present the manner in which tables can be joined in QBE.

- Discuss the relational algebra.

Introduction

You begin this chapter by examining the requirements of a company called Premiere Products, which will be used in many examples throughout this chapter and in the rest of the text. Then, you will move on to study the relational model, the approach to database management taken by most PC-based database management systems (and many mainframe systems, as well). Next, you will examine a very visual way of retrieving data from relational databases, called QBE, which stands for Query-By-Example. Finally, you will learn about the relational algebra, one of the original ways of manipulating relational databases.

■ Premiere Products

Premiere Products is a distributor of appliances, housewares, and sporting goods. Management has determined that the company has grown to the point that the maintenance of customer and order data, as well as the maintenance of their inventory, can no longer be done manually. By placing the data on a computer managed by a full-featured database management system, management will be able to ensure that the data are more current and more accurate than in the present manual system. They also will be able to produce a variety of useful reports. In addition, they want to be able to ask questions concerning the data in the database and obtain answers to these questions easily and rapidly.

In deciding which data must be stored in the database, management has determined that Premiere Products must maintain the following information about its sales reps, customers, and parts inventory:

1. Premiere Products must store the sales rep number, name, address, total commission, and commission rate for each of its sales reps.

Note: All sales rep numbers appear as two-digit codes. Thus, a sales rep number of 3 actually appears as 03.

2. The company must store the customer number, name, address, current balance, and credit limit for each of its customers, as well as the number of the sales rep who represents the customer.

3. The company must store the part number, description, number of units on hand, item class, number of the warehouse where the item is stored, and unit price for each part in inventory.

Premiere Products must also store information on orders. A sample of a printed order is shown in Figure 2.1. Note that there are three components to the order: (1) The heading (top) of the order contains the order number; the date; the customer's number, name, and address; the sales rep number; and the sales rep name. (2) The body of the order contains a number of order lines, sometimes called line items. Each order line contains a part number, a part description, the number of units of the part that was ordered, and the quoted price for the part. It also contains a total, usually called an extension, which is the product of the number ordered and the quoted price. (3) Finally, the footing (bottom) of the order contains the order total. Premiere Products would like to be able to automatically generate orders like the one shown in Figure 2.1 using its database.

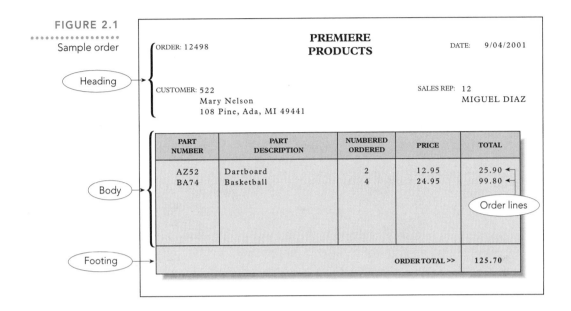

Premiere Products also would like to store the following order information:

1. For each order: the order number, the date the order was placed, and the number of the customer who placed the order. Note that the customer's name and address and the number of the sales rep who represents the customer are stored with customer information. The name of the sales rep is stored with sales rep information.

2. For each order line: the order number, the part number, the number of units ordered, and the quoted price. Remember that the part description is stored with information on parts. The product of the number of units ordered and the quoted price is not stored, since it can be computed easily when needed.

Premiere Products does not want to store the overall order total as part of the database. Instead, the order total will be computed whenever an order is printed or displayed on the screen.

Figure 2.2 shows sample data tables for Premiere Products. In the first table, titled Sales Rep, you see that there are three sales reps whose numbers are 03, 06, and 12. The name of sales rep 03 is Mary Jones. Her street address is 123 Main. She lives in Grant, Michigan and her ZIP code is 49219. Her total commission is $2150.00, and her commission rate is 5% (.05).

SalesRep

Sales Rep Number	Last Name	First Name	Street	City	State	Zip Code	Commission	Rate
03	Jones	Mary	123 Main	Grant	MI	49219	2150.00	.05
06	Smith	William	102 Raymond	Ada	MI	49441	4912.50	.07
12	Diaz	Miguel	419 Harper	Lansing	MI	49224	2150.00	.05

Customer

Customer Number	Last Name	First Name	Street	City	State	Zip Code	Balance	Credit Limit	Sales Rep Number
124	Adams	Sally	481 Oak	Lansing	MI	49224	$818.75	$1000	03
256	Samuels	Ann	215 Pete	Grant	MI	49219	$21.50	$1500	06
311	Charles	Don	48 College	Ira	MI	49034	$825.75	$1000	12
315	Daniels	Tom	914 Cherry	Kent	MI	48391	$770.75	$750	06
405	Williams	Al	519 Watson	Grant	MI	49219	$402.75	$1500	12
412	Adams	Sally	16 Elm	Lansing	MI	49224	$1817.50	$2000	03
522	Nelson	Mary	108 Pine	Ada	MI	49441	$98.75	$1500	12
567	Dinh	Tran	808 Ridge	Harper	MI	48421	$402.40	$750	06
587	Galvez	Mara	512 Pine	Ada	MI	49441	$114.60	$1000	06
622	Martin	Dan	419 Chip	Grant	MI	49219	$1045.75	$1000	03

Orders

Order Number	Order Date	Customer Number
12489	9/02/2001	124
12491	9/02/2001	311
12494	9/04/2001	315
12495	9/04/2001	256
12498	9/05/2001	522
12500	9/05/2001	124
12504	9/05/2001	522

Order Line

Order Number	Part Number	Number Ordered	Quoted Price
12489	AX12	11	$14.95
12491	BT04	1	$149.99
12491	BZ66	1	$399.99
12494	CB03	4	$279.99
12495	CX11	2	$22.95
12498	AZ52	2	$12.95
12498	BA74	4	$24.95
12500	BT04	1	$149.99
12504	CZ81	2	$325.99

Part

Part Number	Part Description	On Hand	Class	Warehouse	Price
AX12	Iron	104	HW	3	$24.95
AZ52	Dartboard	20	SG	2	$12.95
BA74	Basketball	40	SG	1	$29.95
BH22	Cornpopper	95	HW	3	$24.95
BT04	GasGrill	11	AP	2	$149.99
BZ66	Washer	52	AP	3	$399.99
CA14	Griddle	78	HW	3	$39.99
CB03	Bike	44	SG	1	$299.99
CX11	Blender	112	HW	3	$22.95
CZ81	Treadmill	68	SG	2	$349.95

In the second table, you see that there are 10 customers, numbered 124, 256, 311, 315, 405, 412, 522, 567, 587, and 622. The name of customer 124 is Sally Adams. (There are actually two customers named Sally Adams in the table.) Her street address is 481 Oak. She lives in Lansing, Michigan, and her ZIP code is 49224. Her current balance is $818.75, and her credit limit is $1000. The number 03 in the column titled Sales Rep Number indicates that Sally is represented by sales rep 03 (Mary Jones).

Skipping down to the table labeled Part, you see that there are 10 parts, whose part numbers are AX12, AZ52, BA74, BH22, BT04, BZ66, CA14, CB03, CX11, and CZ81. Part AX12 is an iron, and the company has 104 units of this part on hand. These parts are in item class HW (housewares) and are stored in warehouse 3. The price of an iron is $24.95.

Moving back up to the table labeled Orders, you see that there are seven orders, numbered 12489, 12491, 12494, 12495, 12498, 12500, and 12504. Order 12489 was placed on September 2, 2001, by customer 124 (Sally Adams).

Note: In some database management systems, the word order has a special purpose. Having a table with the name Order could cause problems in such systems. For this reason, the name is Orders rather than Order.

The table titled Order Line may seem strange at first glance. Why do you need a separate table for the order lines? Couldn't this type of information concerning the parts that were ordered be included in the Orders table? The answer is yes, they could. The Orders table could be structured in the manner shown in Figure 2.3. Examining this table, you see that the same orders as those shown in Figure 2.2 are present, with the same dates and the same customer numbers. In addition, each row contains all the order lines for a given order. By examining the fifth row of Figure 2.3, you see that order 12498 has two order lines. One of these order lines is for two AZ52s at $12.95 each; the other is for four BA74s at $24.95 each.

FIGURE 2.3

Sample table structure

Orders

Order Number	Order Date	Customer Number	Part Number	Number Ordered	Quoted Price
12489	9/02/2001	124	AX12	11	$14.95
12491	9/02/2001	311	BT04	1	$149.99
			BZ66	1	$399.99
12494	9/04/2001	315	CB03	4	$279.99
12495	9/04/2001	256	CX11	2	$22.95
12498	9/05/2001	522	AZ52	2	$12.95
			BA74	4	$24.95
12500	9/05/2001	124	BT04	1	$149.99
12504	9/05/2001	522	CZ81	2	$325.99

QUESTION   How is identical information represented in Figure 2.2?

ANSWER   Take a look at the Order Line table in Figure 2.2 and examine the sixth and seventh rows. The sixth row indicates that there is an order line on order 12498 for two AZ52s at $12.95 each. The seventh row indicates that there is an order line on order 12498 for four BA74s at $24.95 each. Thus, the same information that you find in Figure 2.3 is represented here in two separate rows rather than one.

At first glance, it would seem to make more sense to use one row (as shown in Figure 2.3) to represent the same information that could be displayed in two rows (as shown in Figure 2.2). There is a problem with the arrangement shown in Figure 2.3, however; the table is more complicated. In Figure 2.2, there is a single item at each position in the table. In Figure 2.3, some of the individual positions within the table contain multiple data entries. Furthermore, there is a connection between these items.

Note: In the row for order 12498, it is crucial to know that the AZ52 corresponds to the 2 in the Number Ordered column, not the 4, and to the $12.95 in the Quoted Price column, not the $24.95.

There are practical issues to consider in the Figure 2.3 setup, such as:

1. How much room do you allow for these multiple entries?

2. What if an order has more order lines than you have allowed room for?

Certainly, neither of these problems is unsolvable. They do add a level of complexity, however, that is not present in the arrangement shown in Figure 2.2. In the structure shown in that figure, there are no multiple entries to consider, nor does it matter how many order lines exist for any order. In general, this simpler structure is preferable, and that is why order lines have been placed in a separate table.

To test your understanding of the Premiere Products data, answer the following questions, using the data in Figure 2.2.

QUESTION   What are the numbers of all the customers represented by Mary Jones?

ANSWER   124, 412, and 622. (Look up the number of Mary Jones in the Sales Rep table and see that her sales rep number is 03. Then, find all customers in the Customer table that have number 03 in the Sales Rep Number column.)

QUESTION   What is the name of the customer who placed order 12491? Who is the sales rep who represents this customer?

ANSWER   Don Charles is the customer and Miguel Diaz is the sales rep. (Look up the customer number in the Orders table and see that the customer number is 311. Then find the customer in the Customer table who has customer number 311. Using this customer's sales rep number, which is 12, find the name of the sales rep in the Sales Rep table.)

QUESTION List all the parts that appear on order 12491. For each part, give the description, number ordered, and quoted price.

ANSWER Part Number: BT04, Part Description: Gas Grill, Number Ordered: 1, Quoted Price: 149.99. Also, Part Number: BZ66, Part Description: Washer, Number Ordered: 1, Quoted Price: 399.99. (Look up each Order Line table row in which the order number is 12491. Each of these rows contains a part number, the number ordered, and the quoted price. The only thing missing is the description of the part. Use the part number to look up the corresponding description in the Part table.)

QUESTION Why is the column Quoted Price part of the Order Line table? Why not take the part number and look up the price in the Part table?

ANSWER If you don't have the Quoted Price column in the Order Line table, you must obtain the price for a part on an order line by looking up the price in the Part table. While this is not problematic, it does prevent Premiere Products from charging different prices to different customers for the same part. Since Premiere Products wants the flexibility to quote different prices to different customers (to allow for volume discounts or other special arrangements), you should include the Quoted Price column in the Order Line table. If you examine the Order Line table, you will see cases in which the quoted price matches the actual price in the Part table and cases in which it differs. For example, you see that in order number 12489, Sally Adams bought 11 irons, and Premiere Products charged her only $14.95 per iron, rather than the regular price of $24.95.

Relational Databases

You have actually just seen a relational database. A relational database is essentially a collection of tables like the ones you just looked at for Premiere Products in Figure 2.2. A relational database is perceived by the user as being just such a collection. (The phrase "perceived by the user" simply indicates that what matters is how things appear to the user, not what the DBMS is actually doing behind the scenes.) You might wonder why this model is not called the "table" model, or something similar, if a database is a collection of tables. Formally, these tables are called relations, and this is where the model gets its name.

How does a DBMS that follows the relational model handle entities, attributes of entities, and relationships between entities? Entities and attributes are fairly simple. Each entity gets a table of its own. Thus, in the database for Premiere Products, there is a table for sales reps, a separate table for customers, and so on. The attributes of an entity become the columns in the table. In the table for sales reps, for example, there is a column for the sales rep number, a column for the sales rep name, and so on.

What about relationships? At Premiere Products there is a one-to-many relationship between sales reps and customers (each sales rep is related to the many customers he or she represents, and each customer is related to the one sales rep who represents him or her). How is this relationship implemented in a relational model database? The answer is through common columns in two or more tables. Consider again Figure 2.2. The Sales Rep Number column of the Sales Rep table and the Sales Rep Number column of the Customer table are used to implement the relationship between sales reps and customers;

that is, given a sales rep, you can use these columns to determine all the customers he or she represents, and, given a customer, you can use these columns to find the sales rep who represents the customer. If the sales rep number was not included in the Customer table, you would not be able to tell who each customer's sales rep is.

Let's now be a little more precise in the description of a relation. As discussed, a relation is essentially a two-dimensional table. If you consider the tables in Figure 2.2, however, you can see that there are certain restrictions you would probably want to place on relations. Each column should have a unique name within the table, and entries within each column should all "match" this column name. For example, if the column name is Credit Limit, all entries in that column should in fact *be* credit limits. Also, each row should be unique. After all, if two rows are absolutely identical, the second row doesn't give any information that you don't already have. In addition, for maximum flexibility, the ordering of the columns and the rows should be irrelevant. Finally, the table will be simplest if each position is restricted to a single entry, that is, if you do not allow multiple entries (often called **repeating groups**) in an individual location in the table. These restrictions lead to the following definitions:

Definition: A **relation** is a two-dimensional table in which:

1. The entries in the table are single-valued, that is, each location in the table contains a single entry;

2. Each column has a distinct name (technically called the attribute name);

3. All the values in a column are values of the same attribute (that is, all entries must match the column name);

4. The order of columns is irrelevant;

5. Each row is distinct; and

6. The order of rows is irrelevant.

Definition: A **relational database** is a collection of relations.

Note: Later in the text, you will encounter situations in which a structure satisfies all the properties of a relation *except for property 1*; that is, some of the entries contain repeating groups and thus are not single-valued. Such a structure is called an **unnormalized relation**. This jargon is certainly a little strange, in that an unnormalized relation is thus not a relation at all. It is the term that is used for such a structure, however. The table shown in Figure 2.3 is an example of an unnormalized relation.

Note: Rows in a table (relation) are often called **records** and columns are often called **fields**. Rows are also called **tuples** and columns are called **attributes**.

There is a commonly accepted shorthand representation of the structure of a relational database. You merely write the name of the table and then within parentheses list all the columns (fields) in the table. Each table should be shown on its own line. Thus, this sample database consists of:

```
Sales Rep (Sales Rep Number, Last Name, First Name, Street, City, State,
     Zip Code, Commission, Rate)
Customer (Customer Number, Last Name, First Name, Street, City, State,
     Zip Code, Balance, Credit Limit, Sales Rep Number)
Orders (Order Number, Order Date, Customer Number)
Order Line (Order Number, Part Number, Number Ordered, Quoted Price)
Part (Part Number, Part Description, On Hand, Class, Warehouse, Price)
```

Notice that there is some duplication of names. The column Sales Rep Number appears in *both* the Sales Rep table *and* the Customer table. Suppose a situation existed wherein the two might be confused. If you merely wrote Sales Rep Number, how would the computer know which Sales Rep Number you meant? How would a person looking at what you had written know which one you meant for that matter? You need a mechanism for indicating the one to which you are referring. One common approach to this problem is to write both the table name and the column name separated by a period. Thus, the Sales Rep Number in the Customer table would be written Customer.Sales Rep Number, whereas the Sales Rep Number in the Sales Rep table would be written Sales Rep.Sales Rep Number. Technically, when you do this you say that you **qualify** the names. It is *always* acceptable to qualify column names, even if there is no possibility of confusion. If confusion may arise, however, it is *essential* to do so.

Note: In some systems, it is not possible to include spaces within table or column names. Some such systems allow uppercase and lowercase. In these systems, a typical approach is to omit the space, but retain the capitalization to indicate the beginnings of the various words within the name, for example, CustomerNumber or SalesRepNumber. Another approach that is especially common in systems that do not support upper and lower case is to replace the spaces with underscores, for example, CUSTOMER_NUMBER or SALES_REP_NUMBER.

Note: Even in systems that allow spaces, there are occasions in which the space can cause confusion. For example, it may not be clear whether Credit Limit refers to a single column named "Credit Limit" or two columns, one named "Credit" and the other named "Limit." If any such confusion is possible, it is common to place the name between square brackets ([ ]). In such a situation, Credit Limit would be represented as [Credit Limit], making it clear that you are referring to a single column.

The **primary key** of a table (relation) is the column or collection of columns that uniquely identifies a given row. In the Sales Rep table, for example, the sales rep's number uniquely identifies a given row. (Sales rep 06 occurs in only one row of the table.) Thus, Sales Rep Number is the primary key.

The primary key provides an important way of distinguishing one row from another. Primary keys are typically indicated in the shorthand representation by underlining the column or collection of columns that comprises the primary key. Thus, the complete shorthand representation for the Premiere Products database would be:

```
Sales Rep (Sales Rep Number, Last Name, First Name, Street, City, State,
     Zip Code, Commission, Rate)
Customer (Customer Number, Last Name, First Name, Street, City, State,
     Zip Code, Balance, Credit Limit, Sales Rep Number)
Orders (Order Number, Order Date, Customer Number)
Order Line (Order Number, Part Number, Number Ordered, Quoted Price)
Part (Part Number, Part Description, On Hand, Class, Warehouse, Price)
```

QUESTION   Why does the primary key to the Order Line table consist of two columns, not just one?

ANSWER   No single column uniquely identifies a given row in the Order Line table. It requires two: a combination of Order Number and Part Number.

■ QBE

When you pose a question to Access a database management system, the question is called a query. A **query** is simply a question represented in a way that the database management system can recognize and process. In this section, you will investigate an approach to queries that is very visual. It is called **Query-By-Example** (**QBE**). Not only are results displayed on the screen in tabular form, but users actually enter their requests by filling in portions of a grid on the screen. Studies have shown that learning and using QBE is as fast or faster than learning and using other methods, and the accuracy of the QBE query results is as good as or better than queries developed through other approaches.

Note: This chapter introduces QBE by using a particular QBE implementation. The examples that follow use the Premiere Products data and are for illustration only; you will not need to do any computer work at this point. The QBE version you'll look at is found in the PC-based DBMS called Access, a product of Microsoft. Although the various versions of QBE are certainly not identical, the differences are relatively minor. If you have mastered one version of it, you should easily be able to learn another.

In Access, queries are specified using a special window called the Select Query window. The upper pane (portion) of the window contains a list of all the fields in the table you want to query. The lower pane contains the **Design grid**, the area where you specify how you want the output to look, fields to be included in the query output, sort order, and the criteria the records you are looking for must satisfy.

The following figures and examples will show you how to retrieve data using the Access version of QBE.

Simple Queries

To include a column in the results of a query, you place it in the Design grid.

EXAMPLE 1   List the customer number, last name, first name, balance, and credit limit of all customers in the database.

To include a field in a query in Microsoft Access, double-click the field in the field list. The field will then appear in the Design grid at the bottom of the screen (Figure 2.4a). The check marks in the Show boxes indicate that the fields will be included in the results of the query. Clicking the Run button on the toolbar causes the query to be run and the results displayed (Figure 2.4b).

FIGURE 2.4
(a and b)

Query to select
only certain fields

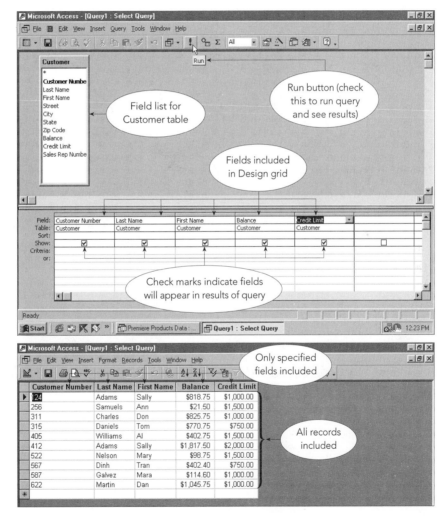

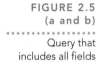

You could certainly put a check mark in each column in the table to obtain this result. There is a shortcut, however. The Access shortcut to include all fields is to double-click the asterisk in the Field list. The asterisk then appears in the Design grid (Figure 2.5a), indicating that all fields will display. The results of executing this query are shown in Figure 2.5b.

FIGURE 2.5
(a and b)
· ·
Query that
includes all fields

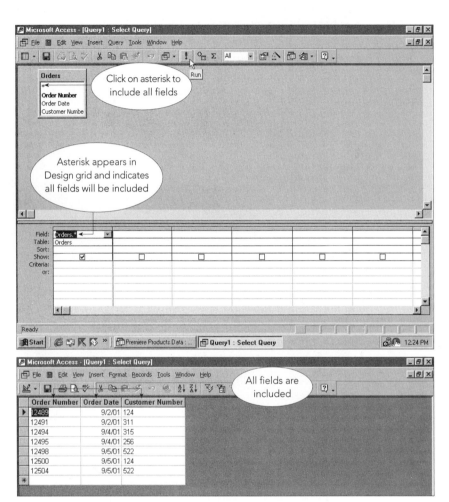

Simple Criteria

To indicate **criteria**, that is, restrictions that the records to be retrieved must satisfy, simply put each criterion (condition) in the appropriate column as illustrated in the following example.

EXAMPLE 3 : Find the last name and first name of customer 124.

To enter a criterion for a field, the field must be included in the Design grid. The criterion is then entered on the row labeled Criteria (Figure 2.6a). Normally, if a field is included in the Design grid, it will appear in the results of the query. In this example, the Customer Number field is not supposed to be included. To indicate that the field is not to display in the results, you remove the check mark from the field's Show check box as shown in the figure. The results are shown in Figure 2.6b.

FIGURE 2.6
(a and b)
....
Query to find the
name of a customer

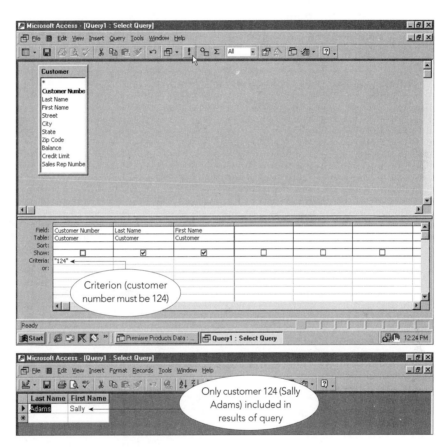

Note: You will notice quotation marks around the 124 in the criteria line of Figure 2-6a. This is because of how the Customer Number field was defined. In general, even though a field contains numbers, if it is not to be used for arithmetic, the field will typically be defined as a text (also called character) field. This is the case with the Customer Number field. When entering a value for a text field, the value typically needs to be enclosed between quotation marks. The user does not need to worry about this, however, since Microsoft Access will automatically place the quotation marks around the value that was entered as soon as any other action is taken. In this case, as soon as the check mark was removed from the Show box, the quotation marks appeared.

If you want something other than an exact match (=), you must enter the appropriate **comparison operator**, also called a **relational operator**, as you will see in the next example. The comparison operators are = (equal to), > (greater than), < (less than), >= (greater than or equal to), <= (less than or equal to), and NOT (not equal to). (It is common in QBE to omit the "=" symbol in "equal" comparisons, although you certainly can use it if you wish.)

Compound Criteria

Not only can you use the comparison operators, but you can also combine criteria to create **compound criteria**. In many query tools, you would do so by placing the word AND or the word OR between the criteria. In QBE, it is done a little differently: If you want to combine criteria with AND, place the criteria on the same criteria row; if you want to combine criteria with OR, place the criteria on different rows in the criteria section of the Design grid.

EXAMPLE 4   List the description of all parts for which there are more than 100 units on hand *and* that are located in warehouse 3.

To indicate that two criteria must both be true, place the criteria on the same row, as shown in Figure 2.7a. In this case, you have requested those parts for which the value in the On Hand field is greater than 100, which requires the use of the > comparison operator, and the value in the Warehouse field is 3. The results are shown in Figure 2.7b.

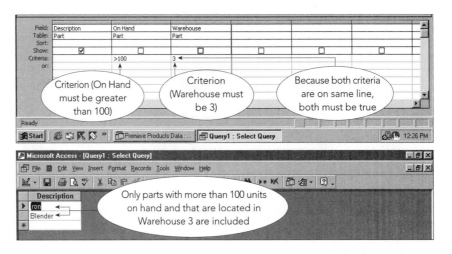

FIGURE 2.7
(a and b)
· · · · · · · · · · · · · · · · · · · ·
Query that involves
AND condition

EXAMPLE 5   List the description of all parts for which there are more than 100 units on hand *or* that are located in warehouse 3.

To combine two criteria with "Or," place the first criterion in the Criteria row and the second in the row labeled "or" (Figure 2.8a). The results are shown in Figure 2.8b.

38

FIGURE 2.8
(a and b)
. . . .
Query that involves
OR condition

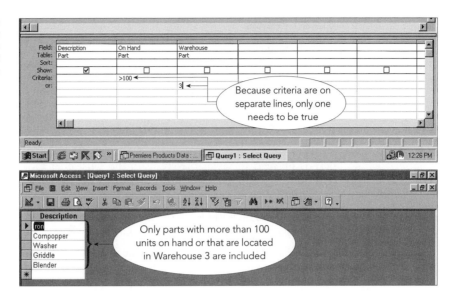

EXAMPLE 6 : List the number, name, and balance for each customer whose balance is between $100 and $500.

At times you need to search for a range of values. For example, in this query, you need to find all customers with balances between $100 and $500. When you ask this kind of question, you are really looking for all balances that are greater than 100 *and* less than 500, which requires using a compound criterion: two criteria in the same field. To place two criteria in the same field, separate the criteria by placing the word "And" between them. Figure 2.9a shows the Balance field selected and the two criteria entered in the field. The results are shown in Figure 2.9b.

FIGURE 2.9
(a and b)
. . . .
Query that involves
two conditions in a
single field

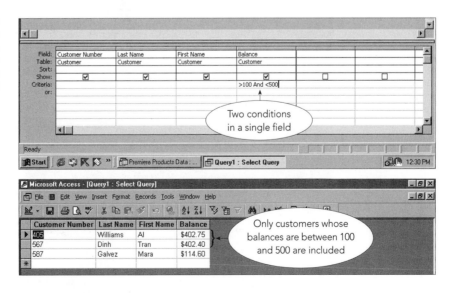

Computed Fields

You can include fields in queries that are not in the database, but that can be calculated from fields that are. Such a field is called a **computed** or **calculated field**. Its use is illustrated in the following example.

EXAMPLE 7 : List the number, name, and available credit for all customers.

There is no field for available credit in the Customer table. You can calculate it from existing fields, however, since the available credit is equal to the credit limit minus the balance. To include computed fields in queries, you enter a name for the computed field, a colon, and then the expression in one of the columns in the Field row. For the available credit, for example, you will type Available Credit:[Credit Limit]-[Balance]. You can type this directly into the Field row. You will not be able to see the entire entry, however, because there is not enough room for it. A better way is to select the column in the Field row, right-click to display the shortcut menu, and then click Zoom. The Zoom dialog box will appear. You then can type the expression in the dialog box (Figure 2.10a). Notice that field names are enclosed between square brackets ([ ]). The results of the query are shown in Figure 2.10b.

FIGURE 2.10
(a and b)

Query that involves
a computed field

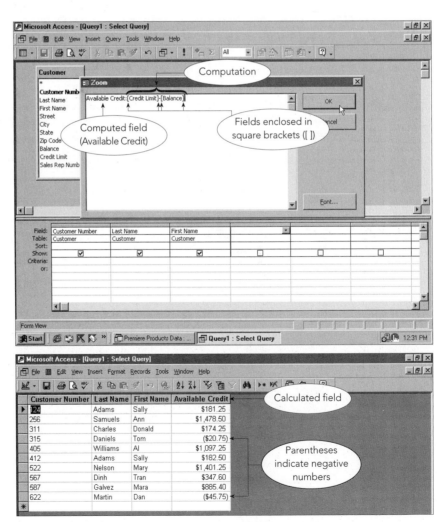

You are not restricted to subtraction in computations. You can use addition (+), multiplication (*), or division (/). Also, you can include parentheses in your computations to indicate which computations should be done first.

Calculating Statistics

All products that support QBE, including Microsoft Access, support the built-in **statistics** (called aggregate functions in Access): Count, Sum, Avg (average), Max (largest value), Min (smallest value), StDev (standard deviation), Var (variance), First, and Last. To use any of these in a query, you include it in the Total row in the design grid. The Total row does not appear automatically in the grid. To include it, you need to take some special action, for example, right-clicking the grid, and then clicking Totals on the shortcut menu.

The following example illustrates how you use these functions by counting the different parts in item class HW.

EXAMPLE 8 : How many parts are in item class HW?

In this case, Count is the appropriate operation. Enter the Part Number and Class columns in the Design grid and then include the Totals row. The entry in the Totals row for the Part Number column should be Count. In the Class column, you would enter Where in the Totals row, which simply indicates that there will also be a criterion. In the Criteria row, the entry is HW. The correct entries appear in Figure 2.11a and the results are shown in Figure 2.11b.

FIGURE 2.11
(a and b)
· · · · · · · · · · · · · · · · · · · ·
Query to count
records

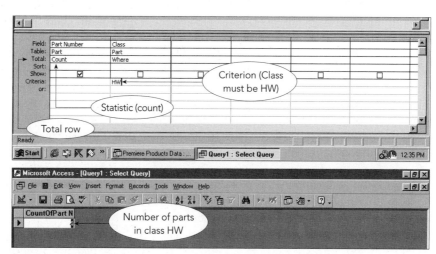

EXAMPLE 9 ⋮ What is the average balance of all customers?

In this example, Avg is the appropriate operation (Figure 2.12a). The results are shown in Figure 2.12b.

FIGURE 2.12
(a and b)
• • • • • • • • • • • • • • • • • •
Query to calculate
an average

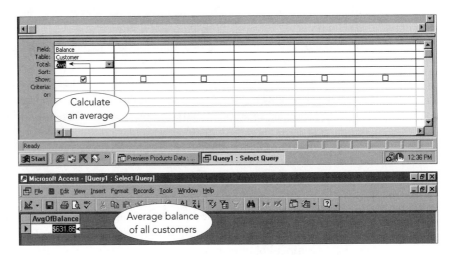

Grouping

Another way statistics are often used is in combination with grouping, in which statistics are calculated for groups of records. For example, you may need to calculate the average balance for the customers of each sales rep. You will want the average for the customers of sales rep 03, the average for customers of sales rep 06, and so on.

Grouping simply means creating groups of records that share some common characteristic. In grouping by Sales Rep Number, for example, the customers of sales rep 03 would form one group, the customers of sales rep 06 would be a second, and the customers of sales rep 12 form a third. The calculations are then made for each group. To indicate grouping in Access, select Group By as the entry in the Total row for the field to be used for grouping.

EXAMPLE 10 ⋮ What is the average balance for customers of each sales rep?

In this example, you will include the Sales Rep Number and Balance fields in the Design grid. Select Group By as the entry in the Total row for Sales Rep Number and Avg for Balance (Figure 2.13a). The results are shown in Figure 2.13b.

FIGURE 2.13
(a and b)
....
Query to perform
multiple
calculations

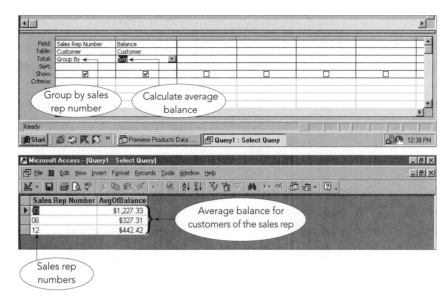

Joining Tables

So far, the queries have all involved only a single table. In many cases, queries require that data be drawn from more than one table. To do so, it is necessary to join the tables, that is to combine tables based on matching fields in corresponding columns. To join tables in Access, first you bring field lists for both tables to the upper pane of the Select Query window. Access will draw a line between matching fields in the two tables indicating that the tables are related. You can then select fields from either table. Access will join the tables automatically if the corresponding fields have the same field name.

EXAMPLE 11   List each customer's number and name, along with the number and name of the corresponding sales rep.

This query cannot be satisfied using a single table. The customer name is in the Customer table, whereas the sales rep name is in the Sales Rep table. The sales rep number can come from either table. Thus, you need to join the tables. To do so, first place Field lists for both tables in the upper pane and then select the desired fields from either list (Figure 2.14a). Notice that the Table row indicates with which table each field is associated. The results are shown in Figure 2.14b.

FIGURE 2.14
(a and b)
·······················
Query to join
tables

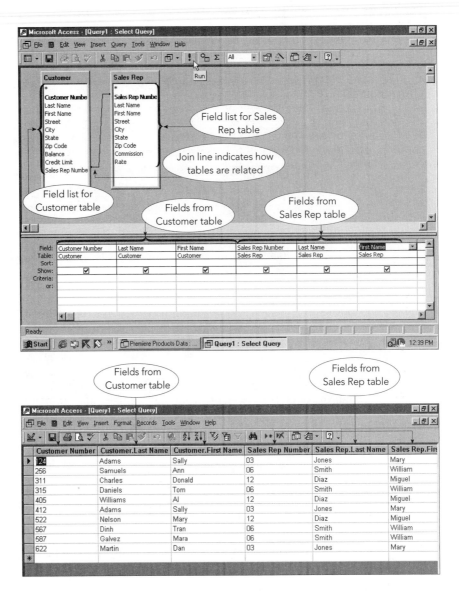

EXAMPLE 12   For each customer whose credit limit is $1000, list his or her number and name, along with the number and name of the corresponding sales rep.

The only difference between this query and the previous one is that there is an extra restriction. The credit limit must be $1000. To accommodate this, include the Credit Limit field in the Design grid, enter 1000 as the criteria, and remove the check mark from the Credit Limit field's Show box (since it is not to appear in the results). The query is shown in Figure 2.15a, and the results are shown in Figure 2.15b. Only the customers whose credit limit is $1000 are included.

FIGURE 2.15
(a and b)

Query to restrict
records in a join

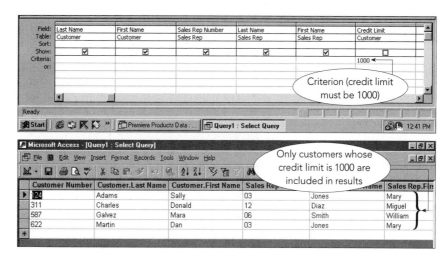

The Relational Algebra

The relational algebra is a theoretical way of manipulating a relational database. In the relational algebra, operations act on existing tables to produce new tables. This is similar to the way the operations of addition and subtraction act on numbers to produce new numbers in the algebra with which you are familiar.

Retrieving data from a relational database through the use of the relational algebra involves issuing relational algebra commands to operate on existing tables to form a new table that contains the desired information. Sometimes you may need to execute a series of commands in order to obtain the final result.

Note: Unlike QBE, the relational algebra is not used in current systems. Its importance is the theoretical base it provided to the relational model. It formed a benchmark by which other approaches to querying relational databases could be judged.

Note: There is no "standard" for the way relational model commands are to be represented. The method used for representing commands in this section, by using uppercase letters, is just one possibility. What is important is not the particular way the commands are represented, but rather what they accomplish.

As you will notice in these examples, each command ends with a clause that reads GIVING, followed by a table name. This clause is requesting that the result of the execution of the command be placed in a table with the name you have specified.

Select

The SELECT command within the relational algebra takes a horizontal subset of a table; that is, it retrieves certain rows from an existing table (based on some user-specified criteria) and saves them as a new table.

EXAMPLE 1 List all information from the Customer table concerning customer 256.

```
SELECT [Customer] WHERE [Customer Number] = 256
    GIVING [Answer]
```

This command will create a new table called Answer, which contains only the single row on which the customer number is 256. All the columns from the Customer table are included in the new Answer table.

EXAMPLE 2 List all information from the Customer table concerning those customers whose credit limit is 1000.

```
SELECT [Customer] WHERE [Credit Limit] = 1000
    GIVING [Answer]
```

This command will create a new table called Answer. The Answer table will contain all the columns from the Customer table, but only those rows on which the credit limit is $1000.

Project

The PROJECT command within the relational algebra takes a vertical subset of a table (that is, it causes only certain columns to be included in the new table).

EXAMPLE 3 List the number, first name, and last name of all customers.

```
PROJECT [Customer] OVER ([Customer Number], [First Name], [Last Name])
    GIVING [Answer]
```

This command will create a new table called Answer. The Answer table will contain only the Customer Number, First Name, and Last Name columns from the Customer table. All the rows from the Customer table will be included in the Answer table, but only the Customer Number, First Name, and Last Name columns.

EXAMPLE 4 List the number, first name, and last name of all customers whose credit limit is $1000.

This requires a two-step process. You first use a SELECT command to create a new table that contains only those customers whose credit limit is $1000. Then you project the new table to restrict the result to only the indicated columns.

```
SELECT [Customer] WHERE [Credit Limit] = 1000
    GIVING [Temp]
PROJECT Temp OVER ([Customer Number], [First Name], [Last Name])
    GIVING [Answer]
```

The first command will create a new table called Temp. The Temp table will contain all the columns from the Customer table, but only those rows in which the credit limit is $1000. The second command will create a new table called Answer. The Answer table will contain all the rows from the Temp table (that is, only customers whose credit limit is $1000), but only the Customer Number, First Name, and Last Name columns.

Join

The **join** operation is at the heart of the relational algebra. It is the command that allows you to pull together data from more than one table. In the most common form of the join, you join two tables together based on the values in matching columns. The join forms a new table containing the columns of both the tables that have been joined. Rows in this new table will be the **concatenation** (combination) of a row from the first table and a row from the second that match on the common column (often called the **join column**). In other words, two tables are joined *on* the join column.

For example, suppose you wish to join the two tables shown in Figure 2.16 on Sales Rep Number (the join column), creating a new table called Temp.

FIGURE 2.16
· · · · · · · · · · · · · · · ·
Customer and
Sales Rep tables

Customer

Customer Number	Last Name	First Name	Sales Rep Number
124	Adams	Sally	03
256	Samuels	Ann	06
311	Charles	Don	12
315	Daniels	Tom	06
405	Williams	Al	12
412	Adams	Sally	03
522	Nelson	Mary	12
567	Dinh	Tran	06
587	Galvez	Mara	06
622	Martin	Dan	03
701	Peters	Art	05

Sales Rep

Sales Rep Number	Last Name	First Name
03	Jones	Mary
06	Smith	William
12	Diaz	Miguel
15	Lewis	Joan

The result of the join is the table shown in Figure 2.17. Note that the column on which the tables are joined appears only once. Other than that, all columns from both tables are present in the result. Each table contains columns labeled Last Name and First Name. To avoid any ambiguity, the names of the second column called Last Name and the second column called First Name have been changed automatically in the Temp table to Last Name 1 and First Name 1, respectively.

FIGURE 2.17

Table produced by
joining Customer
and Sales Rep

Temp

Customer Number	Last Name	First Name	Sales Rep Number	Last Name 1	First Name 1
124	Adams	Sally	03	Jones	Mary
256	Samuels	Ann	06	Smith	William
311	Charles	Don	12	Diaz	Miguel
315	Daniels	Tom	06	Smith	William
405	Williams	Al	12	Diaz	Miguel
412	Adams	Sally	03	Jones	Mary
522	Nelson	Mary	12	Diaz	Miguel
567	Dinh	Tran	06	Smith	William
587	Galvez	Mara	06	Smith	William
622	Martin	Dan	03	Jones	Mary

If there is a row in one table that does not match any row in the other table, it will not appear in the result of the join. Thus, sales rep 15, Joan Lewis, from the Sales Rep table, and customer 701, Art Peters, from the Customer table, do not appear in the join table, since their rows are not common to both tables.

You can restrict the output from the join to include only certain columns by using the PROJECT command, as the following example illustrates:

EXAMPLE 5   For each customer, list the customer number, last name, first name, sales rep number, and sales rep's last name.

```
JOIN [Customer] [Sales Rep] WHERE [Customer].[Sales Rep Number]
     = [Sales Rep].[Sales Rep Number]
     GIVING [Temp]
PROJECT [Temp] OVER ([Customer Number], [Last Name], [First Name],
          [Sales Rep Number], [Last Name 1])
     GIVING [Answer]
```

In the WHERE clause in the JOIN command, the matching fields are both called Sales Rep Number: The field in Sales Rep called Sales Rep Number is supposed to match the field in Customer called Sales Rep Number. In this case, if you merely mention Sales Rep Number, it will not be clear which one you mean. It is necessary to qualify Sales Rep Number, or to specify to which table and field you are referring. You do this by preceding the name of the field with the name of the table, followed by a period. The Sales Rep Number field in the Sales Rep table is Sales Rep.Sales Rep Number. The Sales Rep Number field in the Customer table is Customer.Sales Rep Number.

In this example, the JOIN command will join the Sales Rep and Customer tables to create a new table called Customer Temp. The second join command will create a new table called Answer. The Answer table will contain all the rows from the Customer Temp table, but only the Customer Number, First Name, Sales Rep Number, and Last Name 1 columns.

Although this type of join is by far the most common kind, there is another possibility. The one described above is called the natural join. The other type of join, the outer join, is similar to the natural join except that it also displays records from the original tables that are not common to both tables. Recall that in the natural join these records are eliminated. In the outer join they are maintained, and values of the fields are left vacant, or null, for the records that do not have data common to both tables. In the case of the original example from this section, the outer join operation results in the table shown in Figure 2.18.

FIGURE 2.18

Table produced by an outer join of Customer and Sales Rep

Temp

Customer Number	Last Name	First Name	Sales Rep Number	Last Name 1	First Name 1
124	Adams	Sally	03	Jones	Mary
256	Samuels	Ann	06	Smith	William
311	Charles	Don	12	Diaz	Miguel
315	Daniels	Tom	06	Smith	William
405	Williams	Al	12	Diaz	Miguel
412	Adams	Sally	03	Jones	Mary
522	Nelson	Mary	12	Diaz	Miguel
567	Dinh	Tran	06	Smith	William
587	Galvez	Mara	06	Smith	William
622	Martin	Dan	03	Jones	Mary
701	Peters	Art	05	-	-
-	-	-	15	Lewis	Joan

Normal Set Operations

The relational algebra has the normal set operations: union, intersection, and difference. The union of two tables is a table containing all rows that are in either the first table or the second or both. The intersection of two tables is a table containing all rows that are common to both table A and B. The difference of tables A and B (referred to as A minus B) is the set of all rows that are in table A but are not in table B.

Union
There is an obvious restriction on these operations. It does not make sense, for example, to talk about the union of the Sales Rep table and the Customer table. These tables do not contain the same columns.

The two tables *must* have the same structure in order for the union to be appropriate. The formal term is union-compatible. Two tables are union-compatible if they have the same number of columns and if their corresponding columns represent the same type of data. For example, if the first column in one table contains customer numbers, the first column in the other table should also contain customer numbers.

EXAMPLE 6 : List the number, first name, and last name of those customers who either have orders or are represented by sales rep 12, or both.

You can create a table containing the number, last name, and first name of all customers who have orders by joining the Orders table and the Customer table (Temp1 in the following example) and then projecting the result over Customer Number, Last Name, and First Name (Temp2). You can also create a table containing the number, last name, and first name of all customers represented by sales rep 12 by selecting from the Customer table (Temp3) and then projecting the result (Temp4). The two tables ultimately created by this process (Temp2 and Temp4) have the same structure. They each have three fields: Customer Number, Last Name, and First Name. Because they are union-compatible, it is legitimate to take the union of these two tables. This process is accomplished in the relational algebra by:

```
JOIN [Orders], [Customer]
     WHERE [Orders].[Customer Number] = [Customer].[Customer Number]
     GIVING [Temp1]
PROJECT [Temp1] OVER [Customer Number], [Last Name], [First Name]
     GIVING [Temp2]
SELECT [Customer] WHERE [Sales Rep Number] = '12'
     GIVING [Temp3]
PROJECT [Temp3] OVER [Customer Number], [Last Name], [First Name]
     GIVING [Temp4]
UNION [Temp2] WITH [Temp4] GIVING [Answer]
```

Intersection
The INTERSECT command is used to produce a new table that contains rows common to more than one table.

EXAMPLE 7 : List the number, first name, and last name of those customers who have orders *and* are represented by sales rep 12.

This process is virtually identical to the one encountered in the UNION example. Here, however, at the end, you should INTERSECT the two tables, not take their union. The structure follows:

```
JOIN [Orders], [Customer]
     WHERE [Orders].[Customer Number] = [Customer].[Customer Number]
     GIVING [Temp1]
PROJECT [Temp1] OVER [Customer Number], [Last Name], [First Name]
     GIVING [Temp2]
SELECT [Customer] WHERE [Sales Rep Number] = '12'
     GIVING [Temp3]
PROJECT [Temp3] OVER [Customer Number], [Last Name], [First Name]
     GIVING [Temp4]
INTERSECT [Temp2] WITH [Temp4] GIVING [Answer]
```

Difference
The difference operation is performed by the SUBTRACT statement in the relational algebra.

EXAMPLE 8
List the number, first name, and last name of those customers who have orders *but are not* represented by sales rep 12.

This process is also virtually identical to the one encountered in the UNION example. Here, however, at the end, you should SUBTRACT one of the tables from the other, not take their union or intersection. The structure follows:

```
JOIN [Orders], [Customer]
     WHERE [Orders].[Customer Number] = [Customer].[Customer Number]
     GIVING [Temp1]
PROJECT [Temp1] OVER [Customer Number], [Last Name], [First Name]
     GIVING [Temp2]
SELECT [Customer] WHERE [Sales Rep Number] = '12'
     GIVING [Temp3]
PROJECT [Temp3] OVER [Customer Number], [Last Name], [First Name]
     GIVING [Temp4]
SUBTRACT [Temp4] FROM [Temp2] GIVING [Answer]
```

The next two sections present the final two commands in the relational algebra: product and division. These commands are not used nearly as often as the preceding commands.

Product

The product of two tables (mathematically called the Cartesian product) is the table obtained by concatenating every row in the first table with every row in the second table. Thus, the product of the Orders and Part tables shown in Figure 2.19 would be the final table shown in the figure.

FIGURE 2.19

Product of two tables

Orders

Order Number	Order Date
12489	9/02/2001
12491	9/02/2001
12494	9/04/2001

Part

Part Number	Part Description
BT04	Gas Grill
BZ66	Washer

Product of Orders and Part

Order Number	Order Date	Part Number	Part Description
12489	9/02/2001	BT04	Gas Grill
12491	9/02/2001	BT04	Gas Grill
12494	9/04/2001	BT04	Gas Grill
12489	9/02/2001	BZ66	Washer
12491	9/02/2001	BZ66	Washer
12494	9/04/2001	BZ66	Washer

Every row of the Orders table is matched with every row of the Part table. If the Orders table has *m* rows and the Part table has *n* rows, there would be *m times n* rows in the product. If, as is typically the case, the tables have a large number of rows, the number of rows in the product can be so great that it is not practical to form the product. Usually you would only want combinations that satisfy certain restrictions and so you would almost always use the join operation instead of the product operation.

Division

The division process is best illustrated by considering the division of a table with two columns by a table with a single column. Indeed, that is by far the most common situation in which this operation is used. As an example, consider the first two tables in Figure 2.20. The first table contains two columns: Order Number and Part Number. The second contains only a single column: Part Number.

FIGURE 2.20

Dividing one table by another

Order Line

Order Number	Part Number
12489	AX12
12491	BT04
12491	BZ66
12494	CB03
12495	CX11
12498	AZ52
12498	BA74
12500	BT04
12504	CZ81

Part

Part Number
BT04
BZ66

Result of dividing Order Line by Part

Order Number
12491

The quotient will be a new table with a single column titled Order Number (the column from the first table that is *not* in the second). The rows in this new table will consist of those order numbers from Order Line which are "matched" to *all* the parts appearing in the Part table. For an order number to appear in the quotient, there must be a row in Order Line with this order number in the Order Number column and BT04 in the Part Number column. There must also be a row in Order Line with this same order number in the Order Number column and BZ66 in the Part Number column. It doesn't matter if there are other rows in Order Line containing the same order number as long as the rows with BT04 and BZ66 are present. With the sample data, only order 12491 qualifies. The result would be the final table shown in the figure.

SUMMARY

- Premiere Products is an organization whose requirements include the following entities:
  - sales reps
  - customers
  - orders
  - parts
  - order lines

- A relation is a two-dimensional table in which:
  - the entries are single-valued;
  - each field has a distinct name;
  - all the values in a field are values of the same attribute (the one identified by the field name);
  - the order of fields is irrelevant;
  - each row is distinct; and
  - the order of rows is irrelevant.

- A relational database is a collection of relations.

- An unnormalized relation is a structure in which entries need not be single-valued but which satisfies all the other properties of a relation.

- A field name is qualified by preceding it with the table name and a period, for example, Sales Rep.Sales Rep Number.

- The primary key is the field or fields that uniquely identify a given row within the table.

- QBE is a visual tool for manipulating relational databases. QBE queries are indicated by filling in forms on the screen. The version of QBE shown in this chapter is the one in Microsoft Access.

- To indicate that a field is to be included in a Microsoft Access query, include the field in the design grid and make sure there is a check mark in the Show box.

- To indicate criteria in Microsoft Access, place the criteria in the appropriate columns.

- To indicate AND criteria, place both criteria in the same row; to indicate OR criteria, place the criteria on separate rows.

- To use a built-in function, place it in the Total row of the appropriate column.

- To create a computed field in Microsoft Access, enter an appropriate expression.

- To join tables in Microsoft Access, place field lists for both tables in the upper pane of the Select Query window.

- The relational algebra is another language used to manipulate relational databases.

- The SELECT command in the relational algebra selects only certain rows from a table.

- The PROJECT command in the relational algebra selects only certain columns from a table.

- The JOIN command in the relational algebra combines data from two tables based on common columns.

- The UNION command in the relational algebra forms the union of two tables.

- In order for the Union operation to make sense, the tables must be union-compatible.

- The INTERSECT command in the relational algebra forms the intersection of two tables.

- The SUBTRACT command in the relational algebra forms the difference of two tables.

- The PRODUCT command in the relational algebra forms the Cartesian product of two tables.

- The DIVISION command in the relational algebra forms the division of two tables.

KEY TERMS

attribute
calculated field

comparison operator
compound criteria

computed field	qualify
concatenation	query
criterion	Query-By-Example (QBE)
design grid	record
difference	relation
example	relational algebra
field	relational database
grouping	relational operator
intersection	repeating group
join	statistics
join column	tuple
natural join	union
null	union-compatible
outer join	unnormalized relation
primary key	

■ REVIEW QUESTIONS

1. Using the data for Premiere Products as shown in Figure 2.2, solve each of the following problems:

   a. Find the names of all the customers who have a credit limit of at least $1500.

   b. Give the order numbers of those orders placed by customer 124 on September 5, 2001.

   c. Give the part number, description, and on-hand value (units on hand × price) for each part in item class AP.

   d. Find the number and name of all customers whose last name is Nelson.

   e. Find out how many customers have a credit limit of $1000.

   f. Find the total of the balances for all the customers represented by sales rep 12.

   g. For each order, list the order number, order date, customer number, and customer name.

   h. For each order placed on September 5, 2001, list the order number, order date, customer number, and customer name.

   i. Find the number and name of all sales reps who represent any customer with a credit limit of $1000.

   j. For each order, list the order number, order date, customer number, customer name, along with the number and name of the sales rep who represents the customer.

2. Why are order lines in the Premiere Products database in a separate table rather than being part of the Orders table?

3. What is a relation?

4. What is a relational database?

5. What is an unnormalized relation? Is it a relation according to the definition of the word *relation*?

6. How is the term *attribute* used in the relational model? What is a more common name for it?

7. Describe the shorthand representation of the structure of a relational database. Illustrate this technique by representing the database for Henry's bookstores as shown in Chapter 1.

8. What does it mean to qualify the name of a field? How is this done?

9. What is a primary key? What is the primary key for each of the tables in Henry's database? (See Question 7.)

Questions 10 through 19 are based on the Premiere Products database (see Figure 2.2). In each case, indicate how you could use QBE to obtain the desired results.

10. List the number and name of all sales reps.

11. List the complete Customer table.

12. List the number and name of all customers represented by sales rep 03.

13. List the number and name of all customers who are represented by sales rep 03 and whose credit limit is $1000.

14. List the number and name of all customers who are represented by sales rep 03 or whose credit limit is $1000.

15. For each order, list the order number, order date, the number of the customer who placed the order, and the last name of the customer who placed the order.

16. List the number and name of all customers who are represented by Mary Jones.

17. Find out how many customers have a credit limit of $1000.

18. Find the total of the balances for all the customers represented by sales rep 12.

19. Give the part number, description, and on-hand value (units on hand × price) for each part in item class AP.

Questions 20 through 26 are also based on the Premiere Products database (see Figure 2.2). In each case, indicate how you could use the relational algebra to obtain the desired results.

20. List the number and name of all sales reps.

21. List all information from the part table concerning part BT04.

22. List the order number, order date, customer number, last name, and first name for each order.

23. List the order number, order date, customer number, and customer name for each order placed by any customer represented by the sales rep whose last name is Jones.

24. List the number and date of all orders that were either placed on 9/02/2001 or placed by a customer with a $1000 credit limit.

25. List the number and date of all orders that were placed on 9/02/2001 by a customer with a $1000 credit limit.

26. List the number and date of all orders that were placed on 9/02/2001 but not by a customer with a $1000 credit limit.

CHAPTER 3

The Relational Model 2: SQL

OBJECTIVES

- Introduce the SQL language.

- Discuss the use of simple and compound conditions in SQL.

- Present the use of computed fields in SQL.

- Examine the use of SQL built-in functions.

- Discuss the use of nested SQL queries.

- Examine grouping in SQL.

- Examine the way tables can be joined in SQL.

- Discuss the union operator in SQL.

Introduction

In this chapter, you will examine the language called **SQL (Structured Query Language)**. Like QBE, SQL provides users with a way of querying relational databases. However, in SQL, you must type **commands** to obtain the desired results, rather than filling in entries in a form on the screen, as you do in QBE.

Note: SQL contains commands to create tables, to update tables, and to retrieve data from tables. The commands that are used to retrieve data are usually referred to as **queries**.

SQL was developed under the name SEQUEL at the IBM San Jose research facilities in the mid-1970s. SQL was the data manipulation language for IBM's prototype relational model DBMS, System R. In 1980, it was renamed SQL (and still pronounced "sequel") to avoid confusion with an unrelated hardware product also called SEQUEL. SQL is used as the data manipulation language for IBM's current production offerings in the relational DBMS arena, SQL/DS and DB2. Most relational DBMSs use a version of SQL as a data manipulation language. SQL is the standard language for relational database manipulation.

You will begin by looking at the way databases are created in SQL. You will then examine simple retrieval as well as compound conditions. You will next examine the use of computed fields in SQL and also how to sort data in SQL. Following this, you will see how to use built-in functions, nesting queries, and grouping. After this, you will see how to join tables in SQL and how to use the union operator. The chapter ends with a discussion of how SQL can be used to update data in a database.

Database Creation

The SQL command CREATE TABLE is used to describe the layout of a table. The word TABLE is followed by the name of the table to be created and then by the names and data types of the columns that comprise the table. The rules for naming tables and columns (also called fields) vary slightly from one version of SQL to another. If you have any doubts about the validity of any of the names you have chosen, you should consult a manual.

Typical restrictions are:

1. The table or column name can be no longer than 18 characters.

2. The name must start with a letter.

3. The name can contain letters, numbers, and underscores (_).

4. The name cannot contain spaces.

For each field, you must enter the type of data (either character or numerical) that can be stored in the field. While the actual data types will vary somewhat from one implementation of SQL to another, the following are the types that are often encountered:

1. **INTEGER**. Integers, or numbers, without a decimal part. Range is -2,147,483,648 to 2,147,483,647. The contents of integer fields can be used for arithmetic.

2. **SMALLINT**. Like INTEGER, but does not occupy as much space. Range is –32,768 to 32,767. This is a better choice than INTEGER if you are certain that numbers will be within the indicated range. The contents of SMALLINT fields can be used for arithmetic.

3. **DECIMAL (p,q)**. Decimal number p digits long with q of these being decimal places. For example, DECIMAL (5,2) represents a number with three places to the left of the decimal and two to the right. The contents of decimal fields can be used for arithmetic.

4. **CHAR (n)**. Character string n characters long. This type should be used for fields that contain letters or any other special characters. It is also often used for fields that contain numbers, but will not be used for arithmetic. Since neither sales rep numbers nor customer numbers will be used in any arithmetic operations, for example, they are both assigned CHAR as the data type.

5. **DATE**. Dates in the form DD-MON-YYYY or MM/DD/YYYY. For example, May 12, 2001 could be stored as 12-MAY-2001 or 5/12/2001.

EXAMPLE 1   Describe the layout of the Sales Rep table to the DBMS using SQL.

The CREATE TABLE command for the Sales Rep table is:

```
CREATE TABLE SALES_REP
    (SALES_REP_NUMBER          CHAR(2),
    LAST_NAME                  CHAR(15),
    FIRST_NAME                 CHAR(15),
    STREET                     CHAR(15),
    CITY                       CHAR(15),
    STATE                      CHAR(2),
    ZIP_CODE                   CHAR(5),
    COMMISSION                 DECIMAL(7,2),
    RATE                       DECIMAL(3,2) )
```

In this SQL command, which uses the data definition features of SQL, you are describing a table that will be called Sales Rep. It contains nine fields (columns): Sales Rep Number, Last Name, First Name, Street, City, State, Zip Code, Commission, and Rate. Sales Rep Number is a character field, two positions in length. Last Name is a character field of 15 positions in length. Commission is numeric and is seven digits long, including two decimal places. Similarly, Rate is three digits long, and two of those are decimal places.

Note: Commands are free-format in SQL. No rule says that a particular word must begin in a particular position on the line. The previous SQL command could have been written:

```
CREATE TABLE SALES_REP (SALES_REP_NUMBER CHAR(2), LAST_NAME CHAR(15),
FIRST_NAME CHAR(15), STREET CHAR(15), CITY CHAR(15), STATE CHAR(2),
ZIP_CODE CHAR(5), COMMISSION DECIMAL(7,2), RATE DECIMAL(3,2) )
```

The manner in which it was actually written simply makes the command more readable. In general, you should strive for similar readability when you write SQL commands.

Note: Just as with QBE, Microsoft Access will be the vehicle for illustrating SQL in this book. Unlike some other versions of SQL, Microsoft Access does allow spaces within field names. There is a restriction, however, to the way such names are used in SQL commands. When a name containing a space appears in SQL, it must be enclosed in square brackets. For example, Credit Limit must appear as [Credit Limit] because the name includes a space. On the other hand, Balance does not need to be enclosed in square brackets because its name does not include a space.

■ Simple Retrieval

The basic form of a SQL expression is quite simple: SELECT-FROM-WHERE. After SELECT, you list those fields you wish to display. The fields will appear in the results in the order in which they are listed in the expression. After FROM, you list the table or tables involved in the query. Finally, after the WHERE, you list any conditions, such as the fact that the credit limit must be $1000, that apply to the data you want to retrieve.

There are no special format rules in SQL. In this text, you place the word FROM on a new line indented slightly, then place the word WHERE (when it is used) on the next line indented the same amount. This makes the commands more readable. You can indent using either spaces or tabs.

Note: In the following examples, words that are part of the SQL language are entered in uppercase and others are entered in a combination of uppercase and lowercase. The commands are extended over multiple lines and indented. This command formatting is done strictly to improve readability. Neither are required by SQL.

EXAMPLE 2 : List the number, last name, first name, and balance of all customers.

Since you want all customers listed, there is no need for the WHERE clause (you have no restrictions). The query and results are shown in Figure 3.1.

FIGURE 3.1
(a and b)
. . . .
SQL query to find
customer data

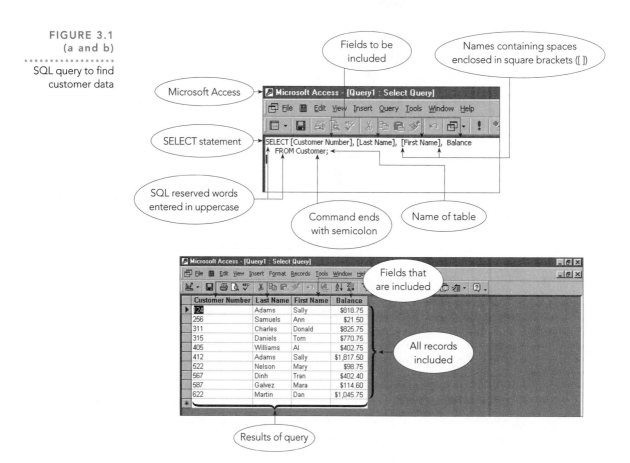

Results of query

60

EXAMPLE 3   List the complete Part table.

You could certainly use the same approach as in Example 2, that is, list each field in the Part table after the word SELECT. However, there is a shortcut. Instead of listing all the field names after SELECT, you can use the "*" symbol. This indicates that you want all fields listed in the order in which you described them to the system during data definition. If you want all the fields, but in a different order, you would have to type the names of the fields in the order you want them to appear. In this case, assuming the default order is appropriate, the query and results would be as shown in Figure 3.2.

FIGURE 3.2
(a and b)
....
SQL query to list
Part table

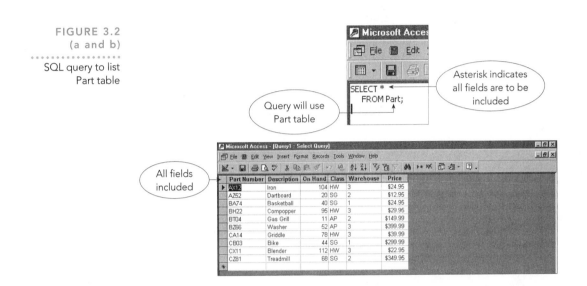

EXAMPLE 4   What is the name (last and first) of any customer with a $1000 credit limit?

You include the following condition in the WHERE clause to restrict the output of the query to those customers with the appropriate credit limit:

```
WHERE Credit Limit = 1000
```

The query and results are shown in Figure 3.3.

The condition in the preceding WHERE clause is called a simple condition. A **simple condition** has the form: field name, comparison operator, then either another field name or a value. The possible comparison operators are shown in Table 3.1. Note that there are two different versions for "not equal to" (<> and !=). You must use the one that is right for your particular implementation of SQL. (If you use the wrong one, your system will instantly let you know. Simply use the other.)

In Example 4, the WHERE clause compares a numeric field, Credit Limit, to a number, 1000. In that command, you simply use the number 1000. No special action has to be taken. When the query involves a character field, such as Customer Number, or Last Name, the value to which the field is being compared must be surrounded by single quotation marks, as illustrated in the next two examples.

FIGURE 3.3
(a and b)
....
SQL query with a
WHERE condition

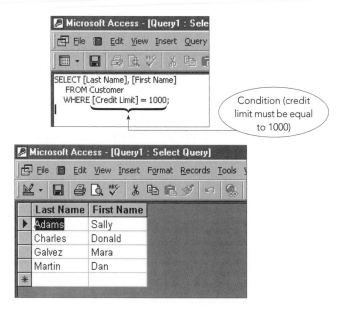

TABLE 3.1
....
Comparison
operators

Comparison Operator	Meaning
=	Equal to
<	Less than
>	Greater than
<=	Less than or equal to
>=	Greater than or equal to
<>	Not equal to (used by most implementations of SQL)
!=	Not equal to (used by some implementations of SQL)

EXAMPLE 5 ⋮ Find the name (last and first) for customer 124.

The query and results are shown in Figure 3.4. Notice that there are quotation marks around the 124, since Customer Number is a text (CHAR) field. Notice also that there is only a single record in the answer. Since the Customer Number field is the primary key for the Customer table, there can be only one customer 124.

EXAMPLE 6 ⋮ Find the customer number for any customer whose last name is Adams.

The query and results are shown in Figure 3.5. Notice that there are multiple records in the answer to the query.

FIGURE 3.4
(a and b)
••••••••••••••••••
SQL query to find
customer 124's
name

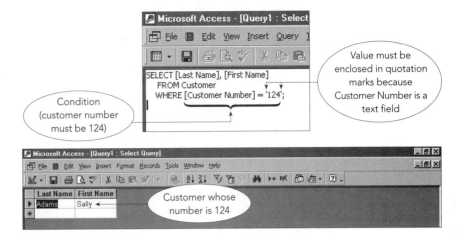

Condition
(customer number
must be 124)

Value must be
enclosed in quotation
marks because
Customer Number is a
text field

Customer whose
number is 124

FIGURE 3.5
(a and b)
••••••••••••••••••
SQL query to find
customer numbers
for customers with
the last name
"Adams"

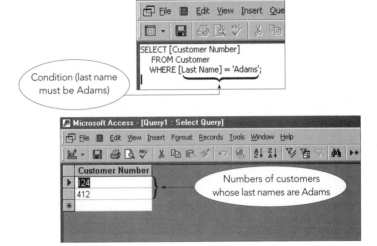

Condition (last name
must be Adams)

Numbers of customers
whose last names are Adams

■ Compound Conditions

The conditions you've seen so far are called simple conditions. The next examples require compound conditions. **Compound conditions** are formed by connecting two or more simple conditions using AND or OR. You can also precede a single condition with the word NOT.

When simple conditions are connected by the word AND, *all* the simple conditions must be true in order for the compound condition to be true. When simple conditions are connected by the word OR, the compound condition will be true whenever *any* of the simple conditions are true. Preceding a condition by NOT reverses the truth or falsity of the original condition. That is, if the original condition is true, the new condition will be false; if the original condition is false, the new one will be true.

EXAMPLE 7 ⋮ List the descriptions of all parts in warehouse 3 that have more than 100 units on hand.

In this example, you want those parts for which *both* the warehouse number is equal to 3 *and* the number of units on hand is greater than 100. Thus, you form a compound condition using the word AND, as shown in Figure 3.6a. The query results are shown in Figure 3.6b.

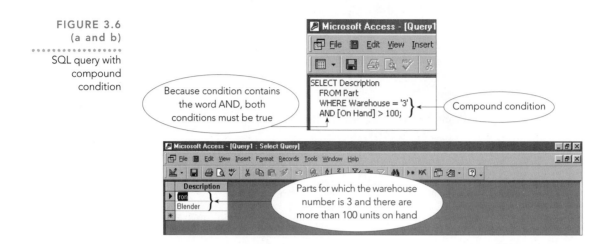

As you would expect, you form compound conditions involving OR in the same fashion. Simply use the word OR instead of the word AND. In that case, the results would contain those records that satisfied either condition.

EXAMPLE 8 ⋮ List the descriptions of all parts that are not in warehouse 3.

For this example, you could use a simple condition with the condition operator "not equal to." As an alternative, you could use "equals" in the condition, but precede the whole condition with the word NOT, as shown in Figure 3.7a. The query results are shown in Figure 3.7b.

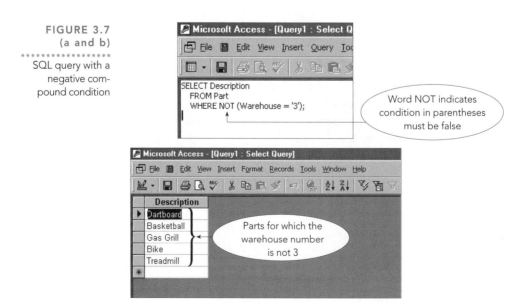

■ Computed Fields

Just as with QBE, you can include fields in queries that are not in the database, but that can be computed from fields that are. Such a field is called a **computed** or **calculated field**. Such computations can involve addition (+), subtraction (-), multiplication (*), or division (/). The query in Example 9, for example, uses subtraction.

EXAMPLE 9   Find the available credit for all customers who have a credit limit of at least $1500.

There is no field for available credit in the database. It is, however, computable from two fields that are present, Credit Limit and Balance (Available Credit = Credit Limit - Balance). The query shown in Figure 3.8a includes this computation. Notice the word AS after the computation followed by [Available Credit]. This is how you assign a name to the newly computed field. As you see in the results, shown in Figure 3.8b, the column heading for these computed amounts is precisely the name you specified after the word AS.

FIGURE 3.8
(a and b)
· ·
Computational
query

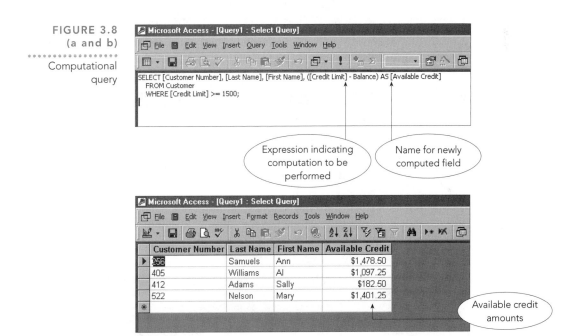

The parentheses around the calculation ([Credit Limit] - Balance) are not essential but improve readability.

■ Sorting

Recall that the order of rows in a table is considered to be irrelevant. From a practical standpoint, this means that in querying a relational database, there are no guarantees concerning the order in which the results will be displayed. The results may be in the order in which the data were originally entered, but even this is not certain. Thus, if the order in which the data are displayed is important, you should *specifically* request that the results be displayed in the desired order. In SQL, this is done with the ORDER BY clause, as shown in Example 10.

EXAMPLE 10   List the number, last name, first name, credit limit, and balance of all customers. Order the customers by balance within credit limit. (This means to order the customers by credit limit. It also means that within each group of customers that have a common credit limit, the customers are to be ordered by balance.)

The field on which data are to be sorted is called a **sort key**, or simply a **key**. If the data are to be sorted on two fields, the more important key is called the **major sort key** (also referred to as the **primary sort key**) and the less important key is called the **minor sort key** (also referred to as the **secondary sort key**). In this case, since the output is to be ordered (sorted) by balance within credit limit, the Credit Limit field is the major sort key and the Balance field is the minor sort key. To sort the output, you include the words ORDER BY in the SQL query, followed by the sort key. If there are two sort keys, as in this example, the major sort key is listed first. The appropriate query is shown in Figure 3.9a. The query results are shown in Figure 3.9b.

FIGURE 3.9
(a and b)
....
SQL query to list customer credit limit and balance information, sorted in order of balance within limit

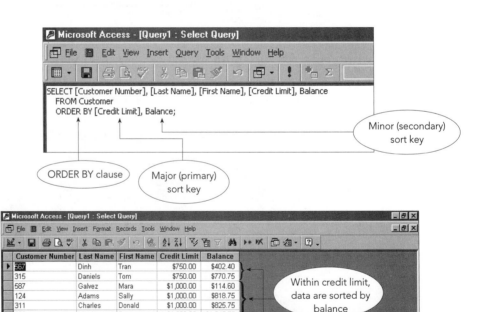

You can specify that the output is to be sorted in descending (high-to-low) order by following the sort key with the letters DESC. To specify that credit limits are to appear in descending order, for example, the ORDER BY clause would read:

```
ORDER BY [Credit Limit] DESC, Balance
```

■ Built-In Functions

SQL has **built-in functions** (sometimes called **aggregate functions**) to calculate the number of entries, the sum or average of all the entries in a given column, and the largest or smallest of the entries in a given column. In SQL, these functions are called COUNT, SUM, AVG, MAX, and MIN, respectively.

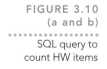 XAMPLE 11 : How many parts are in item class HW?

In this query, you want to know the number of rows in the output table that results from selecting only those parts that are in item class HW. You could count the number of part numbers in this table, or the number of descriptions, or the number of entries in any other field. It doesn't make any difference. Rather than requiring you to pick one of these arbitrarily, some versions of SQL allow you to use the * symbol. In such a version, you can use the query shown in Figure 3.10a. The query results are shown in Figure 3.10b.

FIGURE 3.10
(a and b)
·····················
SQL query to
count HW items

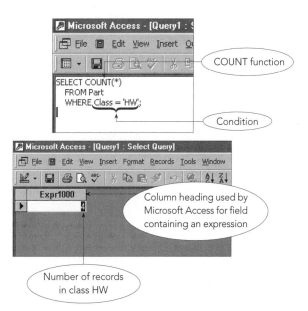

If the * symbol is not allowed, you formulate the query as:

```
SELECT COUNT([Part Number])
    FROM Part
    WHERE Class = 'HW'
```

EXAMPLE 12 : Find the number of customers and the total of their balances.

The only differences between COUNT and SUM — other than the obvious fact that they are computing different statistics — are that in the case of SUM, you *must* specify the field for which you want a total; and the field must be numeric. (It would be impossible to calculate a sum of names or addresses.) This query is shown in Figure 3.11a. The query results are shown in Figure 3.11b.

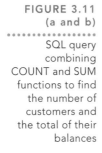

FIGURE 3.11
(a and b)
··················
SQL query
combining
COUNT and SUM
functions to find
the number of
customers and
the total of their
balances

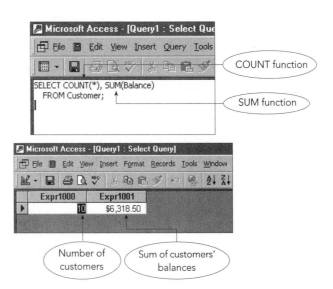

The use of AVG, MAX, and MIN is similar to SUM. The only difference is that a different statistic is calculated.

Just as with computed fields, you can use the word AS to assign names to these computations. If you want the count of customers to be called Customer Count and the sum of the balances to be called Balance Total, for example, the command is:

```
SELECT COUNT(*) AS [Customer Count], SUM(Balance) AS [Balance Total]
    FROM Customer
```

■ Nesting Queries

It is possible to place one query inside another. The inner query is called a subquery. The subquery is evaluated first. Once the subquery has been evaluated, the outer query can be evaluated. The following example illustrates the process.

EXAMPLE 13   List the customer number, last name, and first name of all customers of Premiere Products who have a credit limit that is equal to the largest credit limit awarded to any customer of sales rep 06.

You could do this in two steps. You could first find the largest credit limit awarded to any customer of sales rep 06, as in Figure 3.12.

FIGURE 3.12
(a and b)

Step 1 of nested query to find customers with credit limit equal to largest credit limit for any of sales rep 06's customers

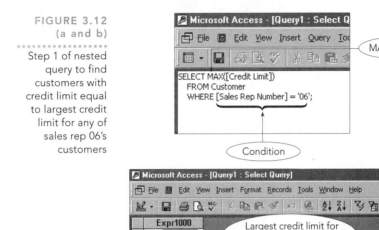

After viewing the answer (1500), you could use a second query, shown in Figure 3.13a, to get the final answer shown in Figure 3.13b.

FIGURE 3.13
(a and b)

Step 2 of nested query

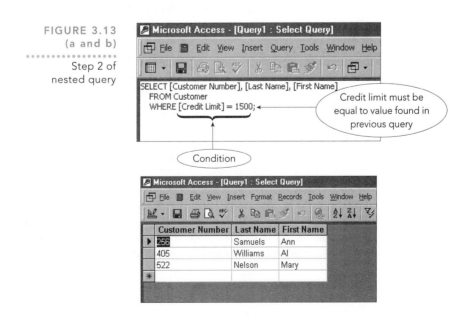

You could actually accomplish this in one step, however, by using subqueries. In this case, the query is the one shown in Figure 3.14a. The portion in parentheses is the subquery. This subquery is evaluated first, producing a temporary table. In this case, the table has one field, MAX(Credit Limit), and a single row containing the number 1500.

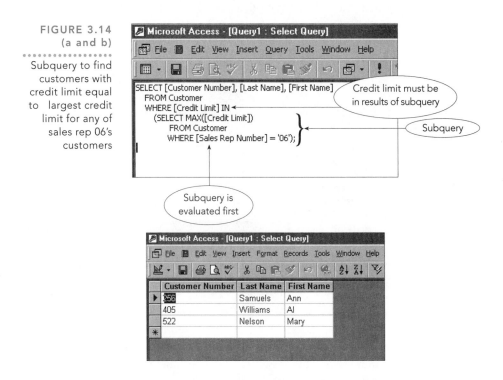

FIGURE 3.14
(a and b)
· · · · · · · · · · · · · · · · · · · ·
Subquery to find
customers with
credit limit equal
to largest credit
limit for any of
sales rep 06's
customers

The outer query can now be evaluated. The query uses the word IN, which indicates that the value must be in the results of the subquery. In this example, the outer query will only obtain the names of customers whose credit limit is *in* the result produced by the subquery. Since that table contains only the maximum credit limit for the customers of sales rep 06, you obtain the desired list of customers, as shown in Figure 3.14b. Incidentally, since the subquery in this case produces a table containing only a single value (the maximum credit limit), this query could have been formulated in another way:

```
SELECT Customer Number, Last Name, First Name
     FROM Customer
     WHERE Credit Limit =
          (SELECT MAX(Credit Limit)
               FROM Customer
               WHERE Sales Rep Number = '06')
```

In this formulation you are asking for those customers whose credit limit *is equal to* the one credit limit obtained by the subquery. In general, unless you know that the subquery *must* produce a single value, the prior formulation using IN would be the one to use.

■ Grouping

Grouping means creating groups of records that share some common characteristic. In grouping customers by sales rep number, for example, the customers of sales rep 03 form one group, the customers of sales rep 06 form a second, and the customers of sales rep 12 form a third.

In the following example, order lines must be grouped by order number to perform the necessary computations.

EXAMPLE 14 : List the order total for each order.

For each order line, you need to calculate the extension (the product of the number of units ordered and the quoted price). To calculate the order total for an order, you add the extensions of each of the order lines on the order. This query thus involves the sum of calculated fields (Number Ordered times Quoted Price). However, there is a little more to it than just including SUM (Number Ordered times Quoted Price) in the query. This only gives the grand total over all order lines; the grand total is not broken down by order.

To get individual totals you use the GROUP BY clause. In this case, GROUP BY Order Number causes the order lines for each order to be "grouped together," that is, all order lines with the same order number form a group. Any statistics, such as totals, requested in the SELECT clause are calculated for each of these groups. It is important to note that the GROUP BY clause does not imply that the information will be sorted. To produce the report in a particular order, you must use the ORDER BY clause. Assuming that the report is to be ordered by order number, you would use the query shown in Figure 3.15a. The query results are shown in Figure 3.15b.

FIGURE 3.15
(a and b)
. . . .
SQL query
combining
GROUP BY and
ORDER BY
clauses

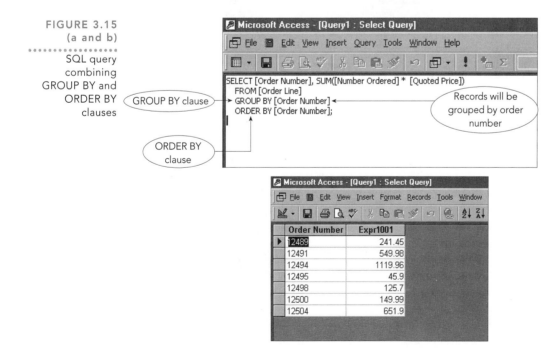

When rows are grouped, one line of output is produced for each group. The only things that may be displayed in the grouped results are statistics calculated for the group or fields whose values are the same for all rows in a group.

QUESTION   Would it be appropriate to display the order number?

ANSWER   Yes, since the output is grouped by order number; thus, the order number on one row in a group must be the same as the order number on any other row in the group.

QUESTION   Would it be appropriate to display a part number?

ANSWER   No, since the part number will vary from one row in a group to another. SQL cannot determine which part number to display for the group.

EXAMPLE 15   List the order total for those orders amounting to more than $200.

This example is similar to the previous one. The only difference is that there is a restriction: you only want to display totals for those orders that amount to more than $200. This restriction does not apply to individual rows, but rather to *groups*. Since the WHERE clause applies only to rows, it is not the appropriate clause to accomplish the kind of selection you have here. Fortunately, there is a clause that is to groups what WHERE is to rows. It is the HAVING clause, as shown in Figure 3.16.

FIGURE 3.16
(a and b)

SQL query using HAVING clause to impart conditions on groups

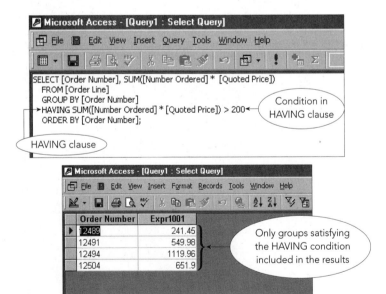

In this case, the row created for a group is displayed because the sum calculated for the group is larger than $200.

72

■ Joining Tables

Many queries require data from more than one table. Just as with QBE and the relational algebra, it is necessary to be able to join tables, that is, to find rows in two tables that have identical values in matching fields. In SQL, this is accomplished through appropriate conditions in the WHERE clause.

EXAMPLE 16 : List the number, last name, and first name of each customer together with the number, last name, and first name of the sales rep who represents the customer.

Since the numbers and names of customers are in the Customer table, while the numbers and names of sales reps are in the Sales Rep table, you need to access both tables in your SQL query:

1. In the SELECT clause, you indicate all the fields you want to display.

2. In the FROM clause, you list all the tables involved in the query.

3. In the WHERE clause, you give the condition that restricts the data to be retrieved to only those rows from the two tables that match; that is, to the rows that have common values in matching fields.

You have a problem, however; the matching fields are both called Sales Rep Number. There is a field in Sales Rep called Sales Rep Number, as well as a field in Customer called Sales Rep Number. In this case, if you merely mention Sales Rep Number, it will not be clear which one you mean. Just as in the relational algebra, it is necessary to qualify Sales Rep Number, or to specify the field to which you are referring. You do this by preceding the name of the field with the name of the table followed by a period. The Sales Rep Number field in the Sales Rep table is Sales Rep.Sales Rep Number. The Sales Rep Number field in the Customer table is Customer.Sales Rep Number. You must also qualify the Last Name and First Name fields in a similar manner. The query and its results are shown in Figure 3.17.

Whenever there is potential ambiguity, you *must* qualify the fields involved. It is permissible to qualify other fields as well, even if there is no confusion. Some people prefer to qualify all fields, and this is certainly not a bad approach. In this text, you will only qualify fields when it is necessary to do so.

FIGURE 3.17
(a and b)
....
SQL query to join
data from two
different tables

SELECT [Customer Number], Customer.[Last Name], Customer.[First Name], [Sales Rep].[Sales Rep Number],
    [Sales Rep].[Last Name], [Sales Rep].[First Name]
FROM Customer, [Sales Rep] ◄
WHERE Customer.[Sales Rep Number] = [Sales Rep].[Sales Rep Number];

Field names are qualified

Condition to relate the tables

Two tables (Customer and Sales Rep) included in query

Customer Number	Customer.L	Customer.F	Sales Rep Number	Sales Rep.L	Sales Rep.F
124	Adams	Sally	03	Jones	Mary
256	Samuels	Ann	06	Smith	William
311	Charles	Donald	12	Diaz	Miguel
315	Daniels	Tom	06	Smith	William
405	Williams	Al	12	Diaz	Miguel
412	Adams	Sally	03	Jones	Mary
522	Nelson	Mary	12	Diaz	Miguel
567	Dinh	Tran	06	Smith	William
587	Galvez	Mara	06	Smith	William
622	Martin	Dan	03	Jones	Mary

Data from Customer table

Data from Sales Rep table

EXAMPLE 17   List the number, last name, and first name of each customer whose credit limit is $1000, together with the number, last name, and first name of the sales rep who represents the customer.

    In Example 16, the condition in the WHERE clause serves only to relate a customer to a sales rep. While relating a customer to a sales rep is essential in the latter example as well, you also want to restrict the output to only those customers whose credit limit is $1000. This is accomplished by including a compound condition, as shown in Figure 3.18a. The query results are shown in Figure 3.18b.

FIGURE 3.18
(a and b)
....
Join query with a
compound
condition

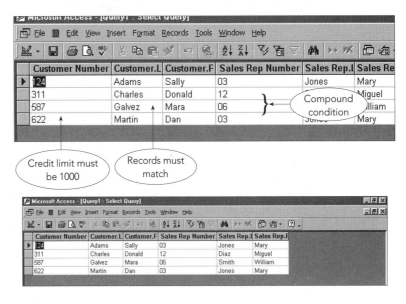

Customer Number	Customer.L	Customer.F	Sales Rep Number	Sales Rep.L	Sales Re
124	Adams	Sally	03	Jones	Mary
311	Charles	Donald	12		Miguel
587	Galvez	Mara	06		lliam
622	Martin	Dan	03		Mary

Compound condition

Credit limit must be 1000

Records must match

Customer Number	Customer.L	Customer.F	Sales Rep Number	Sales Rep.L	Sales Rep.F
124	Adams	Sally	03	Jones	Mary
311	Charles	Donald	12	Diaz	Miguel
587	Galvez	Mara	06	Smith	William
622	Martin	Dan	03	Jones	Mary

Union

SQL supports the union operation. The **union** of two tables is a table containing all rows that are in either the first table, the second, or both. There is an obvious restriction on union. It does not make sense, for example, to talk about the union of the Customer table and the Orders table. The two tables *must* have the same structure. The formal term is union-compatible. Two tables are **union-compatible** if they have the same number of fields and if their corresponding fields represent the same type of data. If, for example, the first field in one table contains customer numbers, the first field in the other table should also contain customer numbers.

EXAMPLE 18   List the number, last name, and first name of all customers who are either represented by sales rep 12, or who currently have orders on file, or both.

You can create a table containing the number, last name, and first name of all customers who are represented by sales rep 12 by selecting customer numbers, last names, and first names from the Customer table in which the sales rep number is 12. Then you can create another table containing the number, last name, and first name of all customers who currently have orders on file by creating a join of the customer table and the order table. The two tables created by this process have the same structure: three fields, a customer number, a last name, and a first name. Since they are union-compatible, it is legitimate to take the union of these two tables. This is accomplished in SQL in the manner shown in Figure 3.19.

FIGURE 3.19
(a and b)
....
UNION operation
to combine into
one table infor-
mation on cus-
tomers who are
represented by
sales rep 12 or
who have orders

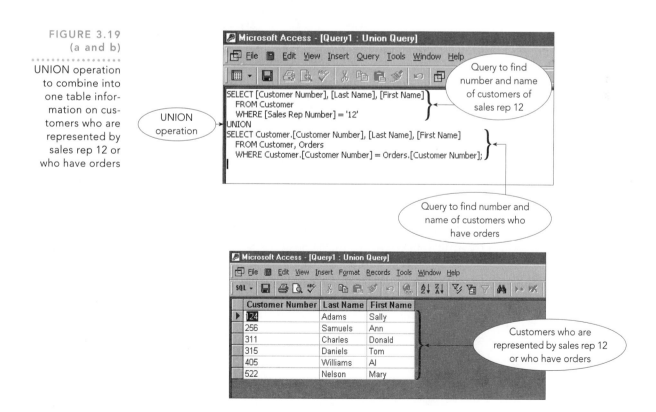

If an implementation truly supports the union operation, it will remove any duplicate rows (i.e., any customers who are represented by sales rep 12 *and* who currently have orders on file will not appear twice). Some implementations of SQL have a "union" operation but will not remove such duplicates.

▌ Updating Tables

There are more uses to SQL than simply retrieving data from a database. SQL has several other capabilities, including the ability to update a database, as demonstrated in the following examples.

EXAMPLE 19 Change the last name of customer 256 to Jones.

The SQL command to make changes to existing data is the UPDATE command. After the word UPDATE, you indicate the table to be updated. After the word SET, you indicate the field to be changed, followed by an equal sign and the new value. Finally, you can place a condition after the word WHERE, in which case only the records that satisfy the condition will be changed. The SQL command for this example is shown in Figure 3.20.

FIGURE 3.20
· · · · · · · · · · · · · · · · · ·
UPDATE
command to
change data

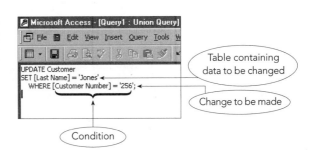

EXAMPLE 20 Add a new sales rep to the Sales Rep table. Her number is 14. Her name is Ann Crane and her address is 123 River, Ada, MI, 42411. So far, she has not earned any commission. Her commission rate is 5 percent (0.05).

Addition of new data is accomplished through the INSERT command. After the words INSERT INTO, you list the name of the table, followed by the word VALUES. You then list the values for each of the columns in parentheses as shown in Figure 3.21. Character values must be enclosed between quotation marks.

FIGURE 3.21
. . . .
Adding new data
using the INSERT
command

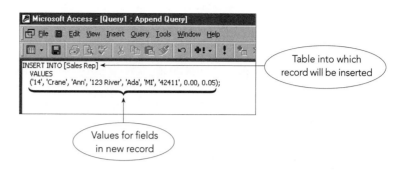

Table into which
record will be inserted

Values for fields
in new record

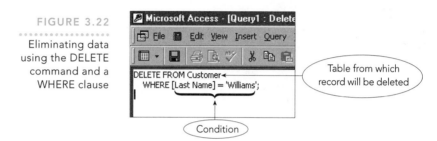

EXAMPLE 21 ⋮ Delete from the database the customer whose last name is Williams.

To delete data from the database, use the DELETE command, which consists of the words DELETE FROM followed by the name of the table. A WHERE clause is used to specify a condition. Any records satisfying the condition will be deleted. The DELETE command for this example is shown in Figure 3.22.

FIGURE 3.22
. . . .
Eliminating data
using the DELETE
command and a
WHERE clause

Table from which
record will be deleted

Condition

Note that this type of deletion can be dangerous. If there happens to be another customer whose last name is also Williams, this customer would be deleted in the process as well. The safest type of deletion occurs when the condition involves the primary key (for example, deleting customer 124). In such a case, since the primary key is unique, you are certain you will not accidentally delete other rows in the table.

■ SUMMARY

- SQL (Structured Query Language) is a language that is used to manipulate relational databases.
- The basic form of a SQL query is SELECT-FROM-WHERE.
- The CREATE command is used to describe the layout of a table.
- In SELECT commands, fields are listed after SELECT, tables are listed after FROM, and conditions are listed after WHERE.
- In conditions, character values must be enclosed between quotation marks.
- Compound conditions are formed by combining simple conditions with AND or OR.
- Sorting is accomplished through the ORDER BY clause. The field on which the records are sorted is called the sort key. If the data are sorted on more than one field, the more important field is called the major sort key, or primary sort key. The less important field is called the minor sort key, or secondary sort key.
- SQL has the built-in (also called aggregate) functions COUNT, SUM, AVG, MAX, and MIN.
- Joining tables is accomplished in SQL through the use of a condition that relates matching rows in the tables to be joined.
- The INSERT command is used to add a new row to a table.
- The UPDATE command is used to change existing data.
- The DELETE command is used to delete records.

■ KEY TERMS

aggregate functions
built-in functions
calculated field
CHAR
command
compound condition
computed field
DATE
DECIMAL
grouping
INTEGER
join
key
major sort key

minor sort key
primary sort key
qualify
query
secondary sort key
simple condition
SMALLINT
sort key
SQL
structured Query Language
subquery
union
union-compatible

▪ REVIEW QUESTIONS

1. Describe the process of creating a table in SQL. Describe the various data types.

2. What is the purpose of the WHERE clause in SQL?

3. What is a compound condition in SQL? When is it true? How do you enter one in a SQL query?

4. How do you sort data in SQL? If there is more than one sort key, how do you indicate which one is the major key?

5. How do you use the SQL built-in functions?

6. When you group in SQL, are there any restrictions on the items that may be listed in the SELECT clause?

7. How do you join tables in SQL?

8. How can you take the union of two tables in SQL? What must be true of the two tables?

9. Describe the three update commands in SQL.

Questions 10 through 25 are based on the Premiere Products database (see Figure 2.2). In each case, write the SQL query and the results that would be produced for each of the following:

10. Find the part number and description of all parts.

11. List the complete sales rep table.

12. Find the names of all the customers who have a credit limit of at least $1500.

13. List the order numbers of those orders placed by customer 124 on September 5, 2001.

14. List the part number, description, and on-hand value (units on hand * price) for each part in item class AP. (Remember that the AP must be enclosed in quotation marks.)

15. Find the number and name of all customers whose last name is Nelson.

16. List all details about parts. The output should be sorted by unit price.

17. Find out how many customers have a credit limit of $1000.

18. Find the total of the balances for all the customers represented by sales rep 12.

19. For each order, list the order number, the order date, the customer number, and the customer name.

20. For each order placed on September 5, 2001, list the order number, the order date, the customer number, and the customer name.

21. Find the number and name of all sales reps who represent any customer with a credit limit of $1000.

22. For each order, list the order number, the order date, the customer number, the customer name, along with the number and name of the sales rep who represents the customer.

23. Change the description of part BT04 to Gas Stove.

24. Add order 12600 to the database. The date of the order is September 6, 2001. The order was placed by customer 311.

25. Delete all customers whose balances are under $100 and who are represented by sales rep 12.

CHAPTER 4

The Relational Model 3: Advanced Topics

OBJECTIVES

- Discuss views: what they are, how they are described, and how they are used.

- Discuss the use of indexes for improving performance.

- Examine the security features of a DBMS.

- Explain entity and referential integrity.

- Discuss the manner in which the structure of a relational database can be changed.

- Define the catalog and explain its use.

- Discuss the integrity support within SQL.

Introduction

In the last chapter, you examined data definition and manipulation within the relational model. In this chapter, you will investigate some other aspects of the relational model. First, you will look at views, which represent a way of giving each user his or her own picture of what the database looks like. In the following section, you will look at indexes and their use in improving performance. Next, you will look at the features of a DBMS that relate to security. Then, two critical integrity rules are presented. The next section covers one of the real strengths of the relational model, the ease with which a database structure can be changed. After that, you will examine the catalog that is provided by many relational DBMSs to give users access to information about the structure of a database. Finally, you will examine additional areas of integrity support provided in SQL.

Note: In the discussion that follows, SQL is the mechanism for illustrating the concepts. It should be emphasized, however, that many systems that do not support the SQL language still provide the features you will encounter. Although the manner in which this is accomplished varies slightly from one system to another, the basic concepts are the same, and it should be easy for you to transfer the knowledge you gain in this chapter to a non-SQL system.

Note: Just as in the previous chapter, the Microsoft Access style will be used for illustrating SQL commands. That is, spaces within names will be allowed, but names that contain spaces will be enclosed in square brackets (for example, [Credit Limit]). Recall that in a system that does not allow spaces, the names contain underscores instead (for example, CREDIT_LIMIT) and are not enclosed in square brackets. You should also keep in mind that some of the SQL commands illustrated in this chapter are handled differently in Access.

Views

Most relational mainframe DBMSs and many of the PC-based DBMSs support the concept of a view. A view is basically a snapshot of certain data in the database at a given moment in time, which can be used in reports, charts, etc. In many cases, a user can access the data in a database via a view. Because a view is usually much less involved than the full database, its use can represent a great simplification. Views also provide a measure of security, because omitting sensitive tables or columns from a view will render them unavailable to anyone who is accessing the database via the view.

To illustrate the idea of a view, let's suppose that Juan is interested in the part number, part description, units on hand, and unit price of those Premiere Products parts that are in item class HW. He is not interested in any of the other columns in the Part table. Nor is he interested in any of the rows that correspond to parts in other item classes. Life would certainly be simpler for Juan if the other rows and columns were not even present. While you cannot change the structure of the Part table and omit some of its rows just for Juan, you can do the next best thing. You can provide him a view that consists of precisely the rows and columns in which he is interested. Using SQL, you do this as follows:

```
CREATE VIEW Housewares AS
    SELECT [Part Number], [Part Description], [On Hand],
        Price
        FROM Part
        WHERE Class = 'HW'
```

The SELECT command, which is called the **defining query**, indicates precisely what is to be included in the view. Notice that it is exactly what Juan wants. Conceptually, given the current data in the Premiere Products database, this view will contain the data shown in Figure 4.1. The data do not really exist in this form, however, nor will they *ever* exist in this form. It is tempting to think that when this view is used, the query is executed and will produce some sort of temporary table, called Housewares, which Juan could then access. This is *not* what happens.

FIGURE 4.1

Housewares view

Housewares

Part Number	Part Description	On Hand	Price
AX12	Iron	104	$24.95
BH22	Cornpopper	95	$24.95
CA14	Griddle	78	$39.99
CX11	Blender	112	$22.95

Instead, the query acts as a sort of window into the database (see Figure 4.2). As far as Juan is concerned, the whole database is just the darker shaded portion. Any change that affects the darker shaded portion of the Part table is seen by Juan. But he is unaware of any changes that affect any other parts of the database.

FIGURE 4.2

Premiere Products
sample data

Sales Rep

Sales Rep Number	Last Name	First Name	Street	City	State	Zip Code	Commission	Rate
03	Jones	Mary	123 Main	Grant	MI	49219	2150.00	.05
06	Smith	William	102 Raymond	Ada	MI	49441	4912.50	.07
12	Diaz	Miguel	419 Harper	Lansing	MI	49224	2150.00	.05

Customer

Customer Number	Last Name	First Name	Street	City	State	Zip Code	Balance	Credit Limit	Sales Rep Number
124	Adams	Sally	481 Oak	Lansing	MI	49224	$818.75	$1000	03
256	Samuels	Ann	215 Pete	Grant	MI	49219	$21.50	$1500	06
311	Charles	Don	48 College	Ira	MI	49034	$825.75	$1000	12
315	Daniels	Tom	914 Cherry	Kent	MI	48391	$770.75	$750	06
405	Williams	Al	519 Watson	Grant	MI	49219	$402.75	$1500	12
412	Adams	Sally	16 Elm	Lansing	MI	49224	$1817.50	$2000	03
522	Nelson	Mary	108 Pine	Ada	MI	49441	$98.75	$1500	12
567	Dinh	Tran	808 Ridge	Harper	MI	48421	$402.40	$750	06
587	Galvez	Mara	512 Pine	Ada	MI	49441	$114.60	$1000	06
622	Martin	Dan	419 Chip	Grant	MI	49219	$1045.75	$1000	03

Orders

Order Number	Order Date	Customer Number
12489	9/02/2001	124
12491	9/02/2001	311
12494	9/04/2001	315
12495	9/04/2001	256
12498	9/05/2001	522
12500	9/05/2001	124
12504	9/05/2001	522

Order Line

Order Number	Part Number	Number Ordered	Quoted Price
12489	AX12	11	$14.95
12491	BT04	1	$149.99
12491	BZ66	1	$399.99
12494	CB03	4	$279.99
12495	CX11	2	$22.95
12498	AZ52	2	$12.95
12498	BA74	4	$24.95
12500	BT04	1	$149.99
12504	CZ81	2	$325.99

Part

Part Number	Part Description	On Hand	Class	Warehouse	Price
AX12	Iron	104	HW	3	$24.95
AZ52	Dartboard	20	SG	2	$12.95
BA74	Basketball	40	SG	1	$29.95
BH22	Cornpopper	95	HW	3	$24.95
BT04	Gas Grill	11	AP	2	$149.99
BZ66	Washer	52	AP	3	$399.99
CA14	Griddle	78	HW	3	$39.99
CB03	Bike	44	SG	1	$299.99
CX11	Blender	112	HW	3	$22.95
CZ81	Treadmill	68	SG	2	$349.95

When a user enters a query that involves a view, the DBMS changes the query to one that instead involves the tables in the database that are included in the view. Suppose, for example, that Juan were to type the following query:

```
SELECT *
    FROM Housewares
    WHERE [On Hand] > 100
```

The query would *not* be executed in this form. Instead, it would be merged with the query that defines the view, forming the query that is actually executed. In this case, the merging of the two would form:

```
SELECT [Part Number], [Part Description], [On Hand],
    Price
    FROM Part
    WHERE Class = 'HW'
    AND [On Hand] > 100
```

Notice the following three things: 1) the selection is from the Part table rather than the Housewares view; 2) the * is replaced by those columns that are in the Housewares view; and 3) the condition involves the condition in the query entered by Juan together with the condition stated in the view definition. This new query is the one that is actually executed.

Juan, however, is unaware that this kind of activity is taking place. It seems to him that he is really using a table called Housewares. One advantage of this approach is that because Housewares never exists in its own right, any update to the Part table is immediately available to Juan's view. If Housewares were an actual stored table, this would not be the case.

What if Juan wants different names for the columns? This can be accomplished by including the desired names in the CREATE VIEW command. For example, if Juan wants the names of the part number, part description, units on hand, and price columns to be Pnum, Desc, OnHd, and Price, respectively, the CREATE VIEW command would be:

```
CREATE VIEW Housewares (Pnum, Desc, OnHd, Price) AS
    SELECT [Part Number], [Part Description], [On Hand],
        Price
        FROM Part
        WHERE Class = 'HW'
```

In this case, when Juan accesses the Housewares view, he refers to Pnum, Desc, OnHd, and Price rather than Part Number, Part Description, On Hand, and Price.

The Housewares view is an example of a row-and-column subset view; that is, it consists of a subset of the rows and columns in some individual table, in this case the Part table. Because the query can be any SQL query, a view can also involve the join of two or more tables.

Suppose, for example, that Francesca needs to know the number and name of each sales rep, along with the number and name of the customers represented by each sales rep. It would be much simpler for her if this information were in a single table instead of two tables that had to be joined together. She would really like a single table that contains a sales rep number, sales rep name, customer number, and customer name. Suppose she would also like these columns to be named Snum, SLast, SFirst, Cnum, CLast, and CFirst, respectively. This can be accomplished by using a join in the CREATE VIEW command, as follows:

```
CREATE VIEW [Sales Cust] (Snum, SLast, SFirst, Cnum, CLast, CFirst) AS
    SELECT [Sales Rep].[Sales Rep Number], [Sales Rep].[Last Name],
        [Sales Rep].[First Name], Customer.[Customer Number],
        Customer.[Last Name], Customer.[First Name]
```

```
FROM [Sales Rep], Customer
WHERE [Sales Rep].[Sales Rep Number] =
      Customer.[Sales Rep Number]
```

Given the current data in the Premiere Products database, this view is conceptually the table shown in Figure 4.3.

FIGURE 4.3
Sales Cust view

Sales Cust

Snum	SLast	SFirst	Cnum	CLast	CFirst
03	Jones	Mary	124	Adams	Sally
03	Jones	Mary	412	Adams	Sally
03	Jones	Mary	622	Martin	Dan
06	Smith	William	256	Samuels	Ann
06	Smith	William	315	Daniels	Tom
06	Smith	William	567	Dinh	Tran
06	Smith	William	587	Galvez	Mara
12	Diaz	Miguel	311	Charles	Don
12	Diaz	Miguel	405	Williams	Al
12	Diaz	Miguel	522	Nelson	Mary

As far as Francesca is concerned, this is a real table; she does not need to know what goes on behind the scenes in order to use it. She can find the number and name of the sales rep who represents customer 256, for example, merely by entering:

```
SELECT Snum, SLast, SFirst
    FROM [Sales Cust]
    WHERE Cnum = 256
```

She is completely unaware that, behind the scenes, her query is actually converted to:

```
SELECT [Sales Rep].[Sales Rep Number], [Sales Rep].[Last Name],
    [Sales Rep].[First Name]
    FROM [Sales Rep], Customer
    WHERE [Sales Rep].[Sales Rep Number] =
          Customer.[Sales Rep Number]
    AND [Customer Number] = 256
```

The use of views provides several advantages:

1. Views provide data independence. If the database structure is changed (columns added, relationships changed, etc.) in such a way that the view can still be derived from existing data, the user can still access and use the same view. If adding extra columns to tables in the database is the only change, and these columns are not required by this user, the defining query may not need to be changed in order for the user to continue using the view he or she created. If relationships are changed, the defining query may be different, but because the user need not be aware of the defining query, this difference is unknown to him or her. The user continues to access the database through the same view, as though nothing has changed.

2. Because each user has his or her own view, the same data can be viewed by different users in different ways.

3. A view should contain only those columns required by a given user. This practice accomplishes two things. First, because the view will, in all probability, contain far fewer columns than the overall database and because the view is effectively a single table, rather than a collection of tables, it greatly simplifies the user's perception of the database. Second, it provides a measure of security. Columns that are not included in the view are not accessible to this user. Omitting the Balance column from the view will ensure that a user of this view cannot access any customer's balance. Likewise, rows that are not included in the view are not accessible. A user of the Housewares view, for example, cannot obtain any information about parts in the AP or SG item classes.

Indexes

If you want to find a discussion of a given topic in a book, you can scan the entire book from start to finish, looking for references to the topic you have in mind. More than likely, however, you won't have to resort to this technique. If the book has a good index, you can use it to rapidly locate the pages on which your topic is discussed.

Within relational model systems on both mainframes and personal computers, the main mechanism for increasing the efficiency with which data are retrieved from the database is the index. Conceptually, these indexes are very much like the index in a book. Consider Figure 4.4, for example, which shows the Customer table for Premiere Products together with one extra column, Record Number. This extra column gives the location of the record in the file (customer 124 is the first record in the table and is on record 1; customer 256 is on record 2; and so on). These record numbers are automatically assigned and used by the DBMS, not by the users, and that is why you do not normally show them. Here, however, you are looking at how the DBMS works, so you do need to be aware of them.

FIGURE 4.4

Customer table with record numbers

Customer

Record Number	Customer Number	Last Name	First Name	...	Balance	Credit Limit	Sales Rep Number
1	124	Adams	Sally	...	$818.75	$1000	03
2	256	Samuels	Ann	...	$21.50	$1500	06
3	311	Charles	Don	...	$825.75	$1000	12
4	315	Daniels	Tom	...	$770.75	$750	06
5	405	Williams	Al	...	$402.75	$1500	12
6	412	Adams	Sally	...	$1817.50	$2000	03
7	522	Nelson	Mary	...	$98.75	$1500	12
8	567	Dinh	Tran	...	$402.40	$750	06
9	587	Galvez	Mara	...	$114.60	$1000	06
10	622	Martin	Dan	...	$1045.75	$1000	03

In order to rapidly access a customer's record on the basis of his or her record number, you might choose to create and use an index as shown in Figure 4.5.

FIGURE 4.5

Customer Number Index

Index for Customer table on Customer Number column

Customer Number	Record Number
124	1
256	2
311	3
315	4
405	5
412	6
522	7
567	8
587	9
622	10

The index has two columns. The first column contains a customer number, and the second column contains the number of the record on which the customer is found. Because customer numbers are unique, there is only a single corresponding record number in this index. This is not always the case, however. Suppose, for example, that you want to rapidly access all customers who have a given credit limit or all customers who are represented by a given sales rep. You might choose to create and use an index on credit limit as well as an index on sales rep number. These two indexes are shown in Figure 4.6.

FIGURE 4.6

Indexes for Customer table on Credit Limit and Sales Rep Number columns

Credit Limit Index

Credit Limit	Record Numbers
$750	4, 8
$1000	1, 3, 9, 10
$1500	2, 5, 7
$2000	6

Sales Rep Number Index

Sales Rep Number	Record Numbers
03	1, 6, 10
06	2, 4, 8, 9
12	3, 5, 7

If you examine the Credit Limit index in Figure 4.6, you see that each credit limit occurs in the index along with the numbers of the records on which that credit limit occurs. Credit limit $1000, for example, occurs on records 1, 3, 9, and 10. Furthermore, the credit limits appear in the index in numerical order. If the DBMS were to use this index to find those records on which the credit limit is $1500, for example, it could rapidly scan the credit limits in the index to find $1500. Once it did, it would determine the corresponding record numbers (2, 5, 7) and then go immediately to those records in the Customer table, thus finding these customers much more quickly than if it had to look through the entire Customer table one record at a time. Thus, indexes can make the process of retrieving records very fast and efficient.

Note: With relatively small tables, the increased efficiency associated with indexes will not be readily apparent. In practice, it is common to encounter tables with thousands, tens of thousands, or even hundreds of thousands of records. In such cases, the increase in efficiency is dramatic. In fact, without indexes, many operations in such databases would simply not be practical. They would take too long to complete.

Typically, an index can be created and maintained for any column or combination of columns in any table. Once an index has been created, it can be used to facilitate retrieval of data. In powerful mainframe relational systems, the decision concerning which index or indexes to use (if any) during a particular type of retrieval is a function of the DBMS. As you would expect, the use of any index is not purely advantageous or disadvantageous. An advantage was already mentioned: an index makes certain types of retrieval more efficient. There are two disadvantages. First, an index occupies space that can be used for something else. Any retrieval that can be made using an index can also be made without the index. The process may be less efficient, but it is still possible. So an index, while it occupies space, is technically not necessary. The other disadvantage is that the DBMS must update the index whenever corresponding data in the database are updated. The main question that you must ask when considering whether or not to create a given index is: Do the benefits derived during retrieval outweigh the additional storage required and the extra processing involved in update operations?

Indexes can be added and dropped at will. You can create an index after the database is built if you decide you need it — it doesn't have to be created at the same time as the database. Likewise, if it appears that an existing index is unnecessary, it can easily be dropped.

The exact process for creating an index varies from one DBMS to another. Figure 4.7 shows the creation of an index on the Last Name field in Microsoft Access. As illustrated in the figure, there are three choices for index options: No, Yes (Duplicates OK), and Yes (No Duplicates).

FIGURE 4.7

Indexing options

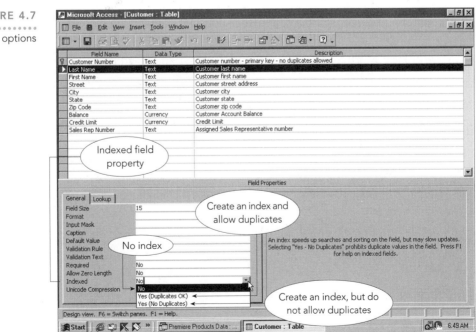

You select No if you do not wish to create an index on the Last Name field or if you wish to remove a previously created index. You select Yes (Duplicates OK) to create an index and to allow duplicates. In that case, Access allows more than one customer with the same last name. If you select Yes (No Duplicates), Access creates the index but you are not able to add a customer whose last name is the same as the last name of a customer already in the database.

■ Security

Security is the prevention of unauthorized access to the database. Within an organization, some person or group will determine the types of access various users can have to the database. Some users may be able to retrieve and update anything in the database. Other users may be able to retrieve any data from the database but not make any changes to the data. Still other users may only be able to access a portion of the database. For example, Jim Turner may be able to retrieve and update sales rep and customer data, but not retrieve data about parts and orders. Marti Simmons may be able to retrieve data on parts and nothing else. Kyung Park may be able to retrieve and update data on parts of type HW, but no others.

Once these rules are determined, it is up to the DBMS to enforce them; in particular, it is up to whatever security mechanism the DBMS provides. In SQL systems, there are two security mechanisms. You have already seen that views provide a certain amount of security. (If someone is accessing the database through a view, he or she cannot access any data that are not part of the view.) The main security mechanism, however, is the GRANT facility.

The basic idea is that different types of privileges can be granted to users and, if necessary, later revoked. These privileges include such things as the right to select rows from a table, the right to insert new rows, the right to update existing rows, and so on. Granting and revoking these privileges is accomplished through GRANT and REVOKE commands. Following are some examples of these commands.

```
GRANT SELECT ON Customer TO TURNER
```

Jim Turner is able to retrieve customer data, but will not be able to take any other action.

```
GRANT INSERT ON Part TO SIMMONS, PARK
```

Marti Simmons and Kyung Park are able to add new parts.

```
REVOKE SELECT ON Customer FROM TURNER
```

Jim Turner no longer has the right to retrieve customer data.

■ Integrity Rules

There are two important integrity rules that should be enforced by a relational DBMS. They were defined by Dr. E. F. Codd[1] and relate to two special types of keys: primary keys and foreign keys. The two integrity rules are called entity integrity and referential integrity.

[1]Codd, E.F. "Extending the Relational Database Model to Capture More Meaning." In *ACM TODS 4*, no. 4, December, 1979

Entity Integrity

In some DBMSs, when you describe a database, you can indicate that certain columns can accept a special value, called null. Essentially, setting the value in a given column to null is similar to not filling it in at all. It is used when a value is unknown or inapplicable. It is *not* the same as blank or zero, which are actual values. For example, a value of zero in Balance indicates that the customer has a zero balance. A value of null, on the other hand, indicates that, for whatever reason, the customer's balance is unknown.

If you indicate that the column Balance can be null, you are saying that this situation (a customer with an unknown balance) is something you want to allow. If you don't want to allow it, you indicate that Balance cannot be null.

The decision whether to allow nulls is generally made on a column-by-column basis. There is one type of column for which you should *never* allow nulls, however, and that is the primary key. After all, the primary key is supposed to uniquely identify a given row, and this cannot happen if nulls are allowed. How, for example, could you tell two customers apart if both have a null customer number? The restriction that the primary key cannot allow null values is called entity integrity.

Definition: Entity integrity is the rule that no column that is part of the primary key may accept null values.

Entity integrity guarantees that each record will indeed have its own identity. In other words, entity integrity prevents the primary key from accepting null values and ensures that one record can be distinguished from another.

Referential Integrity

As you've been examining up until now, relationships between tables in the relational model are not explicit. Relationships between tables are accomplished by having common columns in two or more tables. The relationship between sales reps and customers, for example, is accomplished by including Sales Rep Number, which is the primary key of the Sales Rep table, as a column in the Customer table.

This approach has its drawbacks. First of all, relationships are not very obvious. If you were not already familiar with the relationships within the Premiere Products database, you would have to find the matching columns in separate tables in order to be aware of a relationship. Even then, you couldn't be sure that the matching column names indicate a relationship. Two columns having the same name could be just a coincidence. These columns might have nothing to do with each other. Secondly, what if the primary key to the Sales Rep table were Sales Rep Number, but the corresponding column within the Customer table happened to be called Slsr No? Unless you were aware that these two columns were really the same, the relationship between customers and sales reps would not be clear. In a database having as few tables and columns as the Premiere Products database, these problems might not be major ones. But imagine a database that has 20 tables, each one containing an average of 30 columns. As the number of tables and columns increases, so do the potential problems.

There is also another issue with the relational model. Nothing about the model itself would prevent a user from storing data about a customer whose sales rep number did not correspond to any sales rep already in the database. Clearly this is not a desirable situation.

Fortunately, a solution exists for these two situations, and involves the use of foreign keys.

Definition: A foreign key is a column (or collection of columns) in one table whose value is required to match the value of the primary key for another table.

The Sales Rep Number in the Customer table is a foreign key that must match the primary key of the Sales Rep table. In practice, this simply means that the sales rep number for any customer must be the same as the number of some sales rep who is already in the database.

There is one exception to this. For example, perhaps Premiere Products does not require a customer to have a sales rep — it is strictly optional. This situation could be indicated in the Customer table by setting such a customer's sales rep number to null. Technically, however, a null sales rep number would violate the restrictions that you have indicated for a foreign key. So if you were to use a null sales rep number, you would have to modify the definition of foreign keys to include the possibility of nulls. You would insist, though, that if the foreign key contained a value *other than null*, it would have to match the value of the primary key in some row in the other table. (In the example, for instance, a customer's sales rep number could be null, but if it were not, then it would have to be the number of an actual sales rep.) The general property you have just described is called referential integrity.

Definition: The referential integrity rule states that if table A contains a foreign key that matches the primary key of table B, then values of this foreign key either must match the value of the primary key for some row in table B or must be null.

The problems mentioned above are solved through the use of foreign keys. Indicating that the Sales Rep Number in the Customer table is a foreign key that must match the Sales Rep table makes the relationship between customers and sales reps explicit. You do not need to look for common columns in several tables. Furthermore, with foreign keys, matching columns that have different names no longer poses a problem. For example, it does not matter if the name of the foreign key in the Customer table happens to be Slsr No while the primary key in the Sales Rep table happens to be Sales Rep Number; the only thing that *does* matter is that this column is a foreign key that matches the Sales Rep table. Finally, through referential integrity, it is possible for a customer not to have a sales rep number, but it is not possible for a customer to have an *invalid* sales rep number; that is, a customer's sales rep number *must* either be null or be the number of a sales rep who is already in the database.

The manner in which you specify referential integrity depends on the DBMS you are using. In Microsoft Access, it is specified as part of the process of defining relationships (Figure 4.8).

FIGURE 4.8

. . . .

Defining explicit
relationships
between tables
using primary and
foreign keys

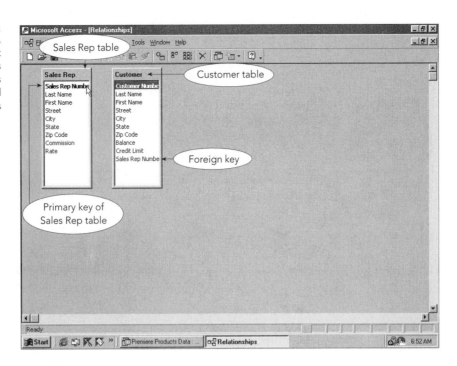

Once you have indicated how two tables are to be related, you can request that Access enforce referential integrity (Figure 4.9). You also can specify whether update or delete is to "cascade." Cascading delete, for example, would mean that whenever a sales rep is deleted, all related customers are also deleted. In the example illustrated in the figure, neither update nor delete is to cascade.

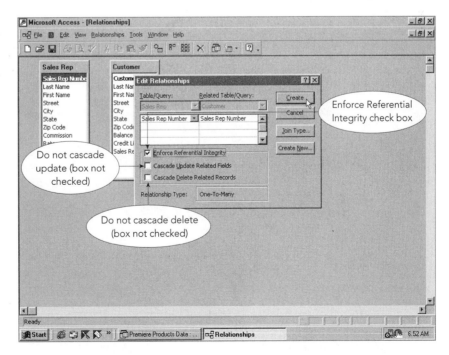

With referential integrity enforced, users are not allowed to add a customer whose sales rep number does not match any sales rep currently in the Sales Rep table. Instead, an error message, such as the one in Figure 4.10, is displayed.

FIGURE 4.10

Referential integrity violation warning when adding data

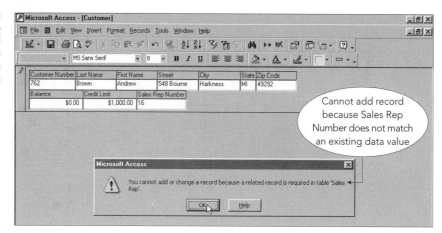

Deleting a sales rep who currently has customers on file also causes referential integrity to be violated, because the sales rep's customers no longer match any sales rep in the Sales Rep table. The DBMS must refuse to carry out this type of deletion; instead it produces an error message, such as the one in Figure 4.11. (If the sales rep were to leave the organization, all of his or her customers would need to be assigned to other sales reps before deleting the sales rep.)

FIGURE 4.11

Referential integrity violation warning when deleting data

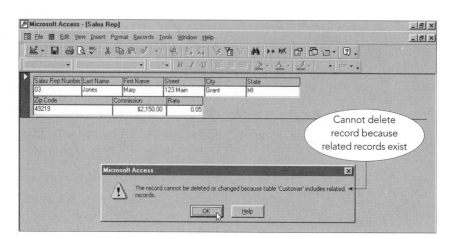

■ Changing the Structure of a Relational Database

An important feature of relational DBMSs is the ease with which the database structure can be changed. New tables can be added and old ones can be removed. Columns can be added or deleted. The characteristics of columns can be changed. New indexes can be created and old ones can be dropped. Though the exact manner in which these changes are accomplished varies from one system to another, most systems allow all of these changes to be made quickly and easily. Because SQL is so widely used, you will use it as a vehicle to illustrate the manner in which these changes may be accomplished.

Alter

Changing a table's structure in SQL is accomplished through the ALTER TABLE command. Virtually every implementation of SQL allows new columns to be added to the end of an existing table. For example, suppose that you now want to maintain a customer type for each customer in the Premiere Products database. You can decide to call regular customers type R, distributors type D, and special customers type S. To implement this change, you need to add a new column to the customer table. This can be done as follows:

```
ALTER TABLE Customer
     ADD [Cust Type]        CHAR (1)
```

At this point, the Customer table contains an extra column, Cust Type. For rows (customers) added from this point on, the value of Cust Type is assigned as the row is added, just like any other field. For existing rows, some value of Cust Type must be assigned. The simplest approach (from the point of view of the DBMS, *not* the user) is to assign the value NULL as a Cust Type on all existing rows. (This requires that Cust Type accepts null values, and some systems do require this. This means that any column added to a table definition *will* accept nulls; the user has no choice in the matter.) A more flexible approach, and one that is supported by a few systems, is to allow the user to specify an initial value. (Many systems, including Access, do not allow this.)

In the example, if most customers are type R, you might set all of the customer types for existing customers to R and later change those customers of type D or type S to the appropriate value. To change the structure and set the value of Cust Type to R for all existing records, you type:

```
ALTER TABLE Customer
     ADD [Cust Type]        CHAR (1)        DEFAULT = 'R'
```

Some systems allow existing columns to be deleted. The syntax for deleting the Warehouse column from the Part table is typically something like this:

```
ALTER TABLE Part
     DELETE Warehouse
```

Finally, some systems allow changes in the data types of given columns. A typical use of such a provision is to increase the length of a character field that is found to be inadequate. Assuming that the Last Name column in the Customer table needs to be increased to 20 characters, the ALTER TABLE command is something like this:

```
ALTER TABLE Customer
     CHANGE COLUMN [Last Name] TO CHAR (20)
```

Drop

A table that is no longer needed can be deleted with the DROP TABLE command. If the Sales Rep table is no longer needed in the Premiere Products database, the command is:

```
DROP TABLE [Sales Rep]
```

The table is erased, as are all indexes and views defined on the table. DROP TABLE deletes the table structure as well as the data. References to the table are removed from the system catalog.

■ The Catalog

Information about tables in the database is kept in the system catalog. The system catalog is a self-maintaining relational database of its own that stores information about the database's structure. This section will describe the types of things kept in a catalog and the way the catalog can be queried to determine information about the database structure. (This description represents the way catalogs are used in DB2, IBM's mainframe relational DBMS.) Although catalogs in individual relational DBMSs will vary from the examples shown here, the general ideas apply to most relational systems.

The catalog you will look at contains two tables, Systables (information about the tables known to SQL) and Syscolumns (information about the columns within these tables). An actual catalog contains other tables as well, such as Sysindexes (information about the indexes that are defined on these tables) and Sysviews (information about the views that have been created). While these tables have many columns, only a few are of concern here.

Systables contains columns Name, Creator, and Colcount (see Figure 4.12). The Name column identifies the name of a table. The Creator column contains an identification of the person or group that created the table. The Colcount column contains the number of columns within the table that is being described. If, for example, the user whose name is Brown creates the sales rep table and the sales rep table has nine columns, there would be a row in the Systables table in which Name is Sales Rep, Creator is Brown, and Colcount is 9. Similar rows would exist for all tables known to the system.

FIGURE 4.12

Systables table

Systables

Name	Creator	Colcount
Customer	Brown	10
Part	Brown	6
Orders	Brown	3
Order Line	Brown	4
Sales Rep	Brown	9

Syscolumns contains columns Colname, Tbname, and Coltype (see Figure 4.13). The Colname column identifies the name of a column in one of the tables. The table in which the column is found is stored in Tbname, and the data type for the column is found in Coltype. There is a row in Syscolumns for each column in the Sales Rep table, for example. On each of these rows, Tbname is Sales Rep. On one of these rows, Colname is Sales Rep Number and Coltype is CHAR (2). On another row, Colname is Last Name and Coltype is CHAR (12).

FIGURE 4.13
....
Syscolumns table

Syscolumns

Colname	Tbname	Coltype
Balance	Customer	DECIMAL(8,2)
City	Customer	CHAR(20)
City	Sales Rep	CHAR(20)
Rate	Sales Rep	DECIMAL (4,2)
Credit Limit	Customer	DECIMAL(5,0)
Customer Number	Customer	CHAR(4)
Customer Number	Orders	DECIMAL(5,0)
First Name	Customer	CHAR(10)
First Name	Sales Rep	CHAR(10)
Class	Part	CHAR(2)
Last Name	Customer	CHAR(12)
Last Name	Sales Rep	CHAR(12)
Number Ordered	Order Line	DECIMAL(4,0)
Order Date	Orders	DATE
Order Number	Orders	CHAR(5)
Order Number	Order Line	CHAR(5)
Part Description	Part	CHAR(15)
Part Number	Order Line	CHAR(4)
Part Number	Part	CHAR(4)
Quoted Price	Order Line	DECIMAL(6,2)
Sales Rep Number	Customer	CHAR(2)
Sales Rep Number	Sales Rep	CHAR(2)
State	Customer	CHAR(2)
State	Sales Rep	CHAR(2)
Street	Customer	CHAR(20)
Street	Sales Rep	CHAR(20)
Commission	Sales Rep	DECIMAL(10,3)
On Hand	Part	DECIMAL(4,0)
Price	Part	DECIMAL(6,2)
Warehouse	Part	CHAR(2)
Zip Code	Customer	CHAR(5)
Zip Code	Sales Rep	CHAR(5)

Because the catalog is a relational database, the same types of queries that are used to retrieve information from relational databases generally can be used to retrieve information from the system catalog. The following queries illustrate this process.

EXAMPLE 1 List the name and creator of all tables known to the system.

```
SELECT Name, Creator
    FROM Systables
```

EXAMPLE 2 List all of the columns in the Customer table as well as their associated data types.

```
SELECT Colname, Coltype
    FROM Syscolumns
    WHERE Tbname = 'Customer'
```

EXAMPLE 3 List all tables that contain a column called Sales Rep Number.

```
SELECT Tbname
    FROM Syscolumns
    WHERE Colname = '[Sales Rep Number]'
```

Thus, information about the tables that exist in your relational database, the columns they contain, and the indexes built on them can be obtained from the catalog by using the same SQL syntax that is used to query any other relational database. You don't need to worry about updating these tables; the system will do it automatically every time a change is made in the database structure.

Integrity in SQL

The original standard for SQL approved by ANSI (the American National Standards Institute) did not contain any provisions for integrity support, that is, provisions to make sure that the data in your database follow rules that you establish. An additional component, called the Integrity Enhancement Feature (IEF), was added later. This is the component that provides support for integrity. The inclusion of the IEF means that data of certain types must meet certain conditions, or that data integrity must be upheld.

The IEF provides three types of integrity support:

1. ***Legal values.*** The CHECK clause ensures that only values that satisfy a particular condition are allowed in a given column. For example, to ensure that the only legal values for credit limits are 750, 1000, 1500, or 2000, the clause is:

```
CHECK ([Credit Limit] IN (750, 1000, 1500, 2000))
```

The general form of the CHECK clause is simply the word CHECK followed by a condition. In the above CHECK clause, the credit limit must be in the set consisting of 750, 1000, 1500, or 2000. If any update to the database would result in the condition being violated, the update is automatically rejected.

2. ***Primary keys.*** The primary key for a table is specified by following the data type for the primary key column with the words PRIMARY KEY in the CREATE TABLE command. As an alternative, you can include the PRIMARY KEY clause in the command. For example, to use the PRIMARY KEY clause to indicate that Customer Number is the primary key for the Customer table, the clause is:

```
PRIMARY KEY ([Customer Number])
```

In general, the PRIMARY KEY clause has the form PRIMARY KEY followed by the name or names in parentheses of the column or columns that make up the primary key. If you include more than one column, separate the columns by commas. Thus, the primary key clause for the Order Line table is:

```
PRIMARY KEY ([Order Number], [Part Number])
```

3. ***Foreign keys.*** Any foreign keys are specified through FOREIGN KEY clauses. To specify a foreign key, you need to specify both the column that is a foreign key and the table whose primary key it is to match. In the Customer table, for example, Sales Rep Number is a foreign key that must match the primary key in the Sales Rep table. This is specified as:

```
FOREIGN KEY ([Sales Rep Number]) REFERENCES [Sales Rep]
```

The general form is FOREIGN KEY, followed by the column or columns that constitute the foreign key, followed by the word REFERENCES, and then by the name of the table containing the primary key that the foreign key is supposed to match.

The following is a complete CREATE TABLE command for the Customer table incorporating all three types of integrity support:

```
CREATE TABLE Customer
       ([Customer Number]    CHAR(4),
       [Last Name]           CHAR(15),
       [First Name]          CHAR(15),
       Street                CHAR(15),
       City                  CHAR(15),
       State                 CHAR(2),
       [Zip Code]            CHAR(5),
       Balance               DECIMAL(7,2),
       [Credit Limit]        DECIMAL(7,2),
       [Sales Rep Number]    CHAR(2) )
       CHECK ([Credit Limit] IN (750, 1000, 1500, 2000) )
       PRIMARY KEY ([Customer Number])
       FOREIGN KEY ([Sales Rep Number]) REFERENCES [Sales Rep]
```

SUMMARY

- Views are used to give each user his or her own picture of the database.
  - A view is defined in SQL through the use of a defining query.
  - When a query referencing a view is entered, it is merged with the defining query to produce the query that is actually executed.

- Indexes are often used to facilitate retrieval of data from the database. Indexes may be created on any column or combination of columns.

- Security is provided in SQL systems through the GRANT and REVOKE commands.

- There are two special integrity rules for relational databases:
  - Entity integrity is the rule that no column that is part of the primary key can accept null values.
  - Referential integrity is the rule that the value in any foreign key either must be null or must match an actual value of the primary key of another table.

- Relational DBMSs provide facilities that allow users to easily change the structure of a database. Two examples of such facilities are as follows:
  - ALTER TABLE allows columns to be added to a table, columns to be deleted, or characteristics of columns to be changed.
  - DROP TAB allows a table to be deleted from a database.

- The catalog is a feature of many relational model DBMSs that stores information about the structure of a database. The system updates the catalog automatically. Users can retrieve data from the catalog in the same manner in which they retrieve data from the database.

- SQL provides support for a variety of integrity constraints through the Integrity Enhancement Feature.

KEY TERMS

ANSI (American National Standards Institute)
catalog
defining query
entity integrity
foreign key
index

Integrity Enhancement Feature
null
referential integrity
security
view

REVIEW QUESTIONS

1. What is a view? How is it defined? Do the data described in a view definition ever exist in that form? What happens when a user accesses a database through a view?

2. Using data from the Premiere Products database, define a view called Small Cust. It consists of the customer number, name, address, balance, and credit limit for all customers whose credit limit is $1000 or less.

   a. Write the view definition for Small Cust.
   b. Write a SQL query to retrieve the number and name of all customers in Small Cust whose balance is over their credit limit.
   c. Convert the query from Step b to the query that will actually be executed.

3. Define a view called Cust Order. It consists of the customer number, name, balance, order number, and order date for all orders currently on file.

   a. Write the view definition for Cust Order.
   b. Write a SQL query to retrieve the customer number, name, order number, and order date for all orders in Cust Order for customers whose balance is more than $100.
   c. Convert the query from Step b to the query that will actually be executed.

4. What are the advantages of using indexes? The disadvantages?

5. Describe the GRANT function and explain how it relates to security. What types of privileges may be granted? How are they revoked?

6. What is the catalog? Name three items about which the catalog maintains information.

7. Why is it a good idea for the DBMS to update the catalog automatically when a change is made in the database structure? Could users cause problems by updating the catalog themselves?

8. What are nulls? Which column should never be allowed to be null?

9. State the two integrity rules. Indicate the reasons for enforcing each rule.

10. The Orders table contains a foreign key, Customer Number, that must match the primary key of the Customer table. What type of update to the Orders table would violate referential integrity? If delete does not cascade, what type of update to the Customer table would violate referential integrity? If delete cascades, what would happen when a customer is deleted?

11. How can the structure of a table be changed in SQL? What general types of changes are possible? Which commands are used to implement these changes?

12. What types of integrity support are provided by SQL? Do all versions of SQL provide this support?

CHAPTER 5

Database Design 1: Normalization

- Present the idea of functional dependence.

- Define first normal form (1NF), second normal form (2NF), and third normal form (3NF).

- Describe the problems associated with tables (relations) that are not in 1NF, 2NF, or 3NF, along with the mechanism for converting to all three.

- Discuss the problems associated with incorrect conversions to 3NF.

- Define fourth normal form (4NF)

- Describe the problems associated with tables (relations) that are not in 4NF and describe the mechanism for converting to 4NF.

Introduction

You have examined the basic relational model, its structure, and the various ways of manipulating data within a relational database. In this chapter, you will learn about the **normalization process** and its underlying concepts and features. The normalization process is a set of steps that enables you to identify the existence of potential problems, called **update anomalies**, in the design of a relational database. This process also supplies methods for correcting these problems.

The process involves converting tables into various types of **normal forms**. A table in a particular normal form possesses a certain desirable collection of properties. There are several normal forms, the most common being first normal form (1NF), second normal form (2NF), third normal form (3NF), and fourth normal form (4NF). They form a progression in which a table that is in 1NF is better than a table that is not in 1NF; a table that is in 2NF is better than one that is in 1NF; and so on. The goal of this process is to allow you to take a table or collection of tables and produce a new collection of tables that represents the same information but is free of problems.

This chapter begins by introducing two crucial concepts that are fundamental to the understanding of the normalization process: functional dependence and keys. Then, first, second, and third normal forms are discussed. Following this, you will examine the issues involved in fourth normal form. You will then be ready to begin your study of the database design process in the next chapter.

Many of the examples in this chapter use data from the Premiere Products database (see Figure 5.1).

FIGURE 5.1

Premiere Products
sample data

Sales Rep

Sales Rep Number	Last Name	First Name	Street	City	State	Zip Code	Commission	Rate
03	Jones	Mary	123 Main	Grant	MI	49219	2150.00	.05
06	Smith	William	102 Raymond	Ada	MI	49441	4912.50	.07
12	Diaz	Miguel	419 Harper	Lansing	MI	49224	2150.00	.05

Customer

Customer Number	Last Name	First Name	Street	City	State	Zip Code	Balance	Credit Limit	Sales Rep Number
124	Adams	Sally	481 Oak	Lansing	MI	49224	$818.75	$1000	03
256	Samuels	Ann	215 Pete	Grant	MI	49219	$21.50	$1500	06
311	Charles	Don	48 College	Ira	MI	49034	$825.75	$1000	12
315	Daniels	Tom	914 Cherry	Kent	MI	48391	$770.75	$750	06
405	Williams	Al	519 Watson	Grant	MI	49219	$402.75	$1500	12
412	Adams	Sally	16 Elm	Lansing	MI	49224	$1817.50	$2000	03
522	Nelson	Mary	108 Pine	Ada	MI	49441	$98.75	$1500	12
567	Dinh	Tran	808 Ridge	Harper	MI	48421	$402.40	$750	06
587	Galvez	Mara	512 Pine	Ada	MI	49441	$114.60	$1000	06
622	Martin	Dan	419 Chip	Grant	MI	49219	$1045.75	$1000	03

(Continued)

Orders

Order Number	Order Date	Customer Number
12489	9/02/01	124
12491	9/02/01	311
12494	9/04/01	315
12495	9/04/01	256
12498	9/05/01	522
12500	9/05/01	124
12504	9/05/01	522

Order Line

Order Number	Part Number	Number Ordered	Quoted Price
12489	AX12	11	$14.95
12491	BT04	1	$149.99
12491	BZ66	1	$399.99
12494	CB03	4	$279.99
12495	CX11	2	$22.95
12498	AZ52	2	$12.95
12498	BA74	4	$24.95
12500	BT04	1	$149.99
12504	CZ81	2	$325.99

Part

Part Number	Part Description	On Hand	Class	Warehouse	Price
AX12	Iron	104	HW	3	$24.95
AZ52	Dartboard	20	SG	2	$12.95
BA74	Basketball	40	SG	1	$29.95
BH22	Cornpopper	95	HW	3	$24.95
BT04	Gas Grill	11	AP	2	$149.99
BZ66	Washer	52	AP	3	$399.99
CA14	Griddle	78	HW	3	$39.99
CB03	Bike	44	SG	1	$299.99
CX11	Blender	112	HW	3	$22.95
CZ81	Treadmill	68	SG	2	$349.95

■ Functional Dependence

The concept of **functional dependence** is crucial to the material in the rest of this chapter. Functional dependence is a formal name for what is basically a simple idea. To illustrate it, suppose that the Sales Rep table for Premiere Products is as shown in Figure 5.2. The only difference between this Sales Rep table and the one you have been looking at previously is the addition of an extra column, Pay Class.

FIGURE 5.2

Sales Rep table with additional column, Pay Class

Sales Rep

Sales Rep Number	Last Name	First Name	Street	City	State	Zip Code	Commission	Pay Class	Rate
03	Jones	Mary	123 Main	Grant	MI	49219	2150.00	1	.05
06	Smith	William	102 Raymond	Ada	MI	49441	4912.50	2	.07
12	Diaz	Miguel	419 Harper	Lansing	MI	49224	2150.00	1	.05

Suppose also that one of the policies at Premiere Products is that all sales reps in any given pay class get the same commission rate. In other words, a sales rep's pay class *determines* his or her commission rate, or a sales rep's commission rate *depends on* his or her pay class. This phrasing uses the words *determines* and *depends on* in exactly the fashion that you will be using them later in the chapter as you experiment with functional dependency. If you wanted to be formal, you would precede either expression with the word *functionally*. Thus you might say, "A sales rep's pay class *functionally determines* his or her commission rate," or "A sales rep's commission rate *functionally depends* on his or her pay class." Another way to describe functional dependency is to say that if you know a sales rep's pay class (A), then you know his or her commission rate (B). The formal definition of functional dependence is as follows:

Definition: A column (attribute), B, is **functionally dependent** on another column, A (or possibly a collection of columns), if a value for A determines a single value for B at any one time.

You can think of functional dependency like this: If you are given a value for A, do you know that you can use it to find a single value for B? If so, B is functionally dependent on A (often written as A → B). If B is functionally dependent on A, you also can say that A functionally determines B.

Now we will apply this theory to the Premiere Products data. In the Customer table, is Last Name (B) functionally dependent on Customer Number (A)? The answer is yes. If you are given customer number 124, for example, you would find a *single* last name, Adams, associated with it.

QUESTION In the same Customer table, is Street functionally dependent on Last Name?

ANSWER   Here the answer is no because, given the last name Adams, you would not be able to find a single street address (there is more than one customer named Adams).

QUESTION In the Order Line table, is the Number Ordered functionally dependent on Order Number?

ANSWER   No. Order Number does not give enough information.

QUESTION Is the Number Ordered functionally dependent on Part Number?

ANSWER   No. Again, not enough information is given. In reality, Number Ordered is functionally dependent on the concatenation (combination) of Order Number and Part Number.

At this point, a question naturally arises: How do you determine functional dependencies? Can you determine them by looking at sample data, for example? The answer is no.

Consider Figure 5.3, in which last names happen to be unique. It is very tempting to say that Last Name functionally determines Street, City, State, and Zip Code (or equivalently, that Street, City, State, and Zip Code are all functionally dependent on Last Name). After all, given the last name of a customer, in this table you can find a single address.

FIGURE 5.3

Customer table

Customer

Customer Number	Last Name	First Name	Street	City	State	Zip Code	Balance	Credit Limit	Sales Rep Number
124	Adams	Sally	481 Oak	Lansing	MI	49224	$818.75	$1000	03
256	Samuels	Ann	215 Pete	Grant	MI	49219	$21.50	$1500	06
311	Charles	Don	48 College	Ira	MI	49034	$825.75	$1000	12
315	Daniels	Tom	914 Cherry	Kent	MI	48391	$770.75	$750	06
405	Williams	Al	519 Watson	Grant	MI	49219	$402.75	$1500	12
522	Nelson	Mary	108 Pine	Ada	MI	49441	$98.75	$1500	12
567	Dinh	Tran	808 Ridge	Harper	MI	48421	$402.40	$750	06
587	Galvez	Mara	512 Pine	Ada	MI	49441	$114.60	$1000	06
622	Martin	Dan	419 Chip	Grant	MI	49219	$1045.75	$1000	03

What happens when customer 412, whose last name also happens to be Adams, is added to the database? You then have the situation illustrated in Figure 5.4. If the last name you are given is Adams, you can no longer find a single address. Thus you were misled by the original sample data. The only way to really determine the functional dependencies that exist is to examine the user's policies. This can involve discussions with users, examination of user documentation, and so on.

FIGURE 5.4

Customer table with second Adams

Customer

Customer Number	Last Name	First Name	Street	City	State	Zip Code	Balance	Credit Limit	Sales Rep Number
124	Adams	Sally	481 Oak	Lansing	MI	49224	$818.75	$1000	03
256	Samuels	Ann	215 Pete	Grant	MI	49219	$21.50	$1500	06
311	Charles	Don	48 College	Ira	MI	49034	$825.75	$1000	12
315	Daniels	Tom	914 Cherry	Kent	MI	48391	$770.75	$750	06
405	Williams	Al	519 Watson	Grant	MI	49219	$402.75	$1500	12
412	Adams	Sally	16 Elm	Lansing	MI	49224	$1817.50	$2000	03
522	Nelson	Mary	108 Pine	Ada	MI	49441	$98.75	$1500	12
567	Dinh	Tran	808 Ridge	Harper	MI	48421	$402.40	$750	06
587	Galvez	Mara	512 Pine	Ada	MI	49441	$114.60	$1000	06
622	Martin	Dan	419 Chip	Grant	MI	49219	$1045.75	$1000	03

▪ Keys

A second underlying concept of the normalization process is that of the primary key. You already encountered the basic concept of a primary key in earlier chapters. In this chapter, however, the discussion now needs to be more precise about its definition. The precise definition is as follows:

Definition: Column (attribute) C (or a collection of columns) is the primary key for a table (relation), T, if:

> Property 1. *All* columns in T are functionally dependent on C.
>
> Property 2. No subcollection of the columns in C (assuming C is a collection of columns and not just a single column) also has Property 1.

For example, is the Last Name column the primary key for the Customer table? No, because the other columns are not functionally dependent on the last name. Given the last name Adams, for example, you could not determine a unique street, city, state, or anything else, since there are two customers who have the last name Adams.

QUESTION
Is Customer Number the primary key for the Customer table?

ANSWER
Yes, because customer numbers are unique. A given customer number cannot appear on more than one row. Thus, all columns in the Customer table are functionally dependent on Customer Number.

QUESTION
Is Order Number the primary key for the Order Line table?

ANSWER
No, because it does not uniquely determine Number Ordered or Quoted Price.

QUESTION
Is the combination of the Order Number and the Part Number the primary key for the Order Line table?

ANSWER
Yes, because all columns can be determined by this combination, and, furthermore, neither the Order Number nor the Part Number alone has this property.

QUESTION
Is the combination of the Part Number and the Part Description the primary key for the Part table?

ANSWER
No. Though it is true that all columns of the Part table can be determined by this combination, the Part Number alone also has this property.

Occasionally (but not often) there might be more than one possibility for the primary key. For example, if the Premiere Products database included an Employee table, either the Employee Number or the Soc Sec Num columns could serve as the primary key. In this case, both columns are referred to as candidate keys. Like a primary key, a candidate key is a column or collection of columns on which all columns in the table are functionally dependent — the definition for primary key really defines candidate key as well. From all the candidate keys, one is chosen to be the primary key. The candidate keys that are not chosen to be the primary key are often referred to as alternate keys.

Note: The primary key is frequently called simply the *key* in other studies on database management and the relational model. You will continue to use the term *primary key* in order to clearly distinguish among the several different concepts of a key that you will encounter throughout this book.

First Normal Form

A table (relation) that contains a repeating group (or multiple entries for a single record) is called an unnormalized relation. Removal of repeating groups is the starting point in the quest for tables that are as free of problems as possible. Tables without repeating groups are in first normal form.

Definition: A table (relation) is in first normal form (1NF) if it does not contain repeating groups.

As an example, consider the following Orders table, in which there is a repeating group consisting of Part Number and Number Ordered. As the example shows, there is one row per order with Part Number, Number Ordered repeated as many times as is necessary.

```
Orders (Order Number, Order Date, (Part Number, Number Ordered) )
```

This notation indicates a table called Orders, consisting of a primary key, (Order Number), and a column called Order Date. The inner parentheses indicate that there is a repeating group. The repeating group contains two columns, Part Number and Number Ordered. This means that for a single order, there can be multiple combinations of a part number and a corresponding number of units ordered. Figure 5.5 shows a sample of this table.

FIGURE 5.5

Sample unnormalized table

Orders

Order Number	Order Date	Part Number	Number Ordered
12489	9/02/2001	AX12	11
12491	9/02/2001	BT04	1
		BZ66	1
12494	9/04/2001	CB03	4
12495	9/04/2001	CX11	2
12498	9/05/2001	AZ52	2
		BA74	4
12500	9/05/2001	BT04	1
12504	9/05/2001	CZ81	2

To convert the table to 1NF, the repeating group is removed, giving the following:

```
Orders (Order Number, Order Date, Part Number, Number Ordered)
```

The corresponding example of the new table is shown in Figure 5.6.

Orders

Order Number	Order Date	Part Number	Number Ordered
12489	9/02/2001	AX12	11
12491	9/02/2001	BT04	1
12491	9/02/2001	BZ66	1
12494	9/04/2001	CB03	4
12495	9/04/2001	CX11	2
12498	9/05/2001	AZ52	2
12498	9/05/2001	BA74	4
12500	9/05/2001	BT04	1
12504	9/05/2001	CZ81	2

Note that the second row of the unnormalized table indicates that part BZ66 and part BT04 are both present for order 12491. In the normalized table, this information is represented by *two* rows, the second and third. The primary key to the unnormalized Orders table was the Order Number alone. The primary key to the normalized table is now the combination of Order Number and Part Number.

In general, in converting a non-1NF table to 1NF, the primary key will typically include the original primary key concatenated with the primary key to the repeating group; i.e., the column that distinguishes one occurrence of the repeating group from another within a given row in the table. In this case, Part Number is the primary key to the repeating group and thus becomes part of the primary key of the 1NF table.

Second Normal Form

Even though the following table is in 1NF, you will want to restructure it because of problems that exist within the table. Consider the table:

```
Orders (Order Number, Order Date, Part Number, Part Description,
     Number Ordered, Quoted Price)
```

with the functional dependencies:

```
Order Number → Order Date
Part Number → Part Description
Order Number, Part Number → Number Ordered, Quoted Price
```

Thus Order Number alone determines Order Date, Part Number alone determines Part Description, but it requires *both* an order number *and* a part number to determine either Number Ordered or Quoted Price. Consider the sample of this table shown in Figure 5.7:

FIGURE 5.7

Sample Orders table

Orders

Order Number	Order Date	Part Number	Part Description	Number Ordered	Quoted Price
12489	9/02/2001	AX12	Iron	11	$14.95
12491	9/02/2001	BT04	Gas Grill	1	$149.99
12491	9/02/2001	BZ66	Washer	1	$399.99
12494	9/04/2001	CB03	Bike	4	$279.99
12495	9/04/2001	CX11	Blender	2	$22.95
12498	9/05/2001	AZ52	Dartboard	2	$12.95
12498	9/05/2001	BA74	Basketball	4	$24.95
12500	9/05/2001	BT04	Gas Grill	1	$149.99
12504	9/05/2001	CZ81	Treadmill	2	$325.99

The description of a specific part, BT04 for example, occurs several times in the table. This redundancy causes several problems. It is certainly wasteful of space, but that is not nearly as serious as some of the other problems. These other problems are called **update anomalies** and they fall into four categories:

1. ***Update.*** A change to the description of part BT04 requires not one change to the table, but several — you have to change each row in which BT04 appears. This certainly makes the update process much more cumbersome; it is more complicated logically and takes more time to update.

2. ***Inconsistent data.*** There is nothing about the design that would prohibit part BT04 from having two different descriptions in the database. In fact, if it occurs in 20 rows, it could conceivably have 20 *different* descriptions in the database!

3. ***Additions.*** You have a real problem when you try to add a new part and its description to the database. Because the primary key for the table consists of both Order Number and Part Number, you need values for both of these to add a new row. If you have a part to add but there are as yet no orders for it, what do you use for an Order Number? The only solution would be to make up a dummy order number and then replace it with a real Order Number once an order for this part had actually been received. Certainly this is not an acceptable solution.

4. ***Deletions.*** In the example above, if you delete order 12489 from the database, you also *lose* all the information about part AX12. For example, you would no longer know that part AX12 is an iron.

These problems occur because you have a column, Part Description, that is dependent on only a portion of the primary key, Part Number, and *not* on the complete primary key. This leads to the definition of second normal form. Second normal form represents an improvement over first normal form because it eliminates update anomalies in these situations. In order to understand second normal form, you first need to understand what a nonkey attribute (column) is.

Definition: A column is a **nonkey attribute** if it is not a part of the primary key.

The following is the definition for second normal form.

Definition: A table (relation) is in **second normal form** (2NF) if it is in first normal form and no nonkey attribute is dependent on only a portion of the primary key.

Note: If the primary key of a table contains only a single column, the table is automatically in second normal form.

For another perspective on 2NF, consider Figure 5.8. This type of diagram, sometimes called a **dependency diagram** indicates by the use of arrows all the functional dependencies in the Orders table. The arrows above the boxes indicate the normal dependencies that should be present; i.e., the primary key functionally determines all other columns. In this case, the concatenation of Order Number and Part Number determines all other columns. The arrows below the boxes are what prevent the table from being in 2NF. These arrows represent what are often termed **partial dependencies**, which are dependencies on only a portion of the primary key. In fact, another definition for 2NF is that a table is in 2NF if it is in 1NF and contains no partial dependencies.

FIGURE 5.8

· · · · · · · · · · · · · · · · · ·

Dependencies in Orders table

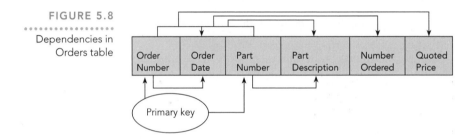

Either way you view 2NF, you can now name the fundamental problem with the Orders table: it is *not* in 2NF. While it may be pleasing to have a name for the problem, what you really need, of course, is a method to *correct* it; you want to be able to convert tables to 2NF. Such a method follows.

First, take each subset of the set of columns that make up the primary key, and begin a new table with this subset as its primary key. For the Orders table, this would yield:

```
(Order Number,
(Part Number,
(Order Number, Part Number,
```

Next, place each of the other columns with the appropriate primary key; that is, place each one with the minimal collection of columns on which it depends. For the Orders table, this would yield:

```
(Order Number, Order Date)
(Part Number, Part Description)
(Order Number, Part Number, Number Ordered, Quoted Price)
```

Each of these new tables can now be given a name that is descriptive of their contents, such as Orders, Part, and Order Line. Figure 5.9 shows samples of the tables involved.

FIGURE 5.9
. . . .
Conversion to 2NF

Orders

Order Number	Order Date	Part Number	Part Description	Number Ordered	Quoted Price
12489	9/02/2001	AX12	Iron	11	$14.95
12491	9/02/2001	BT04	Gas Grill	1	$149.99
12491	9/02/2001	BZ66	Washer	1	$399.99
12494	9/04/2001	CB03	Bike	4	$279.99
12495	9/04/2001	CX11	Blender	2	$22.95
12498	9/05/2001	AZ52	Dartboard	2	$12.95
12498	9/05/2001	BA74	Basketball	4	$24.95
12500	9/05/2001	BT04	Gas Grill	1	$149.99
12504	9/05/2001	CZ81	Treadmill	2	$325.99

is replaced by

Orders

Order Number	Order Date
12489	9/02/2001
12491	9/02/2001
12494	9/04/2001
12495	9/04/2001
12498	9/05/2001
12500	9/05/2001
12504	9/05/2001

Part

Order Number	Part Description
AX12	Iron
AZ52	Dartboard
BA74	Basketball
BH22	Cornpopper
BT04	Gas Grill
BZ66	Washer
CA14	Griddle
CB03	Bike
CX11	Blender
CZ81	Treadmill

Order Line

Order Number	Part Number	Number Ordered	Quoted Price
12489	AX12	11	$14.95
12491	BT04	1	$149.99
12491	BZ66	1	$399.99
12494	CB03	4	$279.99
12495	CX11	2	$22.95
12498	AZ52	2	$12.95
12498	BA74	4	$24.95
12500	BT04	1	$149.99
12504	CZ81	2	$325.99

Note that the update anomalies have been eliminated. A description appears only once for each part, so you do not have the redundancy that you did in the earlier design. Changing the description of part BT04 from Gas Grill to Outdoor Grill is now a simple process involving a single change. Because the description for a part occurs in a single place, it is not possible to have multiple descriptions for a single part in the database at the same time.

To add a new part and its description, you create a new row in the Part table and thus there is no need to have an order already exist for that part. Also, deleting order 12489 does not cause part number AX12 to be deleted from the Part table, and thus you still have its description (Iron) and other information in the database. Finally, you have not lost any information in the process. The data in the original design can be reconstructed from the data in the new design.

■ Third Normal Form

Problems can still exist with tables that are in 2NF. Consider the following Customer table:

```
Customer (Customer Number, Cust Last Name, Cust First Name, Balance,
Credit Limit,
        Sales Rep Number, Slsr Last Name,
        Slsr First Name)
```

Note: This table contains first and last names of both customers and sales reps. To distinguish last names, the customer's last name is denoted Cust Last Name and the sales rep's last name is Slsr Last Name. Similarly, the customer's first name is Cust First Name and the sales rep's first name is Slsr First Name.

The functional dependencies in this table are:

```
Customer Number → Cust Last Name, Cust First Name, Balance, Credit Limit,
        Sales Rep Number, Slsr Last Name, Slsr First Name
Sales Rep Number → Slsr Last Name, Slsr First Name
```

Customer Number determines all the other columns. In addition, Sales Rep Number determines Slsr Last Name and Slsr First Name.

If the primary key of a table is a single column, the table is automatically in second normal form. If the table were not in 2NF, some columns would be dependent on only a *portion* of the primary key, which is impossible when the primary key is just one column. Thus, the Customer table is in 2NF. It is shown in Figure 5.10.

FIGURE 5.10

Sample Customer table

Customer

Customer Number	Cust Last Name	Cust First Name	Balance	Credit Limit	Sales Rep Number	Slsr Last Name	Slsr First Name
124	Adams	Sally	$818.75	$1000	03	Jones	Mary
256	Samuels	Ann	$21.50	$1500	06	Smith	William
311	Charles	Don	$825.75	$1000	12	Diaz	Miguel
315	Daniels	Tom	$770.75	$750	06	Smith	William
405	Williams	Al	$402.75	$1500	12	Diaz	Miguel
412	Adams	Sally	$1817.50	$2000	03	Jones	Mary
522	Nelson	Mary	$98.75	$1500	12	Diaz	Miguel
567	Dinh	Tran	$402.40	$750	06	Smith	William
587	Galvez	Mara	$114.60	$1000	06	Smith	William
622	Martin	Dan	$1045.75	$1000	03	Jones	Mary

As the sample demonstrates, this table possesses problems similar to those encountered earlier, even though it is in 2NF. In this case, the problem is the name of a sales rep that occurs many times in the table; see sales rep 12 (Miguel Diaz), for example. This redundancy results in the same set of problems that was described in the previous Orders table. In addition to the problem of wasted space, you have similar update anomalies, as follows:

1. *Updates.* A change to the name of a sales rep requires not one change to the table, but several. Again, the update process becomes very cumbersome.

114

2. ***Inconsistent data.*** There is nothing about the design that would prohibit a sales rep from having two different names in the database. In fact, if the same sales rep represents 20 customers (and thus would be found on 20 different rows), he or she could appear associated with 20 different names in the database.

3. ***Additions.*** In order to add sales rep 47, whose name is Mary Daniels, to the database, she must represent at least one customer. If she has not yet been assigned any customers, then either you cannot record the fact that her name is Mary Daniels or you have to create a fictitious customer for her to represent. Again, this is not a desirable solution to the problem.

4. ***Deletions.*** If you were to delete all the customers of sales rep 06 from the database, then you would also lose all information concerning sales rep 06.

These update anomalies are caused by the fact that Sales Rep Number determines Slsr Last Name and Slsr First Name, but Sales Rep Number is not the primary key. As a result, the same Sales Rep Number and consequently the same Slsr Last Name and Slsr First Name can appear on many different rows.

You have seen that 2NF is an improvement over 1NF, but in order to eliminate 2NF problems, you need an even better strategy for creating tables in the database. Third normal form provides that strategy. Before looking at third normal form, however, you need to become familiar with the special name that is given to any column that determines another column (like Sales Rep Number in the Customer table).

Definition: Any column (or collection of columns) that determines another column is called a determinant.

Certainly the primary key in a table will be a determinant. In fact, by definition, any candidate key will be a determinant. (Remember that a candidate key is a column or collection of columns that could function as the primary key.) In this case, Sales Rep Number is a determinant, but it is certainly not a candidate key, and that is the problem.

Definition: A table is in third normal form (3NF) if it is in second normal form and if the only determinants it contains are candidate keys.

Again, for an additional perspective, you can use a dependency diagram, as shown in Figure 5.11. As before, the arrows above the boxes represent the normal dependencies of all columns on the primary key. It is the arrow below the boxes that causes the problem. The presence of this arrow means that Sales Rep Number is a determinant. If there were arrows from Sales Rep Number to all the columns, Sales Rep Number would be a candidate key and you would not have a problem. The absence of these arrows indicates that this table possesses a determinant that is not a candidate key. Thus, the table is not in 3NF.

FIGURE 5.11

Dependencies in Customer table

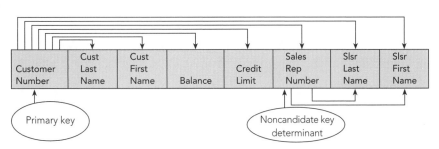

You have now identified the problem with the Customer table: it is not in 3NF. What you need is a scheme to correct the deficiency in the Customer table and in all tables having similar deficiencies. Such a method follows.

First, for each determinant that is not a candidate key, remove from the table the columns that depend on this determinant (but don't remove the determinant). Next, create a new table containing all the columns from the original table that depend on this determinant. Finally, make the determinant the primary key of this new table.

In the Customer table, for example, Slsr Last Name and Slsr First Name are removed because they depend on the determinant Sales Rep Number, which is not a candidate key. A new table is formed, consisting of Sales Rep Number as the primary key, Slsr Last Name and Slsr First Name. Specifically:

```
Customer (Customer Number, Cust Last Name, Cust First Name, Balance,
        Credit Limit, Sales Rep Number, Slsr Last Name,
        Slsr First Name)
```

is replaced by:

```
Customer (Customer Number, Cust Last Name, Cust First Name, Balance,
        Credit Limit, Sales Rep Number)
```

and:

```
Sales Rep (Sales Rep Number, Slsr Last Name, Slsr First Name)
```

Figure 5.12 shows samples of the tables involved.

FIGURE 5.12

Conversion to 3NF

Customer

Customer Number	Cust Last Name	Cust First Name	Balance	Credit Limit	Sales Rep Number	Slsr Last Name	Slsr First Name
124	Adams	Sally	$818.75	$1000	03	Jones	Mary
256	Samuels	Ann	$21.50	$1500	06	Smith	William
311	Charles	Don	$825.75	$1000	12	Diaz	Miguel
315	Daniels	Tom	$770.75	$750	06	Smith	William
405	Williams	Al	$402.75	$1500	12	Diaz	Miguel
412	Adams	Sally	$1817.50	$2000	03	Jones	Mary
522	Nelson	Mary	$98.75	$1500	12	Diaz	Miguel
567	Dinh	Tran	$402.40	$750	06	Smith	William
587	Galvez	Mara	$114.60	$1000	06	Smith	William
622	Martin	Dan	$1045.75	$1000	03	Jones	Mary

(continued)

116

is replaced by

Customer

Customer Number	Cust Last Name	Cust First Name	Balance	Credit Limit	Sales Rep Number
124	Adams	Sally	$818.75	$1000	03
256	Samuels	Ann	$21.50	$1500	06
311	Charles	Don	$825.75	$1000	12
315	Daniels	Tom	$770.75	$750	06
405	Williams	Al	$402.75	$1500	12
412	Adams	Sally	$1817.50	$2000	03
522	Nelson	Mary	$98.75	$1500	12
567	Dinh	Tran	$402.40	$750	06
587	Galvez	Mara	$114.60	$1000	06
622	Martin	Dan	$1045.75	$1000	03

(continued)

and

Sales Rep

Sales Rep Number	Slsr Last Name	Slsr First Name
03	Jones	Mary
06	Smith	William
12	Diaz	Miguel

Note: The first and last names of customers are now in the Customer table. The first and last names of sales reps are now in the Sales Rep table. Thus, there is no longer any need to have special names to distinguish between the fields. (By adhering to the database design process you will see in the next chapter, you would typically rename them at this point to simply First Name and Last Name. For the purposes of this discussion, however, you will keep the current names: Cust Last Name, Cust First Name, Slsr Last Name, and Slsr First Name.)

Have you now corrected all previously identified problems? A sales rep's name appears only once, thus avoiding redundancy and making the process of changing a sales rep's name a very simple one. It is not possible with this design for the same sales rep to have two different names in the database. To add a new sales rep to the database, you add a row in the Sales Rep table, meaning it is not necessary to have a pre-existing customer whom the sales rep represents. Finally, deleting all the customers of a given sales rep will not remove the sales rep's record from the Sales Rep table, so you do retain the sales rep's name; all the data in the original table can be reconstructed from the data in the new collection of tables. All previously mentioned problems have indeed been solved.

Incorrect Decompositions

It is important to note that the decomposition of a table into two or more 3NF tables *must* be accomplished by the method described in the previous sections, even though there are other possibilities that might seem at first glance to be legitimate. Let's examine two other decompositions of the Customer table into 3NF tables in order to understand the difficulties they pose.

What if, in the decomposition process,

```
Customer (Customer Number, Cust Last Name, Cust First Name, Balance,
    Credit Limit, Sales Rep Number, Slsr Last Name,
    Slsr First Name)
```

is replaced by:

```
Customer (Customer Number, Cust Last Name, Cust First Name, Balance,
    Credit Limit, Sales Rep Number)
```

and:

```
Sales Rep (Sales Rep Number, Slsr Last Name, Slsr First Name)
```

Samples of these tables are shown in Figure 5.13. Both new tables are in 3NF. In addition, by joining these two tables together on Customer Number you can reconstruct the original Customer table. The result, however, still suffers from some of the same kinds of problems that the original Customer table did.

FIGURE 5.13

Incorrect
decomposition

Customer

Customer Number	Cust Last Name	Cust First Name	Balance	Credit Limit	Sales Rep Number	Slsr Last Name	Slsr First Name
124	Adams	Sally	$818.75	$1000	03	Jones	Mary
256	Samuels	Ann	$21.50	$1500	06	Smith	William
311	Charles	Don	$825.75	$1000	12	Diaz	Miguel
315	Daniels	Tom	$770.75	$750	06	Smith	William
405	Williams	Al	$402.75	$1500	12	Diaz	Miguel
412	Adams	Sally	$1817.50	$2000	03	Jones	Mary
522	Nelson	Mary	$98.75	$1500	12	Diaz	Miguel
567	Dinh	Tran	$402.40	$750	06	Smith	William
587	Galvez	Mara	$114.60	$1000	06	Smith	William
622	Martin	Dan	$1045.75	$1000	03	Jones	Mary

is replaced by
Customer

Customer Number	Cust Last Name	Cust First Name	Balance	Credit Limit	Sales Rep Number
124	Adams	Sally	$818.75	$1000	03
256	Samuels	Ann	$21.50	$1500	06
311	Charles	Don	$825.75	$1000	12
315	Daniels	Tom	$770.75	$750	06
405	Williams	Al	$402.75	$1500	12
412	Adams	Sally	$1817.50	$2000	03
522	Nelson	Mary	$98.75	$1500	12
567	Dinh	Tran	$402.40	$750	06
587	Galvez	Mara	$114.60	$1000	06
622	Martin	Dan	$1045.75	$1000	03

and
Sales Rep

Customer Number	Slsr Last Name	Slsr First Name
124	Jones	Mary
256	Smith	William
311	Diaz	Miguel
315	Smith	William
405	Diaz	Miguel
412	Jones	Mary
522	Diaz	Miguel
567	Smith	William
587	Smith	William
622	Jones	Mary

Consider, for example, the redundancy in the storage of sales reps' names, the problem encountered in changing the name of a sales rep, and the difficulty of adding a new sales rep for whom there are not yet any customers. In addition, because the sales rep number is in one table and the sales rep name is in another, you have actually *split a functional dependence across two different tables*. Thus, this decomposition, while it may appear to be valid, is definitely not a desirable way to create 3NF tables.

There is another decomposition that you might choose, and that is to replace:

```
Customer (Customer Number, Cust Last Name, Cust First Name, Balance,
     Credit Limit, Sales Rep Number, Slsr Last Name,
     Slsr First Name)
```

with:

```
Customer (Customer Number, Cust Last Name, Cust First Name, Balance,
     Credit Limit, Slsr Last Name, Slsr First Name)
```

and:

```
Sales Rep (Sales Rep Number, Slsr Last Name, Slsr First Name)
```

Samples of these tables are shown in Figure 5.14.

FIGURE 5.14

Second incorrect
decomposition

Customer

Customer Number	Cust Last Name	Cust First Name	Balance	Credit Limit	Sales Rep Number	Slsr Last Name	Slsr First Name
124	Adams	Sally	$818.75	$1000	03	Jones	Mary
256	Samuels	Ann	$21.50	$1500	06	Smith	William
311	Charles	Don	$825.75	$1000	12	Diaz	Miguel
315	Daniels	Tom	$770.75	$750	06	Smith	William
405	Williams	Al	$402.75	$1500	12	Diaz	Miguel
412	Adams	Sally	$1817.50	$2000	03	Jones	Mary
522	Nelson	Mary	$98.75	$1500	12	Diaz	Miguel
567	Dinh	Tran	$402.40	$750	06	Smith	William
587	Galvez	Mara	$114.60	$1000	06	Smith	William
622	Martin	Dan	$1045.75	$1000	03	Jones	Mary

(continued)

is replaced by

Customer

Customer Number	Cust Last Name	Cust First Name	Balance	Credit Limit	Sales Rep Number	Slsr First Name
124	Adams	Sally	$818.75	$1000	Jones	Mary
256	Samuels	Ann	$21.50	$1500	Smith	William
311	Charles	Don	$825.75	$1000	Diaz	Miguel
315	Daniels	Tom	$770.75	$750	Smith	William
405	Williams	Al	$402.75	$1500	Diaz	Miguel
412	Adams	Sally	$1817.50	$2000	Jones	Mary
522	Nelson	Mary	$98.75	$1500	Diaz	Miguel
567	Dinh	Tran	$402.40	$750	Smith	William
587	Galvez	Mara	$114.60	$1000	Smith	William
622	Martin	Dan	$1045.75	$1000	Jones	Mary

(continued)

and

Sales Rep

Sales Rep Number	Slsr Last Name	Slsr First Name
03	Jones	Mary
06	Smith	William
12	Diaz	Miguel

This seems to be a possibility. Not only are both tables in 3NF, but joining them together based on Slsr Last Name and Slsr First Name seems to reconstruct the data in the original table. Or does it? Suppose that the name of sales rep 06 is also Mary Jones. In that case, when you join the two new tables together, you will get a row in which customer 124 (Sally Adams) is associated with sales rep 03 and *another* row in which customer 124 is associated with sales rep 06. Because you obviously want decompositions that preserve the original information, this scheme is not appropriate.

QUESTION   Using the types of entities found in a college environment (faculty, students, departments, courses, etc.), create an example of a table that is in 1NF but not in 2NF and an example of a table that is in 2NF but not 3NF. In each case justify your solutions and show how to convert to the higher forms.

ANSWER   There are many possible solutions. If your answer differs from the following solution, this does not mean that it is an unsatisfactory solution.

To create a 1NF table that is not in 2NF, you need a table that (a) has no repeating groups and (b) has at least one column that is dependent on only a portion of the primary key. For a column to be dependent on a portion of the primary key, the primary key must contain at least two columns. The following is a picture of what you need:

(__1__, __2__, 3 , 4)

This table contains four columns, numbered 1, 2, 3, and 4, in which the combination of columns 1 and 2 functionally determines both columns 3 and 4. In addition, neither column 1 nor column 2 can determine *all* other columns, otherwise the primary key would contain only this one column. Finally, you want part of the primary key, say, column 2, to determine another column, say, column 4. Now that you know the pattern you need, you would like to find columns from within the college environment to fit it. One example would be:

(Student Number, Course Number, Grade, Course Description)

In this example, the concatenation of Student Number and Course Number determines both Grade and Course Description. Both columns are required to determine Grade, and thus the primary key consists of their concatenation. The Course Description, however, is only dependent on the Course Number. This violates second normal form. To convert this table to 2NF, you replace it with the two tables:

```
(Student Number, Course Number, Grade)
```

and:

```
(Course Number, Course Description)
```

You now give these tables appropriate names.

To create a table that is in 2NF but not in 3NF, you need a 2NF table in which there is a determinant that is *not* a candidate key. If you choose a table that has a single column as the primary key, it is automatically in 2NF, so the real problem is the determinant. You need a table like the following:

```
(____1____,      2     ,      3     )
```

This table contains three columns, numbered 1, 2, and 3, in which column 1 determines each of the others and thus is the primary key. In addition, if column 2 determines column 3, it is a determinant. If column 2 does not also determine column 1, then column 2 is not a candidate key. One example that fits this pattern would be:

```
(Student Number, Advisor Number, Advisor Name)
```

Here the Student Number determines both the student's Advisor Number and Advisor Name. Advisor Number determines Advisor Name, but Advisor Number does not determine Student Number, because one advisor can have many advisees. This table is in 2NF but not 3NF. To convert it to 3NF, you replace it with:

```
(Student Number, Advisor Number)
```

and:

```
(Advisor Number, Advisor Name)
```

QUESTION

Convert the following table to 3NF:

```
Student (Student Number, Student Name, Number Credits,
    Advisor Number, Advisor Name, (Course Number,
    Course Description, Grade) )
```

In this table, Student Number determines Student Name, Number Credits, Advisor Number, and Advisor Name. Advisor Number determines Advisor Name. Course Number determines Course Description. The combination of a Student Number and a Course Number determines a Grade.

ANSWER

Step 1. Remove the repeating group to convert to 1NF. This yields:

```
Student (Student Number, Student Name, Number Credits,
    Advisor Number, Advisor Name, Course Number,
    Course Description, Grade)
```

This table is now in 1NF, because it has no repeating groups. It is not, however, in 2NF, because Student Name is dependent only on Student Number, which is only a portion of the primary key.

Step 2. Convert the 1NF table to 2NF. First, for each subset of the primary key, start a table with that subset as its primary key, yielding:

```
(Student Number,
(Course Number,
(Student Number, Course Number,
```

Next, place the rest of the columns with the smallest collection of columns on which they depend, yielding:

```
(Student Number, Student Name, Number Credits,
    Advisor Number, Advisor Name)
(Course Number, Course Description)
(Student Number, Course Number, Grade)
```

Finally, assign names to each of the newly created tables:

```
Student (Student Number, Student Name, Number Credits,
    Advisor Number, Advisor Name)
Course (Course Number, Course Description)
Grade (Student Number, Course Number, Grade)
```

While these tables are all in 2NF, both Course and Grade are also in 3NF. The Student table is not in 3NF, however, because it contains a determinant, Advisor Number, that is not a candidate key.

Step 3: Convert the 2NF Student table to 3NF by removing the column that depends on the determinant Advisor Number and placing it in a separate table:

```
(Student Number, Student Name, Number Credits,
    Advisor Number)
(Advisor Number, Advisor Name)
```

Step 4: Name these tables and put the entire collection together, yielding:

```
Student (Student Number, Student Name, Number Credits,
    Advisor Number)
Advisor (Advisor Number, Advisor Name)
Course (Course Number, Course Description)
Grade (Student Number, Course Number, Grade)
```

■ Multivalued Dependencies and Fourth Normal Form

By converting a given collection of tables to an equivalent 3NF collection, you remove any problems arising from functional dependencies. Usually this means that the types of anomalies discussed in the previous section have been eliminated.

This is not always the case, however. There is a different kind of dependency that can also lead to the same types of difficulties.

To illustrate the problem, suppose you are interested in faculty members at Marvel College, a local college. In addition to faculty members, you are interested in the students they advise, and the committees on which the faculty members serve. Any faculty member can advise many students. A student can have more than one faculty member as an advisor, since students can have more than one major. Any faculty member can serve on more than one committee. Some don't serve on any. Suppose that, as an initial relational design for this situation, you chose the following unnormalized table:

Faculty (<u>Faculty Number</u>, (Student Number), (Committee Code))

The single table Faculty has a primary key of Faculty Number and two separate repeating groups, Student Number (the number that identifies the student) and Committee Code (the code that identifies the committee, e.g., ADV for the Advisory committee, PER for the personnel committee). To convert this table to 1NF, you might be tempted to merely remove the two repeating groups and expand the primary key to include both Student Number and Committee Code. This solution would give this table:

Faculty (<u>Faculty Number</u>, <u>Student Number</u>, <u>Committee Code</u>)

Samples of these tables are shown in Figure 5.15.

FIGURE 5.15

Incorrect way to remove repeating groups — relation is not in 3NF

Faculty

Faculty Number	Student Number	Committee Code
123	12805 24139	ADV PER HSG
444	57384	HSG
456	24139 36273 37573	CUR

is replaced by

Faculty

Faculty Number	Student Number	Committee Code
123	12805	ADV
123	12805	PER
123	12805	HSG
123	24139	ADV
123	24139	PER
123	24139	HSG
444	57384	HSG
456	24139	CUR
456	36273	CUR
456	37573	CUR

You may already have suspected that there are some problems with this approach. If so, you are correct. It is a strange way to normalize the original table. Yet, it is precisely this approach to the removal of repeating groups that leads to the problems alluded to in the beginning of this section concerning multivalued dependencies. You will later examine how this table should have been normalized to avoid the problems altogether. For the moment, however, let's push ahead with this table and discuss what kinds of problems are present.

The first thing you should observe about the new faculty table is that it is in 3NF, since there are no repeating groups, no column is dependent on only a portion of the primary key, and there are no determinants that are not candidate keys. There are several problems, however, with this 3NF table:

1. **Update.** Changing the code of a committee for faculty member 123 requires more than one change. If you change the code from ADV to CUR, the change should be

made in both of the first two rows in the table. After all, it doesn't make sense to say that the committee is ADV when associated with student 12805 and CUR when associated with student 24139. It is the same committee served on by the same faculty member. The faculty member does not serve on one committee when advising one student and a different committee when advising another.

2. ***Additions.*** Suppose that faculty member 665 joins the faculty at Marvel. Also suppose that this faculty member does not yet serve on any committee. When this faculty member begins to advise student 44332, you have a problem, since Committee Code is part of the primary key. You would need to enter a fictitious committee code in this situation.

3. ***Deletions.*** If faculty member 444 no longer advises student 57384 and you delete the appropriate row from the table, you lose the information that faculty member 444 serves on the HSG (housing) committee.

These problems are certainly similar to those encountered in the discussions of both 2NF and 3NF, but there are no functional dependencies among the columns in this table. A given faculty member is not associated with one student, as he or she would be if this were a functional dependence. Each faculty member, however, is associated with a specific collection of students. More importantly, this association is *independent* of any association with committees. It is this independence that causes the problem. This type of dependency is called a multivalued dependency.

Definition: In a table with columns A, B, and C, there is a multivalued dependence of column B on column A (also read as "B is multidependent on A" or "A multidetermines B"), if each value for A is associated with a specific collection of values for B and, furthermore, this collection is independent of any values for C. This is usually written as like this:

A →→ B

Definition: A table is in fourth normal form (4NF) if it is in 3NF and there are no multivalued dependencies.

As you might expect, converting a table to 4NF is similar to the normalization process encountered in the treatments of 2NF and 3NF. You split the table into separate tables, each containing the column that multidetermines the others, in this case the faculty number. This means you replace:

```
Faculty (Faculty Number, Student Number, Committee Code)
```

with:

```
Fac Student (Faculty Number, Student Number)
Fac Committee (Faculty Number, Committee Code)
```

Figure 5.16 shows samples of these tables. As before, the problems have disappeared. There is no problem with changing the committee code ADV to CUR, since it occurs only in one place. To add the information that faculty member 665 advises student 44332, you need only add a row to the Fac Student table. It does not matter whether this faculty member serves on a committee. Finally, to delete the information that faculty member 444 advises student 57384, you need only remove a row from the Fac Student table. In this case, you do not lose the information that this faculty member serves on the HSG committee.

FIGURE 5.16
· · · · · · · · · · · · · · · · · · ·
Conversion to 4NF

Faculty

Faculty Number	Student Number	Committee Code
123	12805	ADV
123	24139	ADV
123	12805	PER
123	24139	PER
123	12805	HSG
123	24139	HSG
456	37573	CUR
456	24139	CUR
456	36273	CUR
444	57384	HSG

is replaced by
Fac Student

Faculty Number	Student Number
123	12805
123	24139
456	37573
456	24139
456	36273
444	57384

and
Fac Committee

Faculty Number	Committee Code
123	ADV
123	PER
123	HSG
456	CUR
444	HSG

The four normal forms are summarized in Table 5.1.

TABLE 5.1
· · · · · · · · · · · · · · · · · · ·
Normal forms

Normal Form	Meaning/Required Conditions	Notes
1NF	No repeating groups	
2NF	1NF and no nonkey column dependent on only a portion of the primary key	Automatically 2NF if the primary key contains only a single column.
3NF	2NF and the only determinants are candidate keys	
4NF	3NF and no multivalued dependencies	

■ Avoiding the Problem

Any table that is not in 4NF suffers some serious problems, but there is a way to avoid dealing with the issue. It is better to have a design methodology for normalizing tables that will prevent this situation from occurring in the first place. You already have most of such a methodology in place from the discussion of the 1NF, 2NF, and 3NF normalization process. All you need is a slightly more sophisticated method for converting an unnormalized table to 1NF.

The conversion of an unnormalized table to 1NF requires the removal of repeating groups. When this was first demonstrated, you merely removed the repeating group symbol and expanded the primary key. You will recall, for example, that

```
Orders (Order Number, Order Date, (Part Number, Number Ordered) )
```

became

```
Orders (Order Number, Order Date, Part Number, Number Ordered)
```

The primary key was expanded to include the primary key of the original table together with the key to the repeating group.

What if there are two or more repeating groups, however? The method you used earlier is inadequate for such situations. Instead, you must place each separate repeating group in a separate table. Each table will contain all the columns that make up the given repeating group, as well as the primary key to the original unnormalized table. The primary key to each new table will be the concatenation of the primary key of the original table and the primary key to the repeating group.

For example, consider the following unnormalized table containing two separate repeating groups:

```
Faculty (Faculty Number, Faculty Name, (Student Number, Student Name),
    (Committee Code, Committee Description) )
```

where Faculty Name is the name of the faculty member and Student Name is the name of the student. The columns Committee Code and Committee Description refer to the committee code and committee description. (For example, one row in this table would have PER in the Committee Code column and "Personnel Committee" in the Committee Description column.) Applying this new method to create 1NF tables would produce:

```
Faculty (Faculty Number, Faculty Name)
Fac Student (Faculty Number, Student Number, Student Name)
Fac Committee (Faculty Number, Committee Code, Committee Description)
```

As you can see, the problems with multivalued dependencies have been avoided. At this point, you have a collection of 1NF tables and you still need to convert them to 3NF. By using the above process, however, you are guaranteed that the result will also be in 4NF.

■ SUMMARY

- Column B is functionally dependent on column (or collection of columns) A if a value of A uniquely determines a value of B at any point in time.

- The primary key is a column (or collection of columns), A, such that all other columns are functionally dependent on A and no subcollection of the columns in A also has this property.

- If there is more than one possible choice for the primary key, one of the possibilities is chosen to be *the* primary key. The others are referred to as candidate keys.

- A table (relation) is in first normal form (1NF) if it does not contain repeating groups.

- A table is in second normal form (2NF) if it is in 1NF and if no column that is not a part of the primary key is dependent on only a portion of the primary key.

- A determinant is any column that functionally determines another column.

- A table is in third normal form (3NF) if it is in 2NF and if the only determinants it contains are candidate keys.

- A collection of tables that is not in 3NF possesses inherent problems (called update anomalies). Replacing this collection by an equivalent collection of tables that is in 3NF removes these anomalies. This replacement must be done carefully, following a method like the one proposed in this text. If not, other problems, such as those discussed in this chapter, may very well be introduced.

- A table is in fourth normal form (4NF) if it is in 3NF and there are no multivalued dependencies.

■ KEY TERMS

alternate key
candidate key
dependency diagram
determinant
first normal form (1NF)
fourth normal form (4NF)
functional dependence
multivalued dependency

nonkey attribute
normalization
partial dependency
primary key
second normal form (2NF)
third normal form (3NF)
unnormalized relation
update anomaly

■ REVIEW QUESTIONS

1. Define functional dependence.

2. Give an example of a column, A, and another column, B, such that B is functionally dependent on A. Give an example of a column, C, and a column, D, such that D is not functionally dependent on C.

3. Define primary key.

4. Define candidate key.

5. Define first normal form.

6. Define second normal form. What types of problems are encountered in tables that are not in second normal form?

7. Define third normal form. What types of problems are encountered in tables that are not in third normal form?

8. Define fourth normal form. What types of problems are encountered in tables that are not in fourth normal form?

9. Consider a student table containing student number, student name, student's major department, student's advisor number, student's advisor name, student's advisor office number, student's advisor phone number, student's number of credits, and student's class standing (freshman, sophomore, and so on). List the functional dependencies that exist, along with the assumptions that would support these dependencies.

10. Using the types of entities found in Henry's system in Chapter 1 (books, authors, and publishers), create an example of a table that is in 1NF but not in 2NF and an example of a table that is in 2NF but not in 3NF. In each case, justify the answers and show how to convert to the higher forms.

11. Convert the following table to an equivalent collection of tables that is in 3NF.

```
Patient (Household Number, Household Name, Household Street,
        Household City, Household State, Household Zip, Balance,
        Patient Number, Patient Name, (Service Code,
        Service Description, Service Fee)
```

This is a table concerning information about patients of a dentist. Each patient belongs to a household. The head of the household is designated as HH in the table. The following dependencies exist in Patient.

```
Patient Number → Household Number, Household Name,
        Household Street, Household City, Household State,
        Household Zip, Balance, Patient Name
Household Number → Household Name, Household Street,
        Household City, Household State, Household Zip, Balance
Service Code → Service Description, Service Fee
```

12. List the functional dependencies in the following table subject to the specified conditions. Convert this table to an equivalent collection of tables that are in 3NF.

```
Invoice (Invoice Number, Customer Number, Last Name, First Name, Street,
        City, State, Zip Code, Invoice Date, (Part Number,
        Part Description, Price, Number Shipped)  )
```

This table concerns invoice information. For a given invoice (identified by the invoice number), there will be a single customer. The customer's number, name, and address appear on the invoice as well as the invoice date. Also, there may be several different parts appearing on the invoice. For each part that appears, the part number, description, price, and number shipped will be displayed. The price is from the current master price list.

13. Using your knowledge of a college environment, determine the functional dependencies that exist in the following table. After these have been determined, convert this table to an equivalent collection of tables that are in 3NF.

```
Student (Student Number, Student Name, Number Credits,
        Advisor Number, Advisor Name, Dept Number, Dept Name,
        (Course Number, Course Description, Course Term,
        Grade) )
```

14. Determine the multivalued dependencies in the following table. Convert this table to an equivalent collection of tables that is in 4NF.

```
Course (Course Number, Textbook, Instructor Number)
```

Each course is associated with a specific set of textbooks unrelated to the instructors who are teaching the course (i.e., even though many instructors may be teaching the course, they will all use the same set of textbooks).

15. The following unnormalized table is similar in content to the table in Question 14. Convert it to 4NF. Did you encounter the table from that problem along the way?

```
Course (Course Number, Course Description, Number of Credits,
        (Textbook), (Instructor Number, Instructor Name) )
```

Note that this table has two separate repeating groups, one listing the textbooks used for the course and the other listing the instructors who are teaching the course.

CHAPTER **6**

Database Design 2: Design Methodology

OBJECTIVES

- Discuss the general process and goals of database design.

- Define user views and explain their function.

- Explain how to produce a pictorial representation of a database design.

- Present a methodology for database design at the information level as well as examples illustrating the use of this methodology.

- Explain the process of creating a design that is appropriate for a relational model system from the information-level design.

- Illustrate the design process with a comprehensive example.

Introduction

Now that you have learned how to identify and correct poor designs, you will turn your attention to the design process itself; that is, the process of determining the tables and columns, formally called attributes, that make up the database and determining the relationships between the various tables.

Database design is often approached as a two-step process. In the first step, a database is designed that satisfies the requirements as cleanly as possible. This step is called **information-level design**, and it is taken *independently* of any particular DBMS that will ultimately be used. In the second step, which is called the **physical-level design**, the information-level design is transformed into a design for the specific DBMS that will be used. Naturally, the characteristics of that DBMS must come into play during this step.

The next section introduces the information-level design process. After that, you will examine the general database design methodology, followed by a study of examples illustrating this methodology. The physical-level design process is presented next. Then you will examine two additional issues — Entity-Relationship diagram alternatives and top-down vs. bottom-up methodology — with respect to database design. Finally, an optional special project—a comprehensive database design example — is presented.

■ Information-Level Design

User Views

No matter which database design approach is adopted, a complete database design that satisfies all the requirements can only rarely be a one-step process. Unless the requirements are exceptionally simple, it is usually necessary to subdivide the overall job of database design into smaller tasks. This is often done through the separate consideration of individual pieces of the design problem. In design problems for large organizations, these pieces are often called user views, and you will use the same terminology here. A **user view** is the set of requirements that is necessary to support the operations of a particular user. For example, for the person in charge of inventory at Premiere Products, the database must be capable of storing the part's number, description, units on hand, item class, the number of the warehouse in which the part is located, and the price for each part in inventory.

For each user view, a database structure to support the view must be designed and then merged into a cumulative design. Each user view, in general, will be much simpler than the total collection of requirements, so working on these individual tasks will be much more manageable than attempting to turn the design of the entire database into one large task.

The General Database Design Methodology

The database design methodology presented in this text involves representing individual user views, refining them to eliminate any problems, and then merging them into a cumulative design. Once all user views have been represented and merged, the cumulative design will be the complete design for the database.

A "user" in this methodology could be a person or a group that will use the system, a report that the system must produce, or a type of transaction that the system must support. In the last two instances, you might think of the user as the person who will use the report or enter the transaction. In fact, if the same individual required three separate reports, for example, you would probably be better off to consider each of the reports as a separate user view, even though only one "user" was involved, because the smaller the user view, the easier it is to work with.

You will now examine the methodology itself. For each user view, you need to complete the following steps:

1. Represent the user view as a collection of tables.

2. Normalize these tables.

3. Identify all keys.

4. Merge the result of the previous steps into the design.

You will now examine each of these steps in detail.

■ The Methodology

Represent the User View as a Collection of Tables

When given a user view or some sort of stated requirement, you must develop a collection of tables that will support it. In some cases, the collection of tables may be obvious to you. Let's suppose, for example, that a given user view involves departments and employees. Let's assume further that each department can employ many employees, but that each employee is assigned to exactly one department (a typical restriction). A design similar to the following may have naturally occurred to you and is an appropriate design.

```
Department (Department Number, Name, Location)
Employee (Employee Number, Last Name, First Name, Street, City, State,
     Zip Code, Wage Rate, Soc Sec Number, Department Number)
```

You will undoubtedly find that the more designs you have done, the easier it will be for you to develop such a collection without resorting to any special procedure. The real question is: What procedure should be followed if a correct design is not so obvious? In this case, you can take the following four steps:

Step 1. Determine the entities involved and create a separate table for each type of entity. At this point, you do not need to do anything more than give the table a name. For example, if a user view involves departments and employees, you can create a Department table and an Employee table. At this point, you write something like this:

```
Department (
Employee (
```

That is, you write the name of a table and a left parenthesis, *and that is all*. Later steps will fill in the columns (attributes) in these tables.

Step 2. Determine the primary key for each of these tables. This fills in one or more columns (depending on how many columns make up the primary key). Other columns will not be filled in until later. It may seem strange, but even though you have yet to determine the columns in the table, you can usually determine the primary key. For example, the primary key to an Employee table will probably be the Employee Number, and the primary key to a Department table will probably be the department number.

The primary key is the unique identifier, so the essential question here is: What does it take to uniquely identify an employee or a department? Even if you are in the process of trying to automate a system that was previously manual, some unique identifier can still usually be found in the manual system. If not, it is probably time to assign one. Let's say that in a particular manual system, customers did not have numbers. The customer base was small enough that the organization felt that customer numbers were not needed. Now is a good time to assign them, because the company is computerizing its records. These numbers would then be the unique identifier you are seeking.

Now add these primary keys to what you have written already. At this point, you have something like the following:

```
Department (Department Number,
Employee (Employee Number,
```

That is, you have the name of the table and the primary key, but that is all. Later steps will fill in the other columns.

Step 3. Determine the properties for each of these entities. You can look at the user requirements and then determine the other properties of each entity that are required. These properties, along with the primary key identified in Step 2, become columns in the appropriate tables. For example, an employee entity may require Last Name, First Name, Street, City, State, Zip Code, and Soc Sec Number (social security number). The department entity may require Name (department name) and Location (department location). Adding these to what is already in place produces the following:

```
Department (Department Number, Name, Location)
Employee (Employee Number, Last Name, First Name, Street, City, State,
    Zip Code, Wage Rate, Soc Sec Number)
```

Step 4. Determine relationships among the entities. The basic relationships are one-to-many, many-to-many, and one-to-one. You will now see how to handle each of these types of relationships.

One-to-many

A one-to-many relationship is implemented by including the primary key of the "one" table as a foreign key in the "many" table. Let's suppose, that each employee is assigned to a single department but that a department can have many employees. Thus *one* department is related to *many* employees. In this case, you would include the primary key of the Department table (the "one") as a foreign key in the Employee table (the "many"). Thus, the tables would now look like this:

```
Department (Department Number, Name, Location)
Employee (Employee Number, Last Name, First Name, Street, City, State,
    Zip Code, Wage Rate, Soc Sec Number, Department Number)
```

Many-to-many

A many-to-many relationship is implemented by creating a new table whose primary key is the combination of the primary keys of the original tables. Suppose that each employee can be assigned to multiple departments and that each department can have many employees.

In this case, you create a new table whose primary key is the combination of Employee Number and Department Number. Because the new table represents the fact that an employee *works in* a department, you might choose to call it Works In, in which case the collection of tables is as follows:

```
Department (Department Number, Name, Location)
Employee (Employee Number, Last Name, First Name, Street, City, State,
     Zip Code, Wage Rate, Soc Sec Number)
Works In (Employee Number, Department Number)
```

In some situations, no other attributes are required in the new table. The other attributes in the Works In table would be those attributes that depended on both the employee and the department, if such attributes existed. One possibility, for example, would be the date when the employee was first assigned to the department, because it depends on *both* the employee *and* the department.

One-to-one

If each employee is assigned to a single department and each department consists of only one employee, the relationship between employees and departments is one-to-one. (Such relationships are rare in practice.) The simplest way to implement a one-to-one relationship is to treat it as a one-to-many relationship. But which is the "one" part of the relationship and which is the "many" part? Sometimes looking ahead helps. For instance, in the example shown here, you might ask: If the relationship changes in the future, is it more likely that one employee will be assigned to many departments or that one department may consist of several employees rather than just one? If you feel, for example, that it is more likely that a department would be allowed to contain more than one employee, you would make Employee the "many" part of the relationship. If the answer is that both things might very well happen, you might even treat the relationship as many-to-many. If neither change was likely to occur, you could arbitrarily choose the "many" part of the relationship.

Normalize these Tables

Normalize each table, with the target being third normal form. (The target is actually fourth normal form, but a little care in the early phases of the normalization process will usually alleviate the need to consider fourth normal form.)

Represent all Keys

Identify all keys. The types of keys you must identify are primary keys, alternate keys, secondary keys, and foreign keys.

1. *Primary*. The primary key has already been determined in the earlier steps.

2. *Alternate*. Recall from Chapter 5 that an alternate key is a column (attribute) or collection of columns that could have been chosen as primary key but was not. It is not common to have alternate keys, but if they do exist, and if the system is to enforce their uniqueness, they should be so noted.

3. *Secondary*. If there are any secondary keys (columns that are of interest strictly for the purpose of retrieval), they should be represented at this point. If a user were to indicate, for example, that rapidly retrieving an employee record on the basis of his or her last name was important, you would designate Last Name as a secondary key.

4. *Foreign*. This is in many ways the most important category, because it is through foreign keys that relationships among tables are established and that certain types of integrity constraints are enforced in the database. Remember that a foreign key is a column (or collection of columns) in one table that is required to either match the value of the primary key for some row in another table or be null. (This is the property called referential integrity.) Consider, for example, the following tables:

```
Department (Department Number, Name, Location)
Employee (Employee Number, Last Name, First Name, Street, City, State,
     Zip Code, Wage Rate, Soc Sec Number, Department Number)
```

As before, Department Number in the Employee table indicates the department to which the employee is assigned. You can say that Department Number in the Employee table is a foreign key that *identifies* Department. Thus, the number in this column on any row in the Employee table must either be the number of a department that is already in the database, or be null. (Null would indicate that, for whatever reason, the employee is not assigned to a department.)

Database Design Language (DBDL)

You need a mechanism for representing the tables and keys together with the restrictions discussed above. The standard mechanism used thus far for representing tables is fine but it does not go far enough. There is no routine way to represent alternate, secondary, or foreign keys. Because the methodology is based on the relational model, however, it is desirable to represent tables with the standard method. You will add additional features capable of representing additional information. The end result is **Database Design Language** (or **DBDL**). Figure 6.1a shows sample DBDL documentation for the Employee table. In DBDL, tables and their primary keys are represented in the usual manner.

FIGURE 6.1a

DBDL for
Employee table

```
Employee (Employee Number, Last Name, First Name, Street, City, State,
   Zip Code,
         Wage Rate, Soc Sec Number, Department Number)
         AK    Soc Sec Number
         SK    Last Name
         FK    Department Number → Department
```

FIGURE 6.1b

Summary of DBDL

DBDL (Database Design Language)

1. Relations (tables), attributes (columns), and primary keys are represented in the usual way.

2. Alternate keys are identified by the letters AK followed by the attribute(s) that comprise the alternate key.

3. Secondary keys are identified by the letters SK followed by the attribute(s) that comprise the secondary key.

4. Foreign keys are identified by the letters FK followed by the attribute(s) that comprise the foreign key. Foreign keys are followed by an arrow pointing to the relation identified by the foreign key.

136

The various types of keys are listed beneath the table. Each is preceded by an abbreviation indicating the type of key (AK - alternate key, SK - secondary key, FK - foreign key). It is sufficient to list the column or collection of columns that forms an alternate or secondary key. In the case of foreign keys, however, you must also represent the table that is identified by the foreign key; i.e., the table whose primary key the foreign key must match. This is accomplished in DBDL by following the foreign key with an arrow pointing to the table that the foreign key identifies.

Figure 6.1b summarizes the details of DBDL. Examples of DBDL are presented throughout this chapter. The only feature of DBDL not listed in the figure is actually more of a tip than a rule: When several tables are listed, a table containing a foreign key should be listed after the table that the foreign key identifies, if possible.

In the example shown in Figure 6.1a, you are saying that there is a table called Employee, consisting of columns Employee Number, Last Name, First Name, Street, City, State, Zip Code, Soc Sec Number, Wage Rate, and Department Number. The primary key is Employee Number. Another possible primary key is Soc Sec Number. You want to retrieve information efficiently, based on the employee's name, so you have designated Last Name as a secondary key. You can always add secondary key designations later in the process. The Department Number is a foreign key identifying the department to which the employee is assigned (it identifies the appropriate department in the Department table).

Entity-Relationship Diagrams

For many people, a pictorial representation, or diagram, of the structure of the database is quite useful. A popular type of diagram for the structure of a database is the Entity-Relationship (E-R) diagram. In such diagrams, rectangles represent the entities (that is, the tables). Foreign key restrictions determine relationships between the tables and these are represented as lines joining the corresponding rectangles.

There are several different styles of E-R diagrams currently in use. (There is a discussion of some alternatives later in this chapter.) The style you will use is illustrated in Figure 6.2 and has the following characteristics:

1. There is a rectangle for each table in the DBDL design; that is, there is a rectangle for each entity. The name of the entity appears just above the rectangle.

2. The primary key appears above the line in the rectangle.

3. The remaining columns appear below the line.

4. Alternate keys, secondary keys, and foreign keys are denoted with the letters AK, SK, or FK, respectively. After foreign keys that appear below the line, you will also see the letters IE, which stand for Inversion Entry. (An inversion entry is technically a non-unique access identifier for the entity. This simply means that this column is apt to be used as a vehicle for accessing the entity. For example, in Figure 6.2, this type of access would mean finding all employees in a particular department. You do not need to concern yourself with this distinction. The FK, or the fact that it is a foreign key, is the important thing.)

5. Each rectangle (table) with a foreign key is connected by a dashed line to the rectangle (table) that contains the associated primary key. There is a dot at the end of the line indicating the "many" part of this one-to-many relationship. (In Figure 6.2b, for example, *one* department is related to *many* employees so the dot is at the end of the line connected to the Employee rectangle.)

FIGURE 6.2a
·····················
DBDL

```
Department (Department Number, Name, Location)

Employee (Employee Number, Last Name, First Name, Street, City, State,
    Zip Code,
        Wage Rate, Soc Sec Number, Department Number)
        AK   Soc Sec Number
        SK   Last Name, First Name
        FK   Department Number → Department
```

FIGURE 6.2b
·····················
Entity-Relationship
diagram

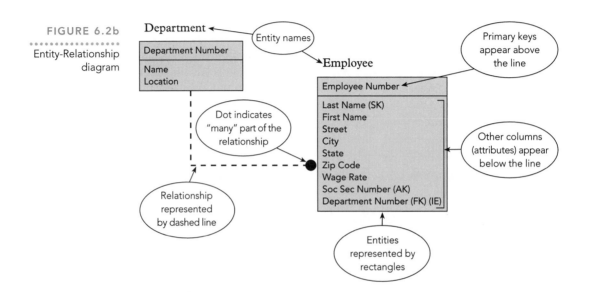

If you are using this style diagram, all the information listed in the DBDL also appears in the diagram. Thus, you would not need to also include the DBDL version of the design. There are other styles, however, that do not include such information within the diagram. In that case, you should represent the design with both the diagram and the DBDL.

Merge the Result into the Design

As soon as you have completed Steps 1 through 3 for a given user view, you can merge these results into the overall design. If the view on which you have been working happens to be the first user view, then the cumulative design will be identical to the design for this first user. Otherwise, you merge all the tables for this user to those that are currently in the cumulative design.

You then combine tables that have the same primary key to form a new table. This table has the same primary key as those tables that have been combined. The new table also contains all the columns from both tables. In the case of duplicate columns, you remove all but one copy of the column. For example, if the cumulative collection already contained the following:

```
Employee (Employee Number, Last Name, First Name, Wage Rate,
        Soc Sec Number, Department Number)
```

and the user view just completed contained the following:

```
Employee (Employee Number, Last Name, First Name, Street, City, State,
    Zip Code)
```

then the two tables would be combined, because they would have the same primary key. All the columns from both tables would appear in the new table, but without duplicates. Thus, Last Name and First Name would appear only once, even though they are in each of the individual tables. The result would be the following:

```
Employee (Employee Number, Last Name, First Name, Wage Rate,
    Soc Sec Number, Department Number, Street, City, State, Zip Code)
```

If you wanted to, you could reorder the columns at this point. You might feel, for example, that placing Street, City, State, Zip Code immediately after First Name would put it in a more natural position. This would give the following:

```
Employee (Employee Number, Last Name, First Name, Street, City, State,
    Zip Code, Wage Rate, Soc Sec Number, Department Number)
```

You would then check the new design to ensure that it was still in third normal form. If it weren't, you would convert it to 3NF before proceeding.

The process, which is summarized in Figure 6.3, is repeated for each user view until all user views have been examined. At that point, the design is reviewed in order to resolve any problems that may remain and to ensure that the needs of all individual users can indeed be met. Once this has been done, the information-level design is complete.

FIGURE 6.3
· · · · · · · · · · · · · · · · · ·
Information-level
design
methodology

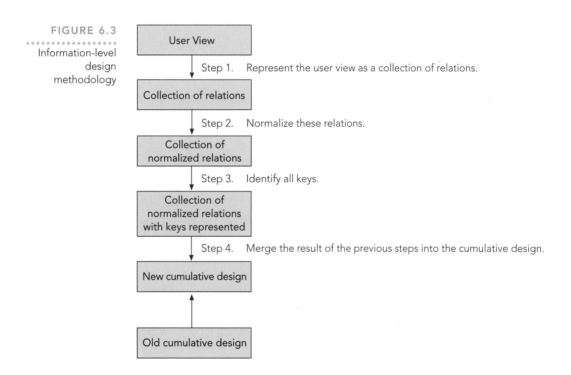

▦ Database Design Examples

You will now look at examples of database design.

<table>
<tr><td>

</td><td>

For an initial example of the design methodology, you will complete an information-level design for a database that must satisfy the following constraints and user view requirements:

User View 1 Requirements. For a sales rep, store the sales rep's number, name, address, total commission, and commission rate.

User View 2 Requirements. For a customer, store the customer's number, name, address, balance, and credit limit. In addition, store the number and name of the sales rep who represents this customer. Upon further checking with the user, you determine that a sales rep can represent many customers, but a customer must have exactly one sales rep (i.e., a customer must have a sales rep and cannot have more than one).

User View 3 Requirements. For a part, store the part's number, description, units on hand, item class, the number of the warehouse in which the part is located, and the price. (**Note:** All units of a particular part will be stored in the same warehouse.)

User View 4 Requirements. For an order, store the order number, order date, the number, name, and address of the customer who placed the order, and the number of the sales rep who represents that customer. In addition, for each line item within the order, store the part number and description, the number of the part that was ordered, and the quoted price. The following information has also been obtained from the user:

</td></tr>
</table>

a. Each order must be placed by a customer who is already in the customer file.

b. There is only one customer per order.

c. On a given order, there is at most one line item for a given part. For example, part BT04 cannot appear on several lines within the same order.

d. The quoted price may be the same as the current price in the Part table, but it need not be. This allows the enterprise the flexibility to sell the same parts to different customers for different prices. It also allows you to change the basic price for a part without necessarily affecting orders that are currently on file.

What are the user views in the preceding example? In particular, how should the design proceed if you are given requirements that are not specifically stated in the form of user views? You might actually be lucky enough to be confronted with a series of well-thought-out user views in a form that can readily be merged into the design. On the other hand, you might only be given a set of requirements, such as the set you have encountered in this example. Or you might be given a list of reports and updates that a system must support. If you happen to be given the job of interviewing users and documenting their needs as a preliminary step to the design process, you can make sure that their views are specified in a form that will be easy to work with when the design process starts. On the other hand, you may just have to take this information as you get it.

If the user views are not spelled out as user views per se, then you should consider each requirement that is specified to be a user view. Thus each report or update transaction that the system must support, as well as any other requirement, such as any of those just stated, can be thought of as an individual user view. In fact, even if the requirements are presented as user views, you may wish to split up a user view that is particularly complex into smaller pieces and consider each piece a user view for the design process.

You will now proceed with the example.

User View 1. This requirement, or user view, poses no particular difficulty. Only one table is required to support this view:

```
Sales Rep (Sales Rep Number, Last Name, First Name, Street, City, State,
     Zip Code, Commission, Rate)
```

This table is in 3NF. Because there are no foreign, alternate, or secondary keys, the DBDL representation of the table is precisely the same as the relational model representation.

Notice that you have assumed that the sales rep's number (Sales Rep Number) is the primary key to the table. This is a fairly reasonable assumption. But because this information was not given in the first requirement, you would need to verify its accuracy with the user. In each of the following requirements, you will assume that the obvious attribute (customer number, part number, and order number) is the primary key. Because this is the first user view, the "merge" step of the design methodology will produce a cumulative design consisting of this one table (It is so simple, you don't need to represent it with a diagram. See Figure 6.4).

FIGURE 6.4

Cumulative design after first user view

```
Sales Rep (Sales Rep Number, Last Name, First Name, Street, City,
     State, Zip Code, Commission, Rate)
```

User View 2. Because the first user view was relatively simple, you were able to come up with the necessary table without having to go through the steps mentioned in the discussion of the design methodology. The second user view is a little more complicated, however, so you should use the steps suggested earlier to determine the tables. (If you have already spotted what the tables should be, you have a natural feel for the process. If so, please be patient and work through the process.)

You will take two different approaches to this requirement so that you can see how they can both lead to the same result. The only difference between the two approaches concerns the entities that you initially identify. In the first approach, suppose you identify two entities: sales reps and customers. You can then begin with the two following tables:

```
Sales Rep (
Customer (
```

After determining the unique identifiers, you add the primary keys, which yields:

```
Sales Rep (Sales Rep Number,
Customer (Customer Number,
```

Adding columns for the properties of each of these tables yields:

```
Sales Rep (Sales Rep Number, Last Name, First Name
Customer (Customer Number, Last Name, First Name, Street, City, State,
     Zip Code, Balance, Credit Limit
```

Finally, you deal with the relationship: *one* sales rep is related to *many* customers. To implement this one-to-many relationship, you include the key of the "one" table in the "many" table as a foreign key. In this case, you include Sales Rep Number in the Customer table. Thus, you have the following:

```
Sales Rep (Sales Rep Number, Last Name, First Name)
Customer (Customer Number, Last Name, First Name, Street, City, State,
     Zip Code, Balance, Credit Limit, Sales Rep Number)
```

Both tables are in 3NF, so you can move on to representing the keys. Before doing that, however, you will investigate another approach that could have been used to determine the tables.

Suppose you didn't realize that there were really two entities and thought there was only a single entity, customers. You thus begin only the single table as follows:

```
Customer (
```

Adding the unique identifier as the primary key yields:

```
Customer (Customer Number,
```

Finally, adding the other properties as additional columns yields:

```
Customer (Customer Number, Cust Last Name, Cust First Name, Street, City,
     State, Zip Code, Balance, Credit Limit, Sales Rep Number,
     Slsr Last Name, Slsr First Name)
```

Note: This table contains first and last names of both customers and sales reps. To distinguish last names, the customer's last name is denoted Cust Last Name and the sales rep's last name is Slsr Last Name. Similarly, the customer's first name is Cust First Name and the sales rep's first name is Slsr First Name.

A problem appears, however, when you examine the functional dependencies that exist in Customer. Customer Number determines all the other columns, as it should. But Sales Rep Number determines Slsr Last Name and Slsr First Name, yet Sales Rep Number is not a candidate key. This table, which is in 2NF, because no column depends on a portion of the key, is not in 3NF. Thus, converting to 3NF produces the following two tables:

```
Customer (Customer Number, Last Name, First Name, Street, City, State,
     Zip Code, Balance, Credit Limit, Sales Rep Number)
Sales Rep (Sales Rep Number, Last Name, First Name)
```

Note: The first and last names of customers are now in the Customer table. The first and last names of sales reps are now in the Sales Rep table. There is no longer any need to have special names to distinguish between the attributes. In both cases, they can simply be called First Name and Last Name.

Notice that these are precisely the same tables that you determined with the other approach. It just took a little longer to get there.

These two tables are what you merge into the design. Besides the obvious primary keys — Customer Number for Customer and Sales Rep Number for Sales Rep — the Customer table now contains a foreign key, Sales Rep Number.

There are no alternate keys, nor did the requirements state anything that would lead to a secondary key. If there were a requirement to retrieve the customer based on his or her last name, for example, you would probably choose to make Last Name a secondary key. (Because last names may not be unique, Last Name could not be an alternate key.)

At this point, you could represent the table Sales Rep in DBDL in preparation for merging this collection of tables into the collection you already have. Looking ahead, however, you see that because this table has the same primary key as the Sales Rep table from the first user view, the two tables will be merged. A single table will be formed that has the common key Sales Rep Number as its primary key and that contains all the other columns from both tables without duplication. For this second user view, the only columns in Sales Rep besides the primary key are Last Name and First Name. These columns were already in the Sales Rep table in the cumulative design. Thus, nothing will be added to the Sales Rep table that is already in place. The cumulative design now contains the two tables Sales Rep and Customer, as shown in Figure 6.5.

FIGURE 6.5

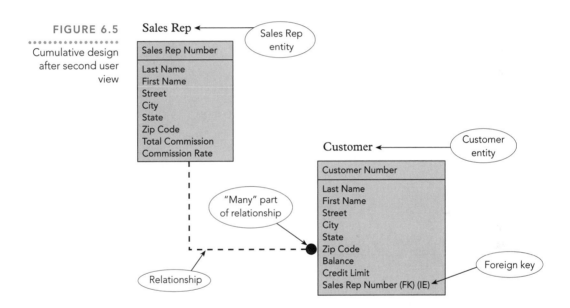

Cumulative design after second user view

User View 3. Like the first user view, this one poses no special problems. Only one table is required to support it:

```
Part (Part Number, Part Description, On Hand, Class, Warehouse, Price)
```

This table is in 3NF. The DBDL representation is identical to the relational model representation.

Because Part Number is not the primary key of any table you have already encountered, merging this table into the cumulative design produces a design with three tables: Sales Rep, Customer, and Part (see Figure 6.6).

FIGURE 6.6

Cumulative design
after third user
view

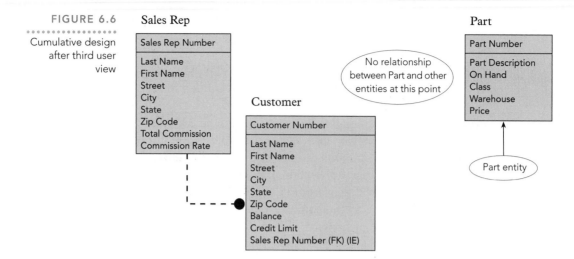

User View 4. This user view is a bit more complicated, and you could approach it in several ways. Suppose you felt that only a single entity was being mentioned, namely Orders. In that case, you would create a single table, as follows:

```
Orders (
```

Because orders are uniquely identified by order numbers, you would add Order Number as the primary key, giving:

```
Orders (Order Number,
```

Examining the various properties of an order, such as the date, the customer number, and so on, as listed in the requirement, you would add appropriate attributes, giving:

```
Orders (Order Number, Order Date, Customer Number, Last Name,
     First Name, Street, City, State, Zip Code, Sales Rep Number,
```

What about the fact that you are supposed to store the part number, description, number ordered, and quoted price for each order line on this order? One way of doing this is to include all these attributes within the Orders table as a repeating group (because there can be many order lines on an order). This yields:

```
Orders (Order Number, Order Date, Customer Number, Last Name,
     First Name, Street, City, State, Zip Code, Sales Rep Number,
     (Part Number, Part Description, Number Ordered, Quoted Price) )
```

At this point, you have a table that does contain all the necessary columns (attributes). Now you must convert this table to an equivalent collection of tables that are in 3NF. Because this table is not even in 1NF, you remove the repeating group and expand the primary key to produce the following:

```
Orders (Order Number, Order Date, Customer Number, Last Name,
     First Name, Street, City, State, Zip Code, Sales Rep Number,
     Part Number, Part Description, Number Ordered, Quoted Price)
```

In the new Orders table, you have the following functional dependencies:

```
Order Number → Order Date, Customer Number, Last Name, First Name,
     Street, City, State, Zip Code, Sales Rep Number
Customer Number → Last Name, First Name, Street, City, State,
     Zip Code, Sales Rep Number
Part Number → Part Description
Order Number, Part Number → Number Ordered, Quoted Price
```

From the discussion of the quoted price in the statement of the requirement, it should be noted that quoted price does indeed depend on *both* the order number and the part number, not on the part number alone. Because some columns depend on only a portion of the primary key, the Orders table is not in 2NF. Converting to 2NF yields the following:

```
Orders (Order Number, Order Date, Customer Number, Last Name,
     First Name, Street, City, State, Zip Code, Sales Rep Number)
Part (Part Number, Part Description)
Order Line (Order Number, Part Number, Number Ordered, Quoted Price)
```

The tables Part and Order Line are in 3NF. The Orders table is not in 3NF, because Customer Number determines Last Name, First Name, Street, City, State, Zip Code, and Sales Rep Number, but Customer Number is not a candidate key. Converting the Orders table to 3NF and leaving the other tables untouched produces the following design for this requirement:

```
Orders (Order Number, Order Date, Customer Number)
Customer (Customer Number, Last Name, First Name, Street, City, State,
     Zip Code, Sales Rep Number)
Part (Part Number, Part Description)
Order Line (Order Number, Part Number, Number Ordered, Quoted Price)
```

This is the collection of tables that will be represented in DBDL and then merged into the cumulative design. Again, however, you can look ahead and see that Customer will be merged with the existing Customer table, and Part will be merged with the existing Part table. In neither case will anything new be added to the Customer or Part tables already in place, so the Customer and Part tables for this user view will not affect the overall design. The representation for Orders and Order Line in DBDL is shown in Figure 6.7.

FIGURE 6.7
. . . .
DBDL for the final
information- level
design

```
Customer (Customer Number, Last Name, First Name, Street, City, State,
     Zip Code, Sales Rep Number)

Part (Part Number, Part Description)

Orders (Order Number, Order Date, Customer Number)
     FK    Customer Number → Customer

Order Line (Order Number, Part Number, Number Ordered, Quoted Price)
     FK    Order Number —> Orders
     FK    Part Number —> Part
```

At this point, you have completed the process for each user view. You should now review the design to make sure that it will cleanly fulfill all the requirements. If problems are encountered or if new information comes to light, the design must be modified accordingly. Based on the assumption that you do not have to further modify the design here, the final information-level design is shown in Figure 6.8.

FIGURE 6.8

Final information-level design

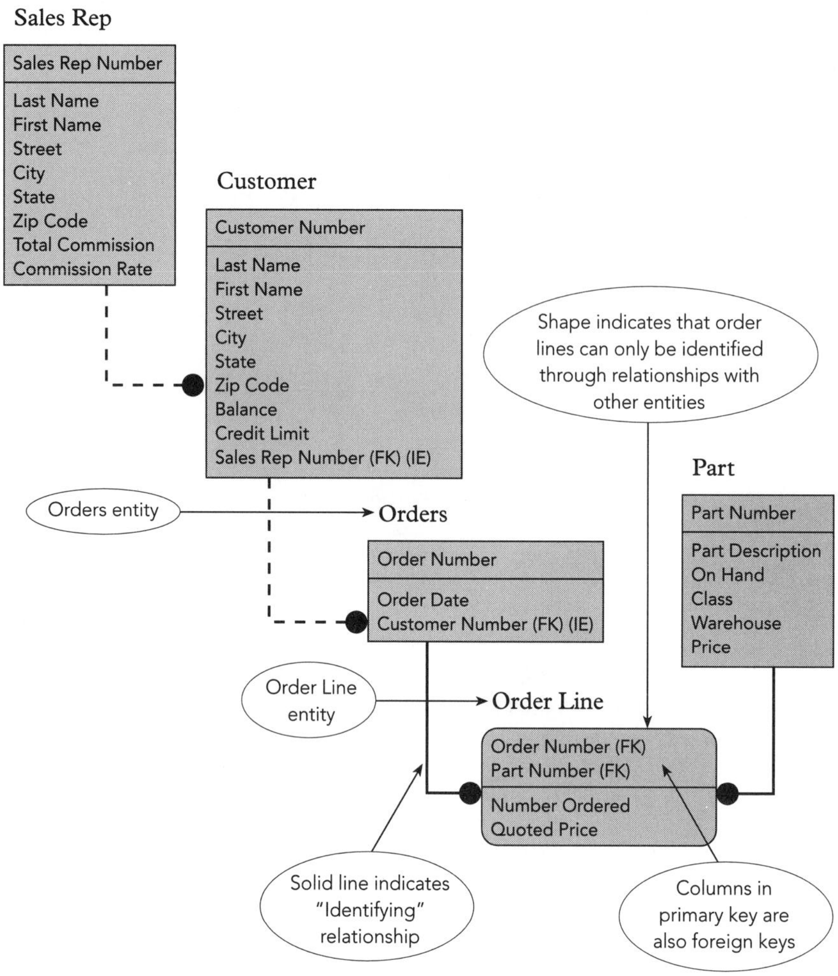

There are some differences between this diagram and the ones you have seen so far. The Order Line entity is not a rectangle; it has curved corners. Furthermore, the relationships from Orders to Order Line and from Part to Order Line are represented with solid, rather than dashed, lines.

Both of these differences result from the fact that the primary key of Order Line contains foreign keys. In Order Line, both columns that comprise the primary key, Order Number and Part Number, are foreign keys. Thus, to identify an order line, it is necessary to know the order and the part to which it corresponds.

This is different from a situation in which the primary key does not contain foreign keys. Consider the Customer table, for example, in which the primary key is Customer Number, which is not a foreign key. The Customer table does contain a foreign key, Sales Rep Number, which identifies the Sales Rep table. To identify a customer, however, all you need is the customer number. You do not need to know the sales rep number. In other words, you do not need to know the sales rep to which the customer corresponds.

An entity that does not require a relationship to another entity for identification is called independent and one that does require such a relationship is called dependent. Thus, Customer is independent, whereas Order Line is dependent. Independent entities have squared corners in the diagram and dependent entities have rounded corners.

A relationship that is necessary for identification is called identifying, whereas one that is not necessary is called nonidentifying. Thus, the relationship between Sales Rep and Customer is nonidentifying, whereas the relationship between Orders and Order Line is identifying. Identifying relationships are represented by solid lines and nonidentifying relationships are represented by dashed lines.

EXAMPLE 2

You will now design a database for Henry. Henry wants to keep information on books, authors, publishers, and branches. The only user is Henry, but you don't want to treat the whole project as a single user view: so let's assume you've asked Henry for all the reports the system is to produce, and you will treat each one as a user view. Suppose that Henry has given the following requirements:

User View 1 Requirements. For each publisher, list the publisher code, the name, and the city in which the publisher is located.

User View 2 Requirements. For each branch, list the number, the name, the location, and the number of employees.

User View 3 Requirements. For each book, list its code, title, the code and name of the publisher, the price, and whether it is paperback.

User View 4 Requirements. For each book, list its code, title, and price. In addition, list how many authors the book has, and their names. (If there is more than one author, they must be listed in the order in which they are listed on the book. This may or may not be an alphabetical listing.)

User View 5 Requirements. For each branch, list the number and name. In addition, list the code and title of each book currently in the branch as well as the number of units of the book the branch currently has.

User View 6 Requirements. For each book, list the code and title. In addition, for each branch that currently has the book in stock, list the number and name of that branch along with the number of copies available.

With these six reports as the user views, let's move on to the design of Henry's database.

User View 1. The only entity in this user view is Publisher. The table to support it is as follows:

```
Publisher (Publisher Code, Name, City)
```

This table is in 3NF. The primary key is Publisher Code. There are no alternate or foreign keys. Let's assume Henry wants to be able to access a publisher rapidly on the basis of its name. Then you will make Name a secondary key.

Because this is the first user view, there is no previous cumulative design. So at this point the new cumulative design consists solely of the design for this user view. It is shown in Figure 6.9. There is no need for a diagram at this point.

FIGURE 6.9

DBDL for Book database after first user view

```
Publisher (Publisher Code, Name, City)
     SK    Name
```

User View 2. The only entity in this user view is *branch*. The table to support it is as follows:

```
Branch (Branch Number, Name, Location, Number Employees)
```

This table is also in 3NF. The primary key is Branch Number, and there are no alternate or foreign keys. Let's assume Henry wants to be able to access a branch rapidly on the basis of its name. Thus you will make Name a secondary key.

Because no table in the cumulative design has Branch Number as its primary key, this table is simply added to the collection of tables in the cumulative design during the merge step. The result is shown in Figure 6.10. Again, there is no need for a diagram with this simple design.

FIGURE 6.10

DBDL for Book database after second user view

```
Publisher (Publisher Code, Name, City)
     SK    Name

Branch (Branch Number, Name, Location, Number Employees)
     SK    Name
```

User View 3. There are two entities here, publishers and books, and a one-to-many relationship between them. This leads to the following:

```
Publisher (Publisher Code, Name)
Book (Book Code, Title, Publisher Code, Price, Paperback)
```

Publisher Code in the Book table is a foreign key identifying the publisher. Merging these tables with those that are already in place does not add any new attributes to the Publisher table, but adds the Book table to the cumulative design. The result of the merge is shown in Figure 6.11. Here you are assuming that Henry will need to access books based on their titles, so Title is designated as a secondary key.

User View 4. There are two entities in this user view, books and authors. The relationship between them is many-to-many (an Author can write many books and a Book can have many Authors). Creating tables for each entity and the relationship gives:

```
Author (Author Number, Name)
Book (Book Code, Title, Price)
Wrote (Book Code, Author Number)
```

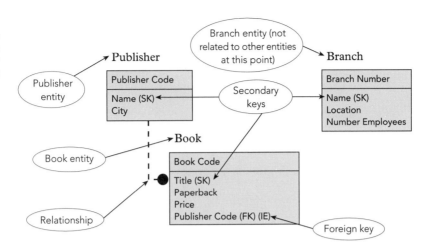

(Because the last table represents the fact that an author *wrote* a particular book, you will call the table Wrote.)

In this user view, you need to be able to list the authors for a book in the appropriate order. To accomplish this, you will add a sequence number attribute to the last table. This completes the tables for this user view, which are:

```
Author (Author Number, Name)
Book (Book Code, Title, Price)
Wrote (Book Code, Author Number, Sequence Number)
```

The Author table is new. Merging the Book table adds nothing new. The Wrote table is new. The result of the merge step is shown in Figure 6.12.

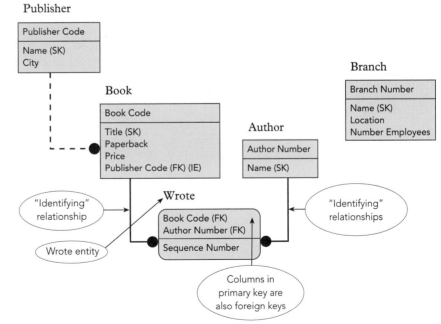

User View 5. Suppose you were to decide that the only entity mentioned in this requirement was *branch*. You would create this table:

```
Branch (
```

You would then add Branch Number as the primary key, producing the following:

```
Branch (Branch Number,
```

The other columns include the branch name as well as the book code, book title, and number of units on hand. Because a branch has several books, the last three columns form a repeating group. You thus have the following:

```
Branch (Branch Number, Name, (Book Code, Title, On Hand) )
```

You convert this table to 1NF by removing the repeating group and expanding the primary key. This gives:

```
Branch (Branch Number, Name, Book Code, Title, On Hand)
```

In this table, you have the following functional dependencies:

```
Branch Number → Name
Book Code → Title
Branch Number, Book Code → On Hand
```

The table is not in 2NF, because some columns depend on just a portion of the key. Converting to 2NF gives:

```
Branch (Branch Number, Name)
Book (Book Code, Title)
Inventory (Branch Number, Book Code, On Hand)
```

The primary keys are indicated. You call the final table Inventory, because it effectively represents each branch's inventory. In the Inventory table, Branch Number is a foreign key that identifies Branch, and Book Code is a foreign key that identifies Book. In other words, in order for a row to exist in the Inventory table, *both* the branch number *and* the book code must already be in the database.

The Branch table will merge with the existing Branch table without adding anything new. Similarly, the Publisher table will not add anything new to the existing Publisher table. The Inventory table is totally new and will appear as part of the new cumulative design, which is shown in Figure 6.13.

QUESTION

How would the design for this user view have turned out if you had started out with two entities, *branch* and *book*, instead of just the single entity *branch*?

ANSWER

In the first step, you would have these two tables:

```
Branch (
Book (
```

Adding the primary keys gives:

```
Branch (Branch Number,
Book (Book Code,
```

Filling in the other columns gives:

```
Branch (Branch Number, Name)
Book (Book Code, Title)
```

150

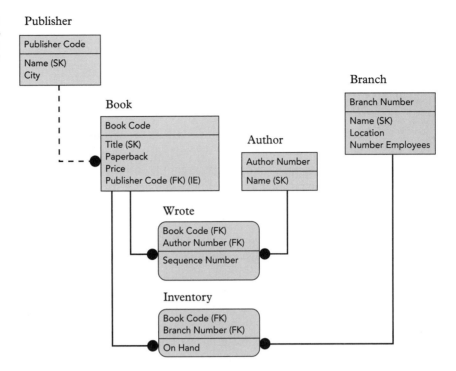

Finally, you must implement the relationship between Branch and Book. Because a branch can have many books and a book can be in stock at many branches, the relationship is many-to-many. To implement a many-to-many relationship, you add a new table whose primary key is the combination of the primary keys of the other tables. Doing this, you produce the following:

```
Branch (Branch Number, Name)
Book (Book Code, Title)
Inventory (Branch Number, Book Code)
```

Finally, you add to the Inventory table any column that depends on both Branch Number and Publisher Code, yielding:

```
Branch (Branch Number, Name)
Book (Book Code, Title)
Inventory (Branch Number, Book Code, On Hand)
```

Thus you end up with exactly the same collection of tables, which illustrates a point made earlier: there's more than one way of arriving at a correct result.

. . . .

User View 6. This user view leads to precisely the same set of tables that were created for User View 5.

You have now reached the end of the requirements, and the design shown in Figure 6.13 represents the complete information-level design. You should take a moment to review each of the requirements to make sure they can all be satisfied.

■ Physical-Level Design

Once the information-level design is complete, you are ready to begin producing the specific design that will be implemented with some typical PC-based DBMSs. This is part of the overall process called physical-level design.

Because most PC-based DBMSs are relational (at least they claim to be), and because the final information-level design is presented in a relational format, the basic job of producing the design for the chosen DBMS is not difficult. You simply use the same tables and columns that you produced in the information-level design process. (At this point, you do need to supply format details, of course, like the fact that Customer Number is a character field, three positions in length, etc., but again, this is not difficult.)

Most database management systems support primary, candidate, secondary, and foreign keys. If you are using such systems, you simply use these features to implement the various types of keys that are listed in the final DBDL version of the information-level design.

Unfortunately, there are systems that don't support all these types of keys. If you are using one of these, you need to devise a scheme for handling these keys. Such a scheme must ensure the uniqueness of primary and candidate keys. It must ensure that values in the foreign keys are legitimate; in other words, that they match the value of the primary key on some row in another table. As far as secondary keys are concerned, you merely need to ensure the efficiency of access to rows on the basis of a value of the secondary key.

For instance, suppose you are implementing the Employee table shown in Figure 6.1, in which Employee Number is the primary key, Soc Sec Number is a candidate key, Last Name is a secondary key, and Department Number is a foreign key that matches the Department Number column in the Department table. You will have to ensure that the following conditions hold true:

1. Employee numbers are unique.

2. Social security numbers are unique.

3. Access to an employee on the basis of his or her last name is rapid. (This restriction differs in that it merely states that a certain type of activity must be efficient, but it is an important restriction nonetheless.)

4. Department numbers are valid; that is, they match the number of a department currently in the database.

The next question is: Who should enforce these restrictions? Two choices are possible, provided the DBMS can't do it. The users of the system could enforce them, or programmers could. In the case of users, they must be careful when entering data not to add two employees with the same Employee Number, not to add an employee whose department number was invalid, and so on. Clearly, this puts a tremendous burden on the user.

Provided the DBMS can't enforce the restrictions, the appropriate place for the enforcement to take place is in programs. Thus, the burden of responsibility for this enforcement should fall on the programmers who write the programs that users will run to update the database. Incidentally, users *must* update the data through these programs and *not* through the built-in features of the DBMS in such circumstances; otherwise, users could bypass all the controls that you are attempting to program into the system.

Thus, it is the responsibility of programmers to include logic in their programs to enforce all the constraints. With respect to the DBDL shown in Figure 6.1, this means the following:

1. Before an employee is added, the program should determine three things:

   a. Whether an employee with the same Employee Number is already in the database; if so, the update should be rejected;

   b. Whether an employee with the same social security number is already in the database; if so, the update should be rejected; and

   c. Whether the department number that was entered matches the number of a department that is already in the database; if it doesn't, the update should be rejected.

2. If the department number is one of the values that is changed when data about an employee are changed, the program should check to make sure that the new number also matches the number of a department that is already in the database. If it doesn't, the update should be rejected.

3. When a department is deleted, the program should check to make sure that the database contains no employees for this department. If the department does contain employees and it is allowed to be deleted, these employees will have department numbers that are no longer valid. In that case, the update should be rejected.

These actions must be performed efficiently, and in most systems this means creating and using indexes on all key columns. Thus, an index will be created for each column (or combination of columns) that is a primary key, a candidate key, a secondary key, or a foreign key.

■ Additional Issues

Entity-Relationship Diagram Alternatives

There are wide variations in the styles people use when drawing Entity-Relationship diagrams. This section examines some of the more common alternatives.

Relationships are often represented explicitly using the diamond shape, as shown in Figure 6.14. In this style, the "one" part of the one-to-many relationship is represented by number 1 and the "many" part is represented by the letter n.

FIGURE 6.14

Symbol for relationship

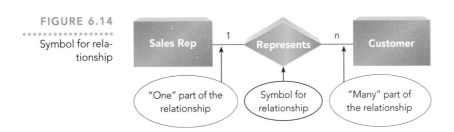

Attributes (columns) are often not represented in entity relationship diagrams. (If they are not, you certainly should include the DBDL along with the diagram.) When they are represented, they can be listed inside the rectangles, as in the diagrams in this text. Alternatively, they can be shown as bubbles, as in Figure 6.15.

FIGURE 6.15

Symbols for
columns

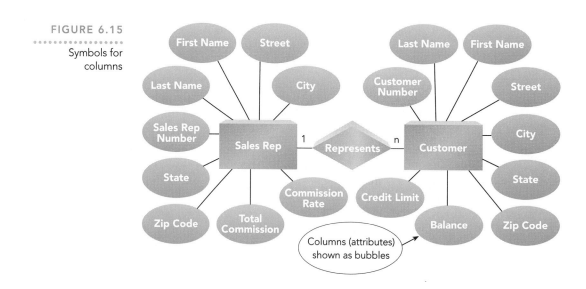

Columns (attributes) shown as bubbles

Recall that when you have a many-to-many relationship, you create an additional table. For example, the many-to-many relationship between orders and parts led to the creation of the Order Line table. Some people emphasize the fact that this *entity* exists to implement a *relationship* by using both the entity symbol (the rectangle) and the relationship symbol (the diamond), as shown in Figure 6.16. This is called a **composite entity**. The letters m and n on the lines between the relationship indicate that it is many-to-many.

FIGURE 6.16

Composite entity

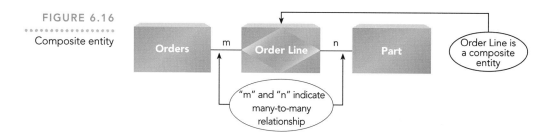

Order Line is a composite entity

"m" and "n" indicate many-to-many relationship

Another popular way to indicate a one-to-many relationship is to not label the "one" end, but to place a crow's foot at the "many" end. This style is illustrated in Figure 6.17.

FIGURE 6.17
· ·
Crow's foot symbol

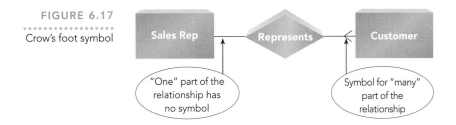

Some people represent **cardinality**, the number of items that must be included in a relationship, in the diagram. The way in which this is done is illustrated in Figure 6.18. The two symbols next to the Sales Rep rectangle are both the number 1. The one closest to the rectangle indicates that the maximum cardinality is 1 (a customer can have *at most* one sales rep). The one closest to the relationship is the minimum cardinality (a customer must have *at least* one sales rep). Together, the two imply that a customer must have exactly one sales rep. (If the minimum cardinality were 0, for example, a customer would not be required to have a sales rep.)

FIGURE 6.18
· ·
Representing
cardinality

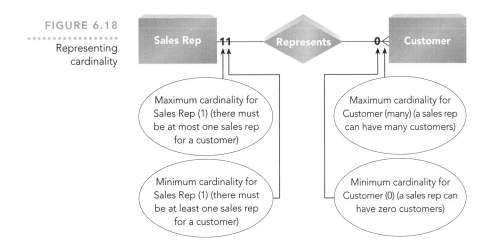

The crow's foot next to the Customer table indicates that the maximum cardinality is "many." The 0 indicates that the minimum cardinality is 0; that is, a sales rep could be associated with 0 customers.

Top-down vs. Bottom-up

The methodology presented here is an example of a bottom-up methodology; that is, starting from specific user requirements, a design is ultimately synthesized. A top-down design methodology is one that begins with a general database design that models the overall enterprise and repeatedly refines the model until a design is achieved that supports all necessary applications.

Both strategies have their advantages. The top-down approach lends a more global feel to the project; you at least have some idea where you are headed, which is not so with a strictly bottom-up approach.

On the other hand, a bottom-up approach provides a rigorous way of tackling each separate requirement and ensuring that it will be met. In particular, tables are created to precisely satisfy each user view or requirement. When these tables are merged into the cumulative design, provided the merge is done correctly, you can be certain that each user view can indeed be satisfied.

The ideal strategy combines the best of both approaches. With a simple modification, the methodology presented here can do this. Assuming that the design problem is sufficiently complicated to warrant the benefits of the top-down approach, you can begin the design process with the following steps:

1. After gathering data on all user views, review them without attempting to create any relations. In other words, try to get a general feel for the task at hand.

2. From this information, determine the basic entities of interest to the enterprise (e.g., sales reps, customers, orders, and parts). Do not be overly concerned that you might miss an entity. If you do, it will show up in later steps of the design methodology.

3. For each entity, start a table. For example, if the entities are sales reps, customers, orders, and parts, you will have:

   ```
   Sales Rep (
   Customer (
   Orders (
   Part (
   ```

4. Determine and fill in a primary key for each table. In this example, you might have:

   ```
   Sales Rep (Sales Rep Number,
   Customer (Customer Number,
   Orders (Order Number,
   Part (Part Number,
   ```

5. (Optional) For each one-to-many relationship that can be identified among these entities, create and document an appropriate foreign key. If there is a one-to-many relationship from Sales Rep to Customer, for example, add the foreign key Sales Rep Number to the Customer entity. Again, don't worry. If this is not done, or if any foreign keys are missed in the process, the situation will be rectified when you treat individual users views later.

You can now apply the methodology that has been discussed earlier for treating individual user views. Keep in mind the tables that you have created and their primary keys as you design each user view. When it is time to determine the primary key for a table, for example, find out whether such a primary key exists in your overall collection. When it is time to determine a foreign key, find out whether the primary key it is required to match exists in the overall collection. In either case, if the primary key exists, give it the name that has already been assigned. This ensures that the tables will merge properly. If, at the end of the design process, there are any tables that were created initially and that have not had any other columns added to them and have no foreign keys matching them, you may consider removing them.

The addition of these steps to the process provides the benefits of the top-down approach. As you proceed through the design process for the individual user views, you have a general idea of the overall picture.

Comprehensive Design Example (Optional)

This section presents a detailed exercise that walks you through the complete design of a database.

Marvel College Requirements

Marvel College is a local college that has decided to computerize its operations. To do so, it has asked you to design a database that will satisfy a number of requirements. The following is an explanation of the requirements the system must satisfy.

General Description

Marvel College is organized by department (math, physics, English, etc.). A department may offer more than one major; for example, the math department might offer majors in mathematics education, applied mathematics, and statistics. Each major, however, is offered by only one department. Each faculty member is assigned to a single department. Students can have more than one major, but most have only one. Each student has a faculty member as an advisor for his or her major; students who have more than one major have a faculty advisor for each one. The faculty member may or may not be assigned to the department offering the major.

Each department is identified by a two- or three-character code (MTH for math, CS for computer science, and ENG for English). Each course is identified by the combination of this code and a three-digit number (MTH 201 for Calculus, and ENG 102 for Creative Writing). The number of credits offered by a particular course does not vary; that is, all students who pass the same course receive the same amount of credit.

Each semester is identified by a two-character code for the term, combined with two digits that designate the year (FA01 for the fall semester of 2001). For a given semester, each section of each course is assigned a four-digit schedule code together with a section letter (schedule code 1295 for section A of MTH 201, 1297 for section B of MTH 201, and 1302 for section C of MTH 201). For a different semester, the schedule codes will be entirely different. The schedule codes are listed in the time schedule, and students use them to indicate the sections in which they wish to enroll. (The enrollment process is described in detail later in this section.)

After the enrollment process has been completed for a given semester, each faculty member receives a class list for each section he or she is teaching. In addition to listing the students who are in that particular section, the class list provides space to indicate the grade each student has earned in the course. At the end of the term, the faculty member will place the student's grades on this list and will return a copy of the list to the records office, where the grades will be entered into the computer. (At some point in the near future, the college plans to automate this part of the process.)

Once the grades have been posted (entered into the computer), report cards are generated and sent to students. The grades become part of the student's permanent record and will appear on the student's transcript, which is generated by the computer upon request.

The preceding description of the requirements is general; the specific information requirements of the college follow.

Report Requirements

The following are the report requirements for Marvel College:

1. **Report card.** At the end of each semester, report cards must be produced. A sample report card is shown in Figure 6.19.

FIGURE 6.19
....
Sample report card
for Marvel College

MARVEL COLLEGE

Department	Course Number	Course Description	Grade	Credits Taken	Credits Earned	Grade Points
Comp. Sci.	CS 162	Intro. to Prog.	A	4	4	16.0
Mathematics	MTH 201	Calculus	B	3	3	12.0

7	7	4.00	28.0
Credits Taken	Credits Erned	GPA	Total Points

Semester: WI02

Current Semester Totals

44	44	3.39	149.2
Credits Taken	Credits Earned	GPA	Total Points

Student Number: 381124188

Cumulative Totals

Student Name & Address	Local Address (IF DIFFERENT)
Brian Connors 686 Franklin Hart, MI 48282	

2. **Class list.** A class list must be produced for each section of each course; a sample class list is shown in Figure 6.20. Note that space is provided for the grades. At the end of the term, the instructor will fill in the grades and return a copy of the class list. The grades will then be posted.

3. **Grade verification report** The grade verification report is identical to the class list shown in Figure 6.20 except that grades have been filled in. It is sent back to the section instructor after the grades have been processed. The instructor can use the report to verify that the grades were entered accurately.

FIGURE 6.20
• • • • • • • • • • • • • • • • • • •
Sample class list
for Marvel College

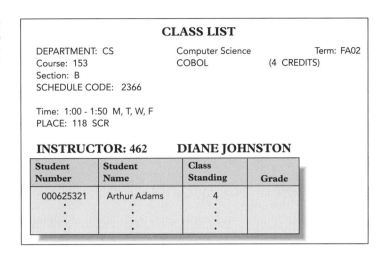

FIGURE 6.21
• • • • • • • • • • • • • • • • • • •
Sample time
schedule for
Marvel College

4. ***Time schedule*** The time schedule, which is shown in Figure 6.21, lists all sections of all courses to be offered during a given semester. Each section has a unique four-digit schedule code. The time schedule lists the schedule code, the department offering the course, the course number, the section letter, the title of the course, the instructor of the course, the time at which the course meets, the room in which the course meets, the number of credits generated by the course, and the prerequisites for the course. In addition to the information shown in the figure, the time schedule includes the date the semester begins, the date the semester ends, the date finals begin, the date finals end, and the last withdrawal date, that is, the last date at which students may withdraw from a course.

TIME SCHEDULE   Term: FA02

Course #	CODE #	SECT	Time	Room	Faculty
		•	•	•	•
		•	•	•	•
		•	•	•	•

CHEMISTRY (CHM) Office: 341 NSB

111 Chemistry I   4 CREDITS

1740	A	10:00-10:50 M, T, W, F	102 WRN	Johnston
1745	B	12:00-12:50 M, T, W, F	102 WRN	Lee
•	•	•	•	•
•	•	•	•	•
•	•	•	•	•

Prerequisite: Mathematics 110

112 Chemistry II   4 CREDITS

1790	A	10:00-11:50 M, W	109 WRN	Adams
1795	B	12:00-1:50 T, R	109 WRN	Nelson
•	•	•	•	•
•	•	•	•	•
•	•	•	•	•

Prerequisite: Chemistry 111

114 . . . .

5. **_Registration request form_** A sample registration request form is shown in Figure 6.22. This form is used by a student to request classes for the following semester. Students indicate the sections for which they wish to register by entering the sections' schedule codes; for each of these sections, they may also enter a code for an alternate section. Students who cannot be placed in the section they request will be placed in the alternate section, provided there is room.

FIGURE 6.22

Sample registration request form for Marvel College

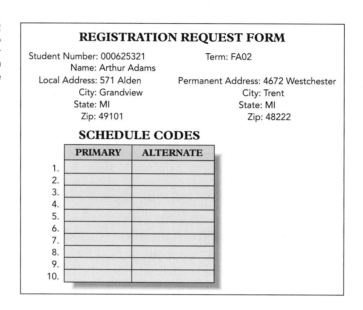

REGISTRATION REQUEST FORM

Student Number: 000625321   Term: FA02
Name: Arthur Adams
Local Address: 571 Alden   Permanent Address: 4672 Westchester
City: Grandview   City: Trent
State: MI   State: MI
Zip: 49101   Zip: 48222

SCHEDULE CODES

	PRIMARY	ALTERNATE
1.		
2.		
3.		
4.		
5.		
6.		
7.		
8.		
9.		
10.		

6. **_Student schedule_** A sample student schedule form is shown in Figure 6.23. This form shows the schedule for an individual student for a given semester.

FIGURE 6.23

Sample student schedule for Marvel College

STUDENT SCHEDULE

Student Number: 000625321   Term: FA02
Name: Arthur Adams
Local Address: 571 Alden   Permanent Address: 4672 Westchester
City: Grandview   City: Trent
State: MI   State: MI
Zip: 49101   Zip: 48222

Schd Code	Crse Numb	Course Description	Sect	Credits	Time	Room
2366	CS 253	COBOL	B	4	1:00-1:50 M, T, W, F	118 SCR
•	•	•	•	•	•	
•	•	•	•	•	•	

Total Credits: 16

7. **Full student information report** A sample of a full student information report is shown in Figure 6.24. It gives complete information about a student, including his or her majors and all grades received to date.

8. **Faculty Information Report** This report lists all faculty by department and contains each faculty member's ID number, name, address, office, phone number, current rank, and starting date of employment. It also lists the number, name, and local and permanent address of each of the faculty member's advisees, along with the code number and description of the major in which the faculty member is advising each advisee, and the code number and description of the department to which this major is assigned. (Remember that this department is not necessarily the one to which the faculty member is assigned.)

9. **Work version of the time schedule** This report is similar to the original time schedule (see Figure 6.21) but is designed for the college's internal use. It shows the current enrollments in each section of each course, as well as the maximum enrollment permitted per section. It is more up-to-date than the time schedule itself. (When students register for courses, enrollment figures are updated on the work version of the time schedule. When room or faculty assignments are changed, this information is also updated. A new version of this report that reflects the updated figures is then printed.)

FIGURE 6.24

Sample full student information report for Marvel College

FULL STUDENT INFORMATION

Student Number: 000625321   Term: FA02
          Name: Arthur Adams
Local Address: 571 Alden   Permanent Address: 4672 Westchester
          City: Grandview   City: Trent
          State: MI   State: MI
          Zip: 49101   Zip: 48222

Major 1: Information Sys.   Department: Computer Science   Advisor: Mark Lee
Major 2: Accounting   Department: Business   Advisor: Jill Thomas
Major 3:   Department: Advisor

Term	Course Number	Course Description	Credits	Grade Earned	Grade Points
FA01	MTH 110	Calculus I	4	A	16
	HST 201	Western Civ	3	B	9
	ENG 101	American Lit.	3	A	12
WI02	MTH 111	Calculus II	4	B	12
	CS 151	Intro. to Prog.	4	B	12

CREDITS ATTEMPTED: 60
CREDITS EARNED: 60
GRADE POINTS: 195
GRADE POINT AVG: 3.25
CLASS Standing: 2

10. ***Course report*** This report lists, for each course, the code and name of the department that is offering the course, the course number, the description of the course, and the number of credits awarded. The department and course number for each prerequisite course are also listed.

Update (Transaction) Requirements

In addition to being able to add, change, and delete any of the entities mentioned in the report requirements, the update requirements accomplish the following:

11. ***Enrollment*** When a student attempts to register for a section of a course, you must determine whether he or she has received credit for all prerequisites to the course. If the student is eligible to enroll in the course and if the number of students currently enrolled in the section is less than the maximum enrollment, enroll the student.

12. ***Post grades*** For each section of each course, post the grades that are indicated on the copy of the class list returned by the instructor, and produce a grade verification report. (Posting the grades is the formal term for the process of entering them permanently into the students' records on the computer.)

13. ***Purge*** Section information, including grades assigned by the section, is retained for two semesters following the end of the semester, at which time the information is removed from the database. (Grades assigned to students are retained by course, but not by section.)

Marvel College Information-Level Design

Some consideration should be given to overall requirements before the methodology is applied to individual user requirements. Scanning the design, you come up with the following list of possible entities: department, major, faculty member, student, course, and semester.

(Your list may be different. You may have included the entity "section," for example, or "grade." On the other hand, you may not have included "semester." In the long run, as long as the list is fairly reasonable, it won't make much difference. In fact, you may remember that this step is really not even necessary. The better you do your job now, however, the simpler the process will be later on.)

You now assign a primary key to each of these entities. In general, this requires some type of consultation with the user. You may need to ask the user directly for the required information, or you may be able to obtain it from some type of survey form. Let's assume that having had such a consultation, you have named a table for each of these entities and have assigned primary keys as follows:

```
Department (Department Code,
Major (Major Number,
Faculty (Faculty Number,
Student (Student Number,
Course (Department Code, Course Number,
Semester (Semester Code,
```

Note that the primary key for the Course table consists of two columns, Department Code (such as CS) and Course Number (such as 153). Both are required. The database could contain, for example, CS 153 and CS 353. Thus the department code alone cannot be the primary key. Similarly, the database could contain ART 101 and MUS 101, two courses with the same course number but different department codes. Thus, the course number alone cannot be the primary key either.

You now begin to examine the individual user views, create relations for them, represent any keys, and merge them into the design. First of all, you must decide exactly what the user views are. In the list of requirements, the term "user view" never appeared. Instead, a general description of the system was given, together with a collection of report requirements and another collection of update requirements. How do these requirements relate to user views?

Certainly, each report requirement and each update requirement can be thought of as a user view. What do you do with the general description? Do you think of each paragraph (or perhaps each sentence) in it as representing a user view, or do you use it to provide additional information about the report and update requirements? Both approaches are acceptable. The second approach is often easier, however, and you will follow it here. Think of the report and update requirements as user views and use the statements in the general description to give additional information about these views wherever needed. You will also consider the general description during the review process to ensure that all the functionality it describes can be satisfied by your final design.

You now turn to the user views. First, let's take one of the simpler user views: Report 10, the course report. (The user views can be examined in any order. Sometimes you take them in the order they are listed. In other cases, you may be able to come up with a better order. Often, examining some of the simpler user views first is a reasonable approach.)

Before you proceed with the design, consider the following: First, with some of the user views, you will take a "good" approach to determining relations; that is, you carefully determine the entities and relationships between them and use this information in creating the tables. This means that from the outset, the collection of tables created will be in or close to 3NF. With other user views, you will create a single table that potentially contains some number of repeating groups. In these cases, as you will see, the normalization process will still produce a correct design, but it will also involve more work. In practice, the more experience a designer has had, the more likely he or she is to create 3NF tables immediately.

Second, the name of an entity (table) or attribute (column) may vary from one user view to another, and this requires resolution. You will attempt to use names that are exactly the same.

User View 1: Course Report (Requirement 10). Forgetting for the moment the requirement to list prerequisite courses, the basic relation necessary to support this report is as follows:

```
Course (Department Code, Department Name, Course Number, Course Title,
    Number Credits)
```

in which the combination of Department Code and Course Number uniquely determines all the other columns. In this relation, Department Code determines Department Name, and thus the table is not in 2NF (a column depends on only a portion of the primary key). To correct this situation, the table is split into:

```
Course (Department Code, Course Number, Course Title, Number Credits)
Department (Department Code, Department Name)
```

The Department Code in the first relation is a foreign key identifying the second.

To maintain prerequisite information, you need the table Prereq:

```
Prereq (Department Code, Course Number, Department Code/1,
     Course Number/1)
```

In this table, columns Department Code and Course Number refer to the current course. Department Code/1 and Course Number/1 refer to the prerequisite course. If CS 362 has a prerequisite of MTH 345, for example, there will be a row in Prereq in which Department Code is CS, Course Number is 263, Department Code/1 is MTH, and Course Number/1 is 345.

Note: Since there are two attributes called Department Code and two called Course Number, there must be a way to distinguish between them. In some cases, you can simply give them different names. In others, you will take an approach like this one, that is, follow one of the names with /1. In this example Department Code/1 and Course Number/1 represent the department code and course number of the *prerequisite* course.

The DBDL version of these tables is shown in Figure 6.25.

FIGURE 6.25

DBDL for User
View 1

```
Department (Department Code, Department Name)


Course (Department Code, Course Number, Course Title, Number Credits)
    FK   Department Code → Department

Prereq (Department Code, Course Number, Department Code/1,
      Course Number/1)
    FK Department Code, Course Number → Course
    FK Department Code/1, Course Number/1 → Course
```

The result of merging these tables into the cumulative design is shown in the E-R diagram in Figure 6.26. Notice that the Department and Course tables have merged with the existing Department and Course tables in the cumulative design. In the process, the attribute Department Name was added to the Department table, and the attributes Course Title and Number Credits were added to the Course. In addition, the attribute Department Code in the Course table was made a foreign key. Since the Prereq table was new, it was added to the cumulative collection in its entirety. Notice also that you do not yet have any relationships involving Student, Major, Faculty, or Semester.

User View 2. Faculty Information Report (Requirement 8). This user view involves three entities: departments, faculty, and advisees. Applying the tips from earlier in the chapter, you can create three tables:

```
Department (
Faculty (
Advisee (
```

The next step is to assign a primary key to each table. Before doing so, however, you should briefly examine the tables in the cumulative collection and use the same names for any tables or columns that are already there. In this case, you would use Department Code as the primary key for the Department table, and Faculty Number as the primary key for the Faculty table. There is no Advisee table in the cumulative collection, but there is a Student table. Since advisees and students are the same, you will rename Advisee as Student and use Student Number as the primary key rather than Advisee Number, yielding:

```
Department (Department Code,
Faculty (Faculty Number,
Student (Student Number,
```

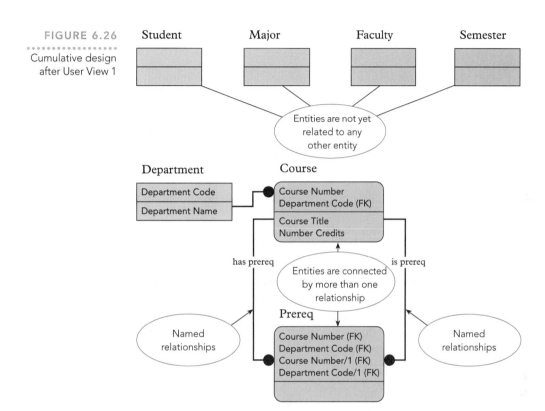

FIGURE 6.26

Cumulative design
after User View 1

Next, add the remaining columns to these tables:

```
Department (Department Code, Department Name)
Faculty (Faculty Number, Last Name, First Name, Street, City, State,
      Zip Code,
      Office Number, Phone, Current Rank, Start Date, Department Code)
Student (Student Number, Last Name, First Name, Local Street,
      Local City,
      Local State, Local Zip Code, Perm Street, Perm City, Perm State,
      Perm Zip Code, (Major Number, Description, Department Code,
      Faculty Number, Last Name, First Name) )
```

The department code is included in the Faculty, since there is a one-to-many relationship between departments and faculty. Since a student can have more than one major, the information concerning majors (number, description, department, and the number and name of the faculty member who advises this student in this major) is a repeating group.

Since the primary key to the repeating group in the student is the major number, removing this repeating group yields:

```
Student (Student Number, Last Name, First Name, Local Street, Local
 City, Local State, Local Zip Code, Perm Street, Perm City, Perm State,
 Perm Zip Code, Major Number, Description, Department Code,
 Faculty Number, Last Name, First Name)
```

Converting this relation to 2NF produces:

```
Student (Student Number, Last Name, First Name, Local Street,
 Local City, Local State, Local Zip Code, Perm Street, Perm City, Perm State,
 Perm Zip Code)
 Major (Major Number, Description, Department Code, Department Name)
 Advises (Student Number, Major Number, Faculty Number)
```

Some dependencies must be removed to create 3NF tables: Office Number determines Phone in the Faculty table, and Department Code determines Department Name in the Major table. Removing these dependencies produces the following collection of tables:

```
Department (Department Code, Department Name)
Faculty (Faculty Number, Last Name, First Name, Street, City, State,
 Zip Code, Office Number, Current Rank, Start Date, Department Code)
 Student (Student Number, Last Name, First Name, Local Street, Local
City, Local State, Local Zip Code, Perm Street, Perm City, Perm State,
 Perm Zip Code)
 Advises (Student Number, Major Number, Faculty Number)
Office (Office Number, Phone)
Major (Major Number, Description, Department Code)
```

The DBDL representation is shown in Figure 6.27, and the result of merging these tables into the cumulative design is shown in Figure 6.28. The Student, Faculty, Major, and Department tables merge into existing tables with the same primary keys and with the same names. Nothing new is added to the Department table in the process, but the other tables receive additional columns. In addition, the Faculty table also receives two foreign keys, Office Number and Department Code. The Major table receives one foreign key, Department Code. The tables Advises and Office are new and are thus added directly to the cumulative collection of tables.

FIGURE 6.27
. . . .
DBDL for User
View 2

```
Department (Department Code, Department Name)

Student (Student Number, Last Name, First Name, Local Street,
        Local City, Local State, Local Zip Code, Perm Street, Perm
        State, Perm Zip Code)

Office (Office Number, Phone)

Faculty (Faculty Number, Last Name, First Name, Street, City, State,
         Zip Code, Office Number, Current Rank, Start Date,
         Department Code)
    FK   Office Number → Office
    FK   Department Code → Department

Major (Major Number, Description, Department Code)
    FK   Department Code → Department

Advises (Student Number, Major Number, Faculty Number)
    FK   Student Number → Student
    FK   Faculty Number → Faculty
    FK   Major Number → Major
```

FIGURE 6.28
· · · · · · · · · · · · · · · · · ·
Cumulative design
after User View 2

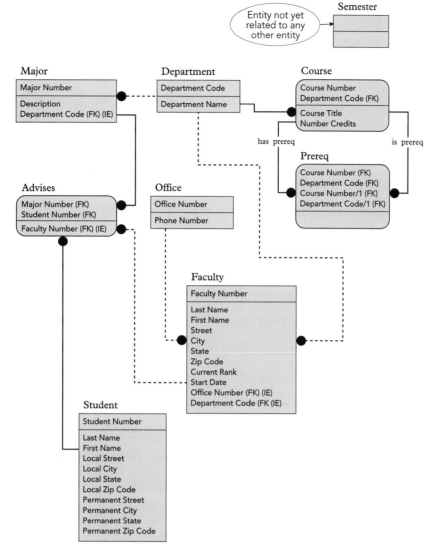

Note: In using software to produce these diagrams, it is possible the software will reverse the order of the fields that make up the primary key from the order you intended. For example, the diagram in Figure 6.28 indicates that the primary key for the Course table is Course Number and then Department Code, even though it was specified in software to be Department Code and then Course Number. This is not a problem. The fields that comprise the primary key are significant, not the order in which they appear.

User View 3. Report Card (Requirement 1). Report cards are fairly complicated documents. The appropriate underlying relations are not immediately apparent. In such a case, it is a good idea to first list all the attributes on the document and give them appropriate names (Figure 6.29). After this has been done, the functional dependencies that exist between these attributes should be listed. The information necessary to determine functional dependencies must ultimately come from the user, although you can often make fairly accurate guesses for most of them.

FIGURE 6.29
·····················
Attributes on
report cards for
Marvel College

```
Department Name
Course Number
Course Title
Grade
Credits Taken in Course
Credits Earned in Course
Grade Points from Course
Credits Taken this Semester
Credits Earned this Semester
GPA this Semester
Total Points this Semester
Point Credits Cumulative
Credits Taken Cumulative
Credits Earned Cumulative
GPA Cumulative
Total Points Cumulative
Semester Code
Student Number
Student Name
Address
City
State
Zip
Local Address
Local City
Local State
Local Zip
```

Let's assume this verification has been done at Marvel College and that Figure 6.30 shows the results. The student number alone determines many of the other attributes. In addition to the student number, the semester must be listed to determine credits taken and earned, grade point average (GPA), and total points this semester. The combination of a department description (such as Computer Science) and a course number (such as 153) determines a course title and the number of credits. Finally, the student number, the semester (season and year), the department, and the course (discipline and course number) are required to determine an individual grade in a course, the credits earned from the course, and the grade points in a course. (The semester is required, since students can take the same course in more than one semester at Marvel College. Furthermore, let's assume that upon checking with the users, you have learned that they want to allow for the possibility that credits offered by a course may vary from one semester to another and even, possibly, from one student to another.)

FIGURE 6.30

Functional dependencies among attributes on report cards

```
Student Number →
     Credits Taken Cumulative
     Credits Earned Cumulative
     GPA Cumulative
     Total Points Cumulative
     Student Name
     Address
     City
     State
     Zip
     Local Address
     Local City
     Local State
     Local Zip

Student Number, Semester Code →
     Credits Taken this Semester
     Credits Earned this Semester
     GPA this Semester
     Total Points this Semester

Department Name, Course Number →
     Course Title
     Credits Taken in Course

Student Number, Semester Code, Department Name, Course Number →
     Grade
     Credits Earned in Course
     Grade Points from Course
```

The next step is to create a collection of tables that will support this user view. A variety of approaches will work. You could combine all the columns into a single table, which would then be converted to 3NF. (In such a table, the combination of discipline, course number, course title, grade, and so on would be a repeating group.) Or you could use the functional dependencies to determine the following collection of tables:

Student (<u>Student Number</u>, Last Name, First Name, Perm Street, Perm City, Perm State, Perm Zip Code, Local Street, Local City, Local State, Local Zip Code, Credits Taken, Credits Earned, GPA, Total Points)
Student Semester (<u>Student Number</u>, <u>Semester Code</u>, Credits Taken, Credits Earned, GPA, Total Points)
Course (<u>Department Code</u>, <u>Course Number</u>, Course Title, Number Credits)
Student Grade (<u>Student Number</u>, <u>Semester Code</u>, <u>Department Name</u>, <u>Course Number</u>, Grade, Credits Earned, Grade Points)

These tables are all in 3NF. The only change you should make concerns the Department Name column in the Student Grade table. In general, if you encounter a column for which there exists a determinant that is not in the table, you should add the determinant. In this case, Department Code is a determinant for Department Name, but it is not in the table, so you should add Department Code. In the normalization process, Department Name will then be removed and placed in another table whose key is Department Code. This other table will merge with the Department table without the addition of any new columns. The resulting Student Grade table is:

```
Student Grade (Student Number, Semester Code, Department Code, Course Number,
 Grade, Credits Earned, Grade Points)
```

Before representing this design in DBDL, let's take a close look at the Student Semester table. It is true that the columns within it (Credits Taken, Credits Earned, GPA, and Total Points), which all refer to the current semester, are attributes that do, in fact, appear on report cards. Let's assume that after further checking, you find that they are all easily calculated from other fields on the report card during the actual production of report cards. Then, rather than store them in the database, you will merely make sure that the program that produces report cards performs the necessary calculations. For this reason, you will remove the Student Semester table from the collection of tables to be documented and merged. (If these attributes are also required by some other user view in which the same computations are not as practical, they may yet find their way into the database when that user view is analyzed.)

QUESTION Write the DBDL representation of these relations, including foreign key specifications. Merge the result into the cumulative design.

ANSWER See Figure 6.31 for the new cumulative design.

FIGURE 6.31

Cumulative design after User View 3

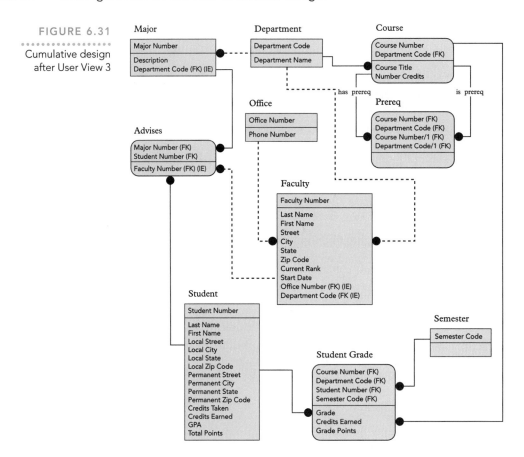

User View 4 Class List (Requirement 2) Let's assume that after examining the sample class list report, you decide to create a single table (actually an unnormalized table) that contains all the attributes on the class list, with the student information (number, name, class standing, and grade) as a repeating group. (Applying the tips for determining the relations to support a given user view would lead more directly to the result, but, for the sake of developing the example, let's assume you haven't done that here.) The unnormalized table created in this fashion would be:

```
Class List (Department Code, Department Name, Semester Code,
  Course Number, Course Title, Number Credits, Section Letter, Schedule Code,
  Time, Room, Faculty Number, Faculty Last Name, Faculty First Name, (Student
  Number, Student Last Name, Student First Name, Class Standing, Grade) )
```

Note: Since column names within a single table must be unique, it is not permissible to have both the faculty and the student last names be called Last Name. Thus, the last and first names of the faculty member are called Faculty Last Name and Faculty First Name. Similarly, the last and first names of the student are called Student Last Name and Student First Name.

Note that you have not as yet indicated the primary key. To identify a given class within a particular semester requires either the combination of department code, course number, and section letter or, more simply, the schedule code. Taking the schedule code as the primary key, however, is not quite adequate. Since the information from more than one semester will be on file at the same time and since the same schedule code could be used in two different semesters to represent completely different courses, the primary key must also contain the semester code. When you remove the repeating group, this primary key expands to contain the key for the repeating group, in this case the student number. Thus, converting to 1NF yields:

```
Class List (Department Code, Department Name, Semester Code,
  Course Number, Course Title, Number Credits, Section Letter, Schedule Code,
  Time, Room, Faculty Number, Faculty Last Name, Faculty First Name,
  Student Number, Student Last Name, Student First Name, Class Standing, Grade)
```

Converting to 3NF yields the following collection of tables:

```
Department (Department Code, Department Name)
Section (Semester Code, Schedule Code, Department Code, Course Number,
      Section Letter, Time, Room, Faculty Number)
Faculty (Faculty Number, Last Name, First Name)
Student Class (Semester Code, Schedule Code, Student Number, Grade)
Student (Student Number, Last Name, First Name, Class Standing)
Course (Department Code, Course Number, Course Title, Number Credits)
```

Note: Since the last name of a faculty member is now in a separate table from the last name of a student, it is no longer necessary to have different names. Thus Faculty Last Name and Student Last Name have both been shortened to Last Name. Similarly, Faculty First Name and Student First Name have both been shortened to First Name.

QUESTION   Why was the grade included?

ANSWER   Although the grade is not actually printed on the class list, it will be entered on the form by the instructor and later returned for posting. A later report, called the grade verification report, differs from the class list only in that the grade is printed. Thus, the grade will ultimately be required and it is legitimate to deal with it here.

QUESTION   Write the DBDL representation of these tables, including foreign key specifications. Merge the result into the cumulative design.

ANSWER   See Figure 6.32 for the new cumulative design.

FIGURE 6.32

Cumulative design after User View 4

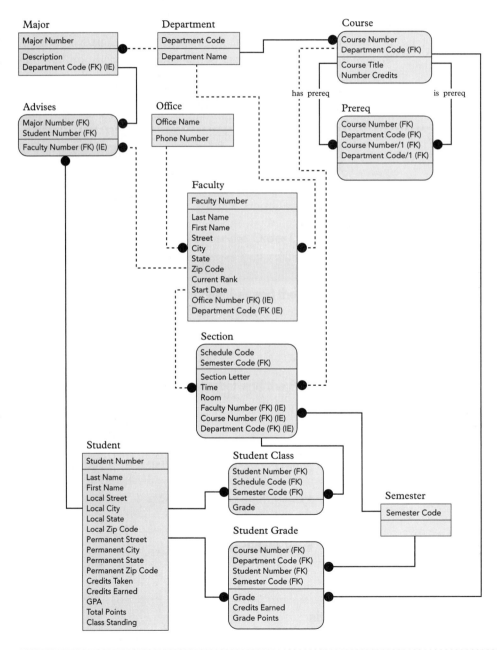

User View 5 Grade Verification Report (Requirement 3) Since the only difference between the class list and the grade verification report is that the grades are printed on the latter, the user views will be quite similar. In fact, since you made a provision for the grade when treating the class list, the views are identical, and no further treatment of this view is required.

User View 6 Time Schedule (Requirement 4) The attributes on the time schedule are as follows: term (which is a synonym for semester), department code, department name, location, course number, course title, number of credits, schedule code, section letter, meeting time, meeting place, and name of instructor. The time schedule also contains the starting and ending date of the semester, the starting and ending date of the exam period, and the last withdrawal date.

You could create a single table containing all these columns and then normalize the table, or you could apply the tips presented in Chapter 5 for determining the collection of tables. In either case, you ultimately create the following collection of tables:

```
Department (Department Code, Department Name, Location)
Course (Department Code, Course Number, Course Title, Number Credits)
Section (Semester Code, Schedule Code, Department Code, Course Number,
     Section Letter, Time, Room, Faculty Number)
Faculty (Faculty Number, Last Name, First Name)
Semester (Semester Code, Start Date, Ending Date, Exam Start Date,
     Exam Ending Date, Withdrawal Date)
```

Note: Actually, given the columns in this user view, the Section table would contain the instructor's name (Last Name and First Name). There was no mention of instructor number. In general, as you saw earlier, it's a good idea to include determinants for columns whenever possible. In this example, since Faculty Number determines Last Name and First Name, you would add Faculty Number to the Section table, at which point the Section table would not be in 3NF. Converting to 3NF will produce the collection of tables shown above.

· ·

QUESTION Write the DBDL representation of these tables, including foreign key specifications. Merge the result into the cumulative design.

ANSWER See Figure 6.33 for the new cumulative design.

User View 7 Registration Request Form (Requirement 5). The collection of tables to support this user view includes a Student table that consists of the primary key, Student Number, and all the columns that depend only on Student Number, such as Last Name, First Name, Local Street, and so on. Since all the columns in this table are already in the Student table in the cumulative collection, this table will not add anything new and there is no need for further discussion of it here.

The portion of this user view that is not already present in the cumulative collection concerns the primary and alternate schedule codes that students request. A table to support this portion of the user view must contain both a primary and an alternate schedule code. It must also contain the number of the student making the request. Finally, to allow the flexibility of retaining this information for more than a single term in order to allow registration for more than one semester at a time, the table must also include the term in which the request is made. This leads to the following table:

```
Registration Request (Student Number, Primary Code, Alternate Code,
     Semester Code)
```

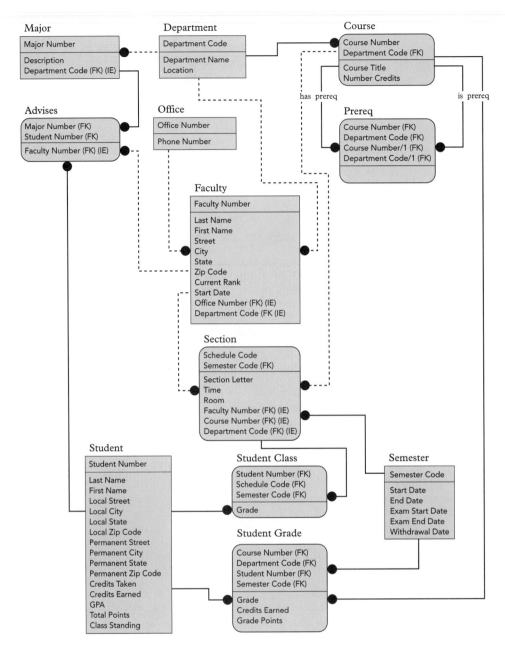

FIGURE 6.33

Cumulative design
after User View 6

For example, if student 123 were to request the section whose schedule code is 2345, with 2396 as an alternate for the FA01 semester, the row (123, 2345, 2396, "FA01") would be stored. The student number, the primary schedule code, and the term are required to uniquely identify a particular row.

QUESTION   Write the DBDL representation of these tables, including foreign key specifications. Merge the result into the cumulative design.

174

ANSWER   See Figure 6.34 for the new cumulative design. Notice that there are two relationships joining Section to Registration Request, so you must name both of them. In this case, you use primary and alternate, indicating that one relationship relates a request to the primary section chosen, the other relates it to the alternate section, assuming there is one.

FIGURE 6.34

Cumulative design after User View 7

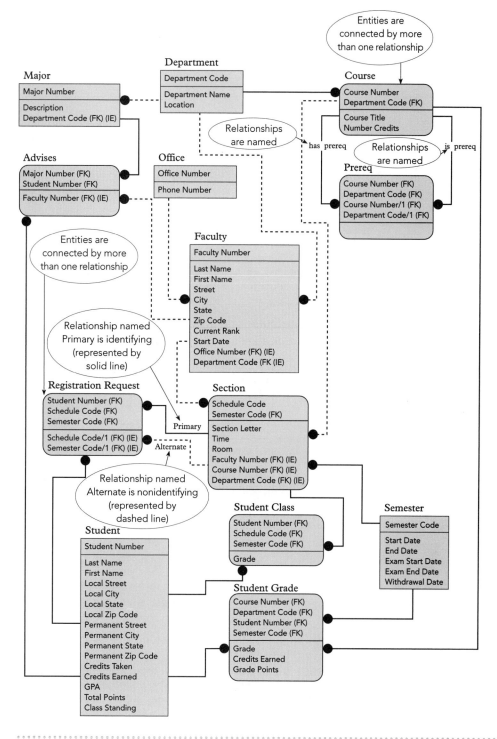

User View 8 Student Schedule (Requirement 6). Suppose you create a single unnormalized table to support the student schedule. This unnormalized table will contain a repeating group representing the lines in the body of the schedule. The table is thus:

```
Student Schedule (Student Number, Semester Code, Last Name, First Name,
     Local Street, Local City, Local State, Local Zip Code,
     Perm Street, Perm City, Perm State, Perm Zip Code,
     (Schedule Code, Department Name, Course Number, Course Title,
     Section Letter, Number Credits, Time, Room) )
```

At this point, you remove the repeating group to convert to 1NF, yielding the following:

```
Student Schedule (Student Number, Semester Code, Last Name, First Name,
     Local Street, Local City, Local State, Local Zip Code, Perm Street,
     Perm City, Perm State, Perm Zip Code, Schedule Code,
     Department Code, Course Number, Course Title, Section Letter,
     Number Credits, Time, Room)
```

Note that the primary key expands to include Schedule Code, which is the primary key to the repeating group. Converting to 2NF produces:

```
Student (Student Number, Last Name, First Name, Local Street,
     Local City, Local State, Local Zip Code, Perm Street, Perm City,
     Perm State, Perm Zip Code)
Student Schedule (Student Number, Semester Code, Schedule Code)
Section (Semester Code, Schedule Code, Department Code, Course Number,
     Course Title, Section Letter, Number Credits, Time, Room)
Course (Department Code, Course Number, Course Title, Number Credits)
```

Removing the attributes that depend on the determinant of Department Code and Course Number from Section to convert to 3NF produces:

```
Student (Student Number, Last Name, First Name, Local Street,
     Local City, Local State, Local Zip Code, Perm Street, Perm City,
     Perm State, Perm Zip Code)
Student Schedule (Student Number, Semester Code, Schedule Code)
Section (Semester Code, Schedule Code, Department Code, Course Number,
     Section Letter, Time, Room)
Course (Department Code, Course Number, Course Title, Number Credits)
```

Merging this collection into the cumulative design does not add anything new. In the process, Student Schedule will merge with Student Class.

User View 9 Full Student Information Report (Requirement 7). Suppose you attempt to place all the attributes on the student information report in a single unnormalized relation. The table has two separate repeating groups, one for the different majors a student may have and the other for all the courses the student has taken.

Note: There are also several attributes, such as name, address, and so on that will not be in the repeating groups. All these attributes are already in the cumulative design, however, and you will not address them here.

The table with repeating groups is:

```
Student (Student Number, (Major Number, Department Code, Last Name,
     First Name), (Semester Code, Department Code, Course Number,
     Course Title, Number Credits, Grade, Grade Points) )
```

Recall from Chapter 5 that you should separate repeating groups when a table has more than one. If you don't do so, you will typically have problems with 4NF. Separating the repeating groups in this example produces:

```
Student Major (Student Number, (Major Number, Department Code,
     Last Name, First Name) )
Student Course (Student Number, (Semester Code, Department Code,
     Course Number, Course Title, Number Credits, Grade, Grade Points) )
```

Converting these to 1NF and including Faculty Number, which is a determinant for Last Name and First Name, produces:

```
Student Major (Student Number, Major Number, Department Code, Faculty Number,
     Last Name, First Name)
Student Course (Student Number, Semester Code, Department Code, Course Number,
     Course Title, Number Credits, Grade, Grade Points)
```

Student Course is not in 2NF, since Course Title and Number Credits depend only on the Department Code, Course Number combination. Student Major is not in 2NF, since Department Code depends on Major Number. Removing these dependencies produces:

```
Student Major (Student Number, Major Number, Faculty Number, Last Name,
     First Name)
Major (Major, Department Code)
Student Course (Student Number, Semester Code, Department Code, Course Number,
     Grade, Grade Points)
Course (Department Code, Course Number, Course Title, Number Credits)
```

Other than Student Major, all these relations are in 3NF. Converting Student Major to 3NF produces the following:

```
Student Major (Student Number, Major Number, Faculty Number)
Faculty (Faculty Number, Last Name, First Name)
```

Merging this collection into the cumulative design does not add anything new. (Student Major merges with the Advises table and does not add any new columns.)

User View 10 Work Version of the Time Schedule (Requirement 9). The only difference between the work version of the time schedule and the time schedule itself (see User View 6) is the addition of two attributes for each section: current enrollment and maximum enrollment. Since these two attributes depend only on the combination of the term and the schedule code, they are placed in the Section table of User View 6 and, after the merge, are in the Section table in the cumulative design. The cumulative design thus far is shown in Figure 6.35.

FIGURE 6.35
· · · · · · · · · · · · · · · · · · · ·
Cumulative design
after User View 10

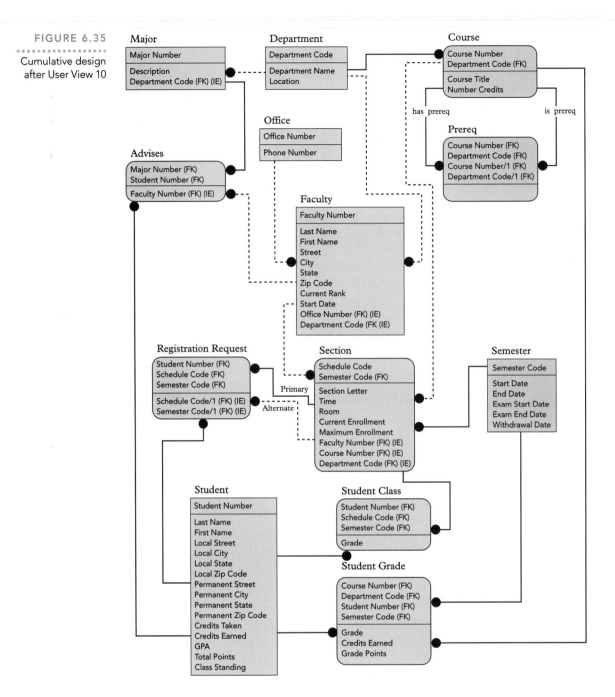

Since the process of determining whether a student has had the prerequisites for a given course involves examining the grades (if any) received in these prior courses, it makes sense to analyze the user view that involves grades before treating the user view that involves enrollment.

User View 11 Post Grades (Requirement 12). There is a slight problem with posting grades. Grades must somehow be posted by section to produce the grade report (e.g., you must record the fact that student 000625321 received an A in the section of CS 153 whose schedule code was 2366 during the fall 2001 semester). On the other hand, for the full student information report, there is no need to have any of the grades related to an actual section of a course. Further, since section information, including these grades, is only to be kept for two semesters (see the description of PURGE in the user requirements), grades would be lost after two semesters if they were kept by section only, since section information would be purged at that time.

A viable alternative is to post two copies of the grade; one copy would be associated with the student, the term, and the section, and the other copy would be associated only with the student and the term. The first copy would be used for the grade verification report and the second for the full student information report. Report cards would probably utilize the second copy, although not necessarily.

Thus, you would have two grade tables:

```
Grade Section (Student Number, Department Code, Course Number, Schedule Code,
    Semester Code, Grade)
Grade Student (Student Number, Department Code, Course
    Number, Semester Code, Grade)
```

Since the Department Code and Course Number in Grade Section depend only on the concatenation of Schedule Code and Semester Code, they are removed from Grade Section during the normalization process and are placed in a table whose primary key is the concatenation of Schedule Code and Semester Code. This table is combined with the Section table in the cumulative design without adding new fields. The Grade Section table that is left will merge with Student Class without adding new fields. Finally, the Grade Student table is combined with the Student Grade table in the cumulative design without adding any new fields. Thus, treatment of this user view does not change the cumulative design.

User View 12 Enrollment (Requirement 11). With the data already in place in the overall design, you can determine what courses a student has taken. You can also determine the prerequisites for a given course. The only remaining issue is the ability to enroll a student in a course. Since information must be retained for more than one semester, you must include the semester code in the table. (You must have the information that student 123 enrolled in section 2345 in SU01 rather than in FA01, for example.) The additional table is as follows:

```
Enroll (Student Number, Semester Code, Schedule Code)
```

The primary key of this table matches the primary key of the table Student Class in the cumulative design. The columns occur in a different order here, but that makes no difference. Thus, this table will merge with Student Class. There are no new columns to be added, so the cumulative design remains unchanged.

User View 13 Purge (Requirement 13). Periodically, certain information that is more than two terms old needs to be removed from the database. This includes all information concerning sections of courses, such as the time, the room, and the instructor, as well as information about the students in the section and their grades. The grade each student received will remain in the database by course, but not by section. For example, you will always retain the fact that student 123 received an A in CS 153 during the Fall semester of 2001, but once the data for that term are purged, you will no longer know the precise section of CS 153 that awarded this grade.

If you examine the current collection of tables, you see that all the data to be purged are already included in the cumulative design, so nothing new needs to be added at this point.

Final Information-Level Design

The design that has been produced is now reviewed to ensure that the user views can be met. You should conduct this review on your own to make certain you understand how the requirements of each user can indeed be satisfied. You will assume that this review has taken place and that no changes have been made. Thus, Figure 6.35 shows the final information-level design.

SUMMARY

- Database design is the process of determining an appropriate database structure to satisfy a given set of requirements. It is a two part process:
    - The information-level design, wherein a clean DBMS-independent design is created to satisfy the requirements.
    - The physical-level design, wherein the final information-level design is converted into an appropriate design for the particular DBMS that will be used.
- A user view is the set of requirements that is necessary to support the operations of a particular user. In order to simplify the design process, the overall set of requirements is split into user views.
- The information-level design methodology involves applying the following steps to each user view:
    - Represent the user view as a collection of tables.
    - Normalize these tables; that is, convert this collection into an equivalent collection that is in 3NF.
    - Represent all keys: primary, alternate, secondary, and foreign.
    - Merge the results of the previous step into the cumulative design.
- The design is represented in a language called DBDL (Database Design Language).
- Designs can be represented pictorially using Entity-Relationship diagrams. Such diagrams have the following characteristics:
    - There is a rectangle for each entity. The name of the entity appears just above the rectangle.
    - The primary key appears above the line in the rectangle.
    - The remaining attributes appear below the line.
    - Alternate keys, secondary keys, and foreign keys are denoted with the letters AK, SK, and FK, respectively.
    - Each rectangle (table) with a foreign key is connected by a dashed line to the rectangle (table) that contains the associated primary key. There is a dot at the end of the line indicating the "many" part of this "one-to-many" relationship.
- Assuming that a relational or relational-like PC-based DBMS is going to be used, the physical-level design process consists of creating a table for each table in the DBDL design. Any constraints (primary key, alternate key, or foreign key) that the DBMS cannot enforce must be enforced by the programs in the system, so this fact must be documented for the programmers.

KEY TERMS

cardinality
composite entity
Database Design Language (DBDL)
dependent entity
Entity-Relationship (E-R) diagram
identifying relationship

independent entity
information-level design
nonidentifying relationship
physical-level design
secondary key
user view

1. Define the term *user view* as it applies to database design.

2. What is the purpose of breaking down the overall design problem into a consideration of individual user views?

3. Under what circumstances would you not have to break down the overall design into a consideration of individual user views?

4. The information-level design methodology presented in this chapter contains a number of steps that must be repeated for each user view. List the steps and briefly describe the kinds of activities that must take place at each step.

5. Describe the function of each of the following types of keys: primary, alternate, secondary, and foreign.

6. Describe the process of creating a design that is appropriate for a relational model system from the information-level design.

7. Suppose that a given user view contains information about employees and projects. Suppose also that each employee has a unique Employee Number and that each project has a unique project number. Explain how you would implement the relationship between employees and projects in each of the following scenarios:

   a. Many employees can work on a given project, but each employee can work on only a *single* project.

   b. An employee can work on many projects but each project has a *unique* employee assigned to it.

   c. An employee can work on many projects, and a project can be worked on by many employees.

8. A database at a college is required to support the following requirements:

   a. For a department, store its number and name.

   b. For an advisor, store his or her number and name and the number of the department to which he or she is assigned.

   c. For a course, store its code and description (for example, MTH110, ALGEBRA).

   d. For a student, store his or her number and name. For each course the student has taken, store the course code, the course description, and the grade received. Also, store the number and name of the student's advisor. Assume that an advisor may advise any number of students but that each student has just one advisor.

   Complete the information-level design for this set of requirements. Use your own experience to determine any constraints you need that are not stated in the problem. Represent the answer in DBDL.

9. List the changes that would need to be made in your answer to Question 8 if a student could have more than one advisor.

10. Suppose that in addition to the requirements specified in Question 8, you must store the number of the department in which the student is majoring. Indicate the changes this would cause in the design in these two situations:

    a. The student must be assigned an advisor who is in the department in which the student is majoring.

    b. The student's advisor does not necessarily have to be in the department in which the student is majoring.

11. Use the design shown in Figure 6.13 to create a design that is appropriate for a relational model system. List the relations. Identify the keys. List the special restrictions that programs will have to enforce.

12. In Example 2 of the section on database design examples, the claim was made that User View 6 led to the same set of tables that had been created for User View 5. Show that this is true.

13. Discuss the effect of the following changes on the design for the Marvel College requirements:

    a. A given section of a course may have more than one instructor, and each instructor is to be listed on the time schedule.

    b. Each department offers only a single major.

    c. Each department offers only a single major, and each faculty member may only advise students in the major that is offered by the department to which the faculty member is assigned.

    d. Each department offers only a single major, and each faculty member may only advise students in the major that is offered by the department to which the faculty member is assigned. In addition, a student may only have a single major.

    e. There is an additional transaction requirement: Given a student's name, find the student's number.

    f. More than one faculty member may be assigned to one office.

    g. The number of credits earned in a particular course may not vary from student to student or from semester to semester.

    h. Instead of a course number, course codes are used to uniquely identify courses (i.e., department numbers are no longer required for this purpose). However, it is still important to know which courses are offered by which departments.

    i. On the registration request, a student may designate a number of alternates along with his or her primary choice. These alternates are listed in a priority order, with the first one being the most desired and the last one being the least desired.

Special Project

Complete the information-level design for the following set of requirements.

Holt Distributors has determined that a database needs to be designed to handle the following new requirements.

General Description

Holt Distributors buys products from its vendors and sells these products to its customers. The Holt Distributors operation is divided into territories. Each customer is represented by a single sales rep, who must be assigned to the territory in which the customer resides. Although each sales rep is assigned to a single territory, more than one may be assigned to the same territory.

When a customer places an order, the order is assigned a number. The customer number, the order number, the customer purchase order (PO) number, and date are entered. (Customers can place orders by sending in a purchase order. For orders that are placed in this fashion, the PO number is recorded.) For each part that is ordered, the part number, quantity, and quoted price are entered. (When it is time for the user to enter the quoted price, the price from the master price list for parts is displayed on the screen. If the quoted price is the same as the actual price, no special action is required. If not, the user enters the quoted price.) The order may also contain special charges, for which a description of the charge and the amount of the charge is entered. Finally, an order may include comments, in which case the comment is entered. Following this, a form is printed that is a combination order acknowledgment/picking list. This form, which is shown in Figure 6.36, is sent to the customer as a record of the order he or she has placed. A copy of the form is also used when the time comes to "pick" the merchandise that was ordered in the warehouse.

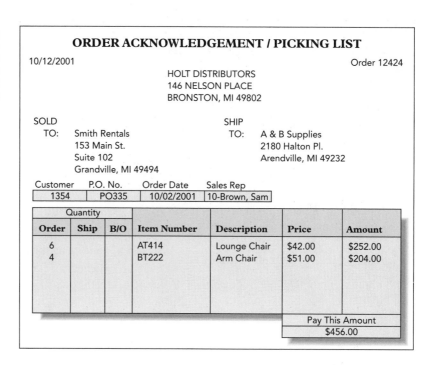

ORDER ACKNOWLEDGEMENT / PICKING LIST

10/12/2001   Order 12424

HOLT DISTRIBUTORS
146 NELSON PLACE
BRONSTON, MI 49802

SOLD
TO: Smith Rentals
      153 Main St.
      Suite 102
      Grandville, MI 49494

SHIP
TO: A & B Supplies
      2180 Halton Pl.
      Arendville, MI 49232

Customer	P.O. No.	Order Date	Sales Rep
1354	PO335	10/02/2001	10-Brown, Sam

Quantity						
Order	**Ship**	**B/O**	**Item Number**	**Description**	**Price**	**Amount**
6			AT414	Lounge Chair	$42.00	$252.00
4			BT222	Arm Chair	$51.00	$204.00

Pay This Amount
$456.00

Until the order is filled, it is considered to be an open order. When the order is filled (which may be some time later), it is said to be released. At this point, an invoice (bill) is printed and sent to the customer, and the customer's balance is increased by the amount of the invoice. The order may have been filled completely or it may have been partially filled (for less than the full amount originally requested). In either case, since the goods have been shipped, the order is considered to have been filled and is no longer considered an open order. (Another possibility is to allow back orders when the order cannot be completely filled. In this case, the order would remain open but only for the back-ordered portion.) When an invoice (see Figure 6.37) is generated, the order is removed from the file of open orders. Summary information is stored concerning the invoice (number, date, customer, invoice total, and freight) until the end of the month.

FIGURE 6.37
....
Invoice for Holt
Distributors

```
10/15/2001                                                    Invoice 11025
                           HOLT DISTRIBUTORS
                           146 NELSON PLACE
                           BRONSTON, MI 49802

   SOLD                              SHIP
    TO:   Smith Rentals               TO:   A & B Supplies
          153 Main St.                      2180 Halton Pl.
          Suite 102                         Arendville, MI 49232
          Grandville, MI 49494
```

Customer	P.O. No.	Our Order No.	Order Date	Ship Date	Sales Rep
1354	PO335	12424	10/02/2001	10/15/2001	10-Brown, Sam

Quantity						
Order	Ship	B/O	Item Number	Description	Price	Amount
6	5	1	AT414	Lounge Chair	$42.00	$210.00
4	4	0	BT222	Arm Chair	$51.00	$204.00
				Freight		$42.50

	Pay This Amount
	$456.50

Companies like Holt Distributors basically employ two methods for accepting payments from customers: open items and balance forward. In the open-item approach, customers make payments on specific invoices. An invoice remains on file until it is completely paid. In the balance-forward approach, customers simply have balances. When an invoice is generated, the customer's balance is increased by the amount of the invoice. When a payment is made, the customer's balance is decreased by the amount of the invoice. Holt Distributors uses the balance-forward approach.

At the end of each month, customers' accounts are updated and aged. (The description of month-end processing in the requirements that follow contains details of the update and aging process.) Statements, an aged trial balance (defined under report requirements), a monthly cash receipts journal, a monthly invoice register, and a sales rep commission report are printed. Cash receipts and invoice summary records are then removed from the database. Month-to-date fields are set to zero. If it is also the end of the year, year-to-date fields are set to zero.

Transaction Requirements

The following are the transaction requirements:

1. Enter/edit territories (territory number and name).

2. Enter/edit sales reps (sales rep number, name, address, city, state, zip code, MTD sales, YTD sales, MTD commission, YTD commission, and commission rate). Each sales rep represents a single territory. (MTD stands for month-to-date and YTD stands for year-to-date.)

3. Enter/edit customers (customer number, name, first line of address, second line of address, city, state, zip code, MTD sales, YTD sales, current balance, and credit limit). A customer may have a different name and address to which goods

will be shipped, called the "ship-to" address.) Each customer has a single sales rep and resides in a single territory. The sales rep must represent the territory in which the customer resides.

4. Enter/edit parts (part number, description, price, MTD and YTD sales, units on hand, units allocated, and reorder point). Units allocated are the number of units that are currently "spoken for" — the number of units of this part that are currently present on some open orders. The reorder point is the lowest value acceptable for units on hand without reordering the product. On the stock status report, which will be described later, any part for which the number of units on hand is less than the reorder point will be indicated by an asterisk.

5. Enter/edit vendors (vendor number, name, address, city, state, zip code). In addition, for each part supplied by the vendor, enter/edit the part number, the price the vendor charges for the part, the minimum order quantity that the vendor will accept for this part, and the expected lead time for delivery of this part from this vendor.

6. Order entry (order number, date, customer, customer PO number, and the order detail lines). An order detail line consists of a part number, description, number ordered, and quoted price. Each order detail line includes a sequence number that is entered by the user. Detail lines on an order must print in the order of this sequence number. The system should calculate and display the order total. After all orders for the day have been entered, order acknowledgments (see Figure 6.36) are printed. In addition, for each part ordered, the units allocated for the part must be increased by the number of units that were ordered.

7. Invoicing cycle:

   a. Enter the numbers of the orders to be released. For each order, enter the ship date for invoicing and the amount of the freight. Indicate whether the order is to be shipped in full or partially shipped. If it is to be partially shipped, enter the number shipped for each order detail line. The system will generate a unique invoice number for this invoice.
   b. Print invoices for each of the released orders. A sample invoice is shown in Figure 6.37.
   c. Update files with information from the invoices just printed. For each invoice, the invoice total is added to the current invoice total, the current balance, and MTD and YTD sales for the customer who placed the order. The total is also added to MTD and YTD sales for the sales rep who represents the customer, and the total, multiplied by the sales rep's commission rate, is added to MTD commission earned and YTD commission earned. For each part shipped, units on hand and units allocated are decreased by the number of units of the part that was shipped. MTD and YTD sales of the part are increased by the product of the number of units shipped and the quoted price.
   d. Create an invoice summary record for each invoice printed. These records contain the invoice number, date, customer, sales rep, invoice total, and freight.
   e. Delete all the released orders.

8. Receive payments on account (customer number, date, amount). Each payment is assigned a number. The amount of the payment is added to the total of current payments for the customer and is subtracted from the current balance of the customer.

Report Requirements

The following are the report requirements:

1. **Territory list**   For each territory, list the number and name of the territory, the number, name, and address of each of the sales reps in the territory, and the number, name, and address of each of the customers represented by these sales reps.

2. **Customer master list**   For each customer, list the number and both the address and the ship-to address. Also list the number, name, address, city, state, and zip code of the sales rep who represents the customer, and the number and name of the territory in which the customer resides.

3. **Open orders by customer**   This report lists open orders organized by customer and is shown in Figure 6.38.

FIGURE 6.38

Open orders report (by customers)

10/08/2001	**HOLT DISTRIBUTORS** **CUSTOMER OPEN ORDER REPORT**				PAGE 1
Order Number	**Item Number**	**Item Description**	**Order Date**	**Order Qty**	**Quoted Price**
Customer 1354 - Smith Rentals					
12424	AT414	Lounge Chair	10/02/2001	6	$42.00
12424	BT222	Arm Chair	10/02/2001	4	$51.00
Customer 1358 -					
. . .	. . .	. . .	. . .	. . .	. . .

4. **Open orders by item**   This report lists open orders organized by item and is shown in Figure 6.39.

FIGURE 6.39
....
Open orders
report (by item)

10/08/2001			**HOLT DISTRIBUTORS** **ITEM OPEN ORDER REPORT**				PAGE 1
Item Number	**Item Description**	**Cust Numb**	**Customer Name**	**Order Number**	**Order Date**	**Order Qty**	**Quoted Price**
AT414	Lounge Chair	1354	Smith Rentals	12424	10/02/2001	6	$42.00
		54	Kayland Enterprises	12489	10/03/2001	8	$42.00
				Total on order —		14	
BT222	Arm Chair	1354	Smith Rentals	12424	10/02/2001	4	$51.00
			•	•	•	•	•
			•	•	•	•	•
			•	•	•	•	•

5. ***Daily invoice register*** For each invoice produced on a given day, list the invoice number, the invoice date, the customer number, the customer name, the sales amount, the freight, and the invoice total. A sample of this report is shown in Figure 6.40.

FIGURE 6.40
....
Daily invoice
register

10/16/2001		**HOLT DISTRIBUTORS** **DAILY INVOICE REGISTER FOR 10/15/2001**				PAGE 1
Invoice Number	**Invoice Date**	**Customer Number**	**Customer Name**	**Sales Amount**	**Freight**	**Invoice Amount**
11025	10/15/2001	1354	Smith Rentals	$414.00	$42.50	$456.50
•	•	•	•	•	•	•
•	•	•	•	•	•	•
•	•	•	•	•	•	•
•	•	•	•	$2840.50	$238.20	$3078.70

6. ***Monthly invoice register*** The monthly invoice register has the same format as the daily invoice register but includes all invoices for the month.

7. ***Stock status report*** For each part, list the part number, description, price, MTD and YTD sales, units on hand, units allocated, and reorder point. For each part for which the number of units on hand is less than the reorder point, an asterisk should appear at the far right of the report.

8. ***Reorder point list*** This report has the same format as the stock status report. Other than the title, the only difference is that parts for which the number of units on hand is greater than or equal to the reorder point should not appear on this report.

9. ***Vendor report*** For each vendor, list the vendor number, name, address, city, state, and zip code. In addition, for each part supplied by the vendor, list the part number, description, the price the vendor charges for the part, the minimum order quantity that the vendor accepts for this part, and the expected lead time for delivery of this part from this vendor.

10. ***Daily cash receipts journal*** For each payment received on a given day, list the number and name of the customer who made the payment, together with the amount of the payment. A sample of the report is shown in Figure 6.41.

FIGURE 6.41
·····················
Daily cash receipts
journal

10/05/2001	**HOLT DISTRIBUTORS** **DAILY CASH RECEIPTS JOURNAL**		PAGE 1
Payment Number	**Customer Number**	**Customer Name**	**Payment Amount**
5807	1354	Smith Rentals	$1000.00
			$12,235.50

11. ***Monthly cash receipts journal*** The monthly cash receipts journal has the same format as the daily cash receipts journal but includes all cash receipts for the month.

12. ***Customer mailing labels*** A sample of the three-across mailing labels the system is to print is shown in Figure 6.42.

FIGURE 6.42
·····················
Customer mailing
labels

Smith Rentals 153 Main St. Suite 102 Grandville, MI 49494	Kayland Enterprises 267 29th St Wyoming, MI 48222	John & Sons, Inc. 5563 Crestview Ada, MI 49292

13. **Statements** Monthly statements are to be produced; a sample is shown in Figure 6.43.

FIGURE 6.43
....
Statements

HOLT DISTRIBUTORS
146 NELSON PLACE
BRONSTON, MI 49802

Smith Rentals   Customer Number: 1354
153 Main St.   Sales Rep: 10 - Sam Brown
Suite 102
Grandville, MI 49494   Limit: $5000.00

Invoice Number	Date	Description	Total Amount
10945	10/02/2001	Invoice	$1230.00
	10/05/2001	Payment	$1000.00CR
11025	10/15/2001	Invoice	$456.50
	10/22/2001	Payment	$500.00CR

Over 90 $0.00	Over 60 $148.50		
Over 30 $490.20	Current $1686.50	Total Due >>>>>>	$2325.20
Previous Balance	Current Invoices	Current Payments	
$2138.70	$1686.50	$1500.00	

14. **Monthly sales rep commission report** For each sales rep, list his or her number, name, address, MTD sales, YTD sales, MTD commission earned, YTD commission earned, and the commission rate.

15. **Aged trial balance** The aged trial balance is a report containing the same information that is printed on the statements.

Month-End Processing

Month-end processing consists of taking the following actions at the end of each month:

1. Update customer account information. In addition to the customer's actual balance, the system must maintain a record stating how much of what the customer owes is current debt incurred within the last 30 days, how much is owed for more than 30 but less than 60 days, more than 60 but less than 90 days, and more than

90 days. While the actual balance, current invoice total, and current payment total are updated whenever an invoice is produced or a payment is received, these aging figures are updated only at month end. The actual update process is as follows:

a. The payments within the last month are credited to the over-90 figure. Any excess is credited first to the over-60 figure, then to the over-30 figure, and then to the current figure. If there is still an excess, it is credited to the current month's invoices.

b. The figures are then rolled. The over-60 amount is added to the over-90 amount. The over-30 amount becomes the new over-60 amount. The current amount becomes the new over-30 amount. Finally, the current month's invoice total becomes the new current amount.

c. Statements and the aged trial balance are printed.

d. The current invoice total is set to zero, the current payment total is set to zero, and the previous balance is set to the current balance in preparation for the coming month.

To illustrate, let's assume that before the update begins, the figures for customer 1354 are as follows:

```
Current Balance:  2375.20        Previous Balance: 2138.70
Current Invoices: 1686.50               Current:   490.20
Current Payments: 1500.00               Over 30:   298.50
                                        Over 60:   710.00
                                        Over 90:   690.00
```

The current payments ($1500.00) are subtracted from the over-90 figure ($690.00), reducing the over-90 figure to zero and leaving an excess of $810.00. This excess is subtracted from the over-60 figure ($710.00), reducing the over-60 figure to zero and leaving an excess of $100.00. This excess is subtracted from the over-30 figure ($298.50), reducing this figure to $198.50. At this point, all the figures are rolled and the Current figure is set to the current invoice total. This produces the following:

```
Current Balance:  2375.20        Previous Balance: 2138.70
Current Invoices: 1686.50               Current:  1686.50
Current Payments: 1500.00               Over 30:   490.20
                                        Over 60:   198.50
                                        Over 90:     0.00
```

Statements and the aged trial balance are now produced, after which the Previous Balance, Current Invoices, and Current Payments figures are updated, yielding:

```
Current Balance: 2375.20        Previous Balance: 2375.20
Current Invoices:   0.00                 Current: 1686.50
Current Payments:   0.00                 Over 30:  490.20
                                         Over 60:  198.50
                                         Over 90:    0.00
```

2. Print the monthly invoice register and the monthly cash receipts journal.

3. Print a monthly sales rep commission report.

4. Zero out all MTD fields. If it also happens to be year end, zero out all YTD fields.

5. Remove all cash receipts and invoice summary records. (In practice, such records would be moved to a historical type of database in order to allow for the possibility of future reference. For the purposes of this assignment, you may disregard this fact.)

CHAPTER 7

Functions of a Database Management System

OBJECTIVE

- Discuss the following nine functions, or services, that should be provided by a DBMS, and the manner in which these services are typically provided:

    a. data storage, retrieval, and update;

    b. a user-accessible catalog;

    c. shared update support;

    d. backup and recovery services;

    e. security services;

    f. integrity services;

    g. data independence support;

    h. replication support; and

    i. utility services.

Introduction

When you left Henry and his chain of bookstores in Chapter 6, his consultant had designed a database to fulfill Henry's business needs. Henry now wants to know what features he can expect to find in a DBMS that he and his staff use on their PC network. The consultant describes to Henry nine features that a DBMS should provide. This chapter provides an overview of all the features that are required to provide optimal DBMS functionality. Some of these features have been introduced in previous chapters; however, they are re-emphasized here because they are key components of a DBMS. The nine features are:

1. **Data storage**, **retrieval**, and **update**: the ability to store, retrieve, and update the data that are in the database.

2. A user-accessible **catalog**: where descriptions of database components are stored and are accessible to users.

3. **Shared update** support: a mechanism to ensure accuracy when several users are updating the database at the same time.

4. **Backup** and **recovery** services: mechanisms for recovering the database in the event that the database is damaged in any way.

5. **Security** services: mechanisms to ensure that only authorized users can access the database or certain parts of the database.

6. **Integrity** services: mechanisms to ensure that certain rules are followed with regard to data in the database and any changes that are made in the data.

7. **Data independence** support: facilities to support the independence of programs from the structure of the database.

8. **Replication** support: a facility to manage copies of the same data at multiple locations.

9. **Utility** services: DBMS-provided services that assist in the general maintenance of the database.

Data, Storage, Retrieval, and Update

A DBMS must provide users with the ability to store, retrieve, and update the data that are in the database.

This statement about storage, retrieval, and update almost goes without saying. It defines the fundamental capability of a DBMS. Unless a DBMS provides this facility, further discussion of what a DBMS can do is irrelevant. In storing, retrieving, and updating data, it should not be necessary for the user to be aware of the system's internal structures or the procedures used to manipulate these structures. This manipulation is strictly the responsibility of the DBMS.

Catalog

A DBMS must provide a catalog (described and illustrated in Chapter 4) in which descriptions of data items are stored and that is accessible to users.

This catalog contains crucial information for those who are in charge of a database or who are going to write programs to access a database. Such persons must be able to easily determine what the database "looks like." Specifically, they need to be able to get quick answers to questions such as the following:

1. What tables and fields are included in the current structure? What are their names?

2. What are the characteristics of these fields? For example, is the Street field within the Customer table 20 characters long or 30? Is the Customer Number field a numeric field or is it a character field? How many decimal places are in the Price field in the Part table?

3. What are the possible values for the various fields? Are there any restrictions on the possibilities for Credit Limit, for example?

4. What are the meanings of the various fields? For example, what exactly is Item Class and what does an Item Class of HW mean?

5. What relationships are present? What is the meaning of each relationship? Must the relationship always exist? For example, must a customer always have a sales rep?

6. Which programs within the system access which data within the database? How do they access it? Do these programs merely retrieve the data, or do they update it? What kinds of updates do the programs do? Can a certain program add a new customer, for example, or can it merely make changes regarding information about customers whose names are already in the database? When it makes a change with regard to a customer, can it change all the fields or only the address?

Mainframe DBMSs often are accompanied by a separate entity called a **data dictionary**, which contains answers to all of the preceding questions and more. The data dictionary forms a sort of super catalog; users access the data dictionary using programs that are supplements to the DBMS. PC-based DBMSs do not offer a data dictionary, but they often have built-in capabilities that provide answers to many of these questions. At a minimum, the capabilities they provide allow users to obtain the answers to questions 1 through 5 in the preceding list.

Shared Update

A DBMS must provide a mechanism to ensure accuracy when several users are updating the database at the same time.

Sometimes a person uses a database stored on a single computer. At other times, several people may be allowed to update a database, but only one person at a time may do so. For example, several people might take turns with one PC to access the database. These situations are easily handled by all DBMSs. However, the use of networks and DBMSs that are capable of running on these networks—allowing several users to access the same database—raises a problem that the DBMS must address: shared update.

Shared update means that two or more users are involved in making updates to the database at the same time. On the surface, it might seem that shared update won't present a problem. Why can't two, three, or 50, for that matter, users update the database simultaneously without incurring a problem?

The Problem

To illustrate the problems involved in shared update, let's assume that you have two users, Ryan and Elena, who both work at Henry's downtown branch. Ryan is currently accessing the database to process incoming book shipments, which includes increasing the number of books on hand by the number in each book shipment. For the downtown store, Ryan is going to increase the number of copies on hand for *The Stranger* by five. Elena, on the other hand, is accessing the database to post sales, which includes decreasing the number of books on hand by the number sold that day. As it happens, the bookstore sold five copies of *The Stranger* that day, so Elena decreases its number on hand by 5. The number on hand for *The Stranger* was 10 prior to the start of Ryan's and Elena's work and, because the amount of the increase exactly matches the amount of the decrease, the number on hand should still be 10 after their work has been completed. But will it? That depends on how the database handles the updates.

How exactly does Ryan make the required update? First, the data concerning *The Stranger* are read from the database into Ryan's work area in memory (RAM). Second, any changes are made in the data in his work area are in memory; in this case, 5 is added to the number on hand of 10, bringing the balance to 15. This change has *not* yet taken place in the database, *only* in Ryan's work area in memory. Finally, the information is written to the database and the change is now made in the database itself (Figure 7.1).

FIGURE 7.1

Ryan updates the database

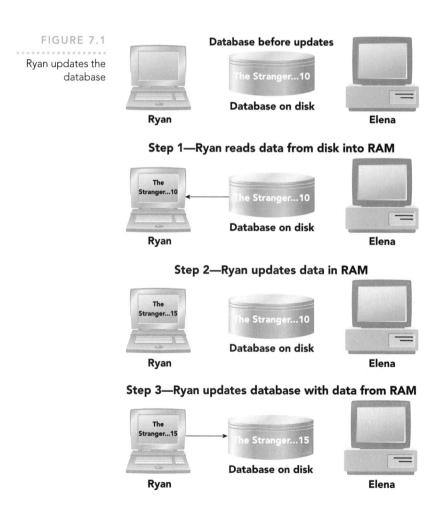

Database before updates

The Stranger...10

Database on disk

Ryan   Elena

Step 1—Ryan reads data from disk into RAM

The Stranger...10 ← The Stranger...10

Database on disk

Ryan   Elena

Step 2—Ryan updates data in RAM

The Stranger...15   The Stranger...10

Database on disk

Ryan   Elena

Step 3—Ryan updates database with data from RAM

The Stranger...15 → The Stranger...15

Database on disk

Ryan   Elena

Suppose that Elena begins her update at this point. The data for *The Stranger* are read from the database, including the new number on hand of 15. The number of copies of the book sold that day, 5, is then subtracted from the number on hand, thus giving a number on hand of 10 in Elena's work area in memory. Finally, this changed value is written to the database, and the number of copies on hand for *The Stranger* is 10, which is correct (Figure 7.2).

FIGURE 7.2

Elena updates the database

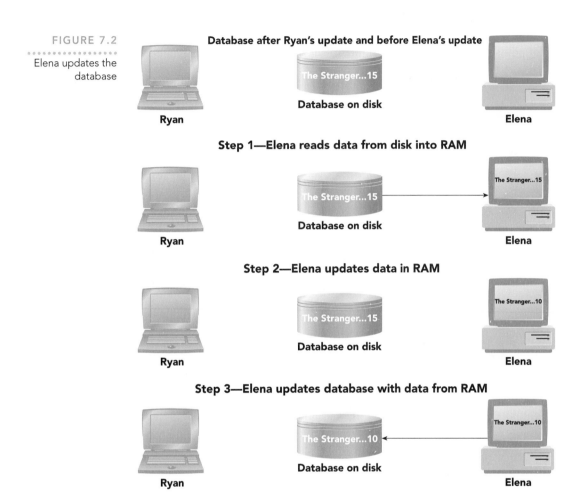

Database after Ryan's update and before Elena's update

The Stranger...15

Database on disk

Ryan

Elena

Step 1—Elena reads data from disk into RAM

The Stranger...15

Database on disk

The Stranger...15

Ryan

Elena

Step 2—Elena updates data in RAM

The Stranger...15

Database on disk

The Stranger...10

Ryan

Elena

Step 3—Elena updates database with data from RAM

The Stranger...10

Database on disk

The Stranger...10

Ryan

Elena

In the preceding scenario, things worked out correctly. But they don't always. Do you see how things could happen in a way that would lead to an incorrect result? What if the scenario shown in Figure 7.3 occurs instead? Here, Ryan reads the data from the database into his work area in memory, and at about the same time, Elena reads the data from the database into her work area in memory. At this point, both Ryan and Elena have the correct data for *The Stranger*, including a number on hand of 10. Ryan adds 5 to the number on hand in his work area, and Elena subtracts 5 from the number on hand in her work area. At this point, in Ryan's work area in memory the number on hand is 15, while in Elena's work area in memory it is 5. Ryan now writes to the database. At this moment, *The Stranger* has a number on hand of 15 in the database. Then Elena writes to the database. Her update overrides Ryan's. Now the number on hand for *The Stranger* in the database is 5! Had the updates to the database taken place in the reverse order, the final number on hand would have been 15. In either case, you now have incorrect data in your database—one of the updates has been "lost." This must not be permitted to happen.

FIGURE 7.3

Ryan and Elena
update the
database in a
manner that leads
to inconsistent
data

Database before updates

Ryan   Elena

Step 1—Ryan reads data from database into RAM

Ryan   Elena

Step 2—Elena reads data from database into RAM

Ryan   Elena

Step 3—Ryan updates data in RAM

Ryan   Elena

Step 4—Elena updates data in RAM

Ryan   Elena

Step 5—Ryan updates the database with data from RAM

Ryan   Elena

Step 6—Elena updates the database with data from RAM; Ryan's update is lost!

Ryan   Elena

Avoiding the Problem

One way to prevent this situation from occurring is to prohibit shared update. This may seem drastic, but it is not really so farfetched. You can permit several users to access the database at the same time, but for retrieval only; that is, they are be able to read information from the database but they are not able to write anything to the database. When these users enter some kind of transaction to update the database (such as decreasing the number of copies on hand for a book), the database itself is not updated. Instead, a record is placed in a separate file of transactions. A record in this file might indicate, for example, that five copies of *The Stranger* had been received on a certain date. Periodically, a single update program reads the *batch* of records in this transaction file and performs the appropriate updates to the database; this processing technique is called batch processing. Because this program is the only one to update the database, you eliminate the problems associated with shared update.

While this approach avoids one set of problems, it creates another problem. From the time users start updating, that is, placing records in the update files, until the time the batch-processing program actually runs, the data in the database are out of date. Where the number of copies of a book in the database is five, the actual number would be zero if a transaction had been entered that decreased the number by 5. If customers call and are told there are copies of the book available, they might drive to the bookstore and become upset upon discovering that the book is not actually in stock. This scheme for avoiding the problems of shared update will not work in any situation—such as credit card processing, banking, inventory control, and airline reservations—that requires the data in the database to be current. Other simple alternate solutions to the shared update problem, such as permitting only one user to update the database, also will not work in these situations because many users are needed to perform the updates in a timely way.

Locking

Assuming you cannot solve the shared update problem by avoiding it, you need a mechanism for dealing with the problem. You need to be able to keep Elena from even beginning the update on *The Stranger* until Ryan has completed his update, or vice versa. This can be accomplished by some kind of locking scheme. Suppose once Ryan reads the data for *The Stranger*, the data are locked, preventing access by any other user, and remain locked until Ryan completes the update. For the duration of the lock, any attempt by Elena to read the data is rejected, and she is notified that the data are locked. If she chooses to do so, she can keep attempting to read the data until the lock is released, at which time her update can be completed. This scenario is demonstrated in Figure 7.4. In at least this simple case, the problem of a "lost update" seems to have been solved.

FIGURE 7.4
....
Ryan and Elena
update the
database using a
locking scheme,
which prevents
inconsistent data.

Step 1—Ryan reads data from database into RAM and locks record

Step 2—Elena tries to read data from database into RAM and fails

Step 3—Ryan updates data in RAM; Elena again tries to read data from the database and again fails

Step 4—Ryan updates the database with data from RAM; Elena again tries to read data from the database and again fails

Step 5—Ryan unlocks record; Elena successfully reads data into RAM and locks record

(continued)

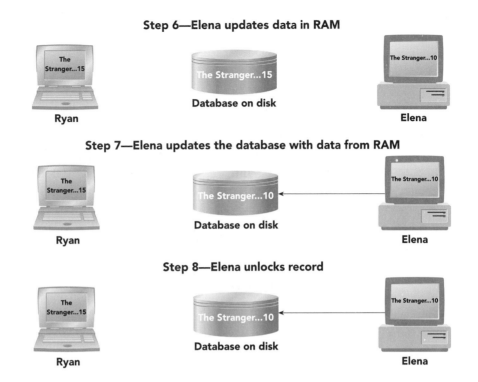

Step 6—Elena updates data in RAM

Ryan · The Stranger...15

The Stranger...15 · Database on disk

Elena · The Stranger...10

Step 7—Elena updates the database with data from RAM

Ryan · The Stranger...15

The Stranger...10 · Database on disk

Elena · The Stranger...10

Step 8—Elena unlocks record

Ryan · The Stranger...15

The Stranger...10 · Database on disk

Elena · The Stranger...10

Two-Phase Locking

How long should a lock be held? If the update involves just changing some values in a single row in a single table, such as changing the name of a book publisher, the lock no longer is necessary once this row has been updated. Sometimes, however, the situation is more involved.

Consider, for example, the process of filling an order for Premiere Products. If you are a user sitting at a workstation, this may seem to involve a single action. You merely indicate that an order currently in the database now needs to be filled. Or you may also be required to enter certain data on the order. In either case, the process still feels like a single action to the user. Behind the scenes, though, lots of activity might be taking place. You might have to update the On Hand field in the Part table for each part that is on the order to reflect the number of units of those parts that were shipped and that are consequently no longer on hand. You might also have to update the Balance field in the Customer table for the customer who placed the order, increasing it by the total amount of the order. You might also have to update the Commission field in the Sales Rep table for the sales rep who represents this customer, increasing it by the amount of commission generated by the order.

In circumstances like these, where a single action on the part of a user requires several updates in the database, what do you do about locks? How long do you hold each one? For safety's sake, locks should be held until all the required updates have been completed. This approach is called two-phase locking. There is a growing phase in which more and more rows are locked but none of the locks are released. After all locks are acquired, the database is updated. Once all the database updates are successfully completed, there is a shrinking phase in which all locks are released and no new ones are added. This two-phase approach solves the lost update problem.

Deadlock

Because users can hold more than one lock at a time, another problem can occur. Suppose that two book orders arrive—Elena will process an order for one copy of *The Stranger* and one copy of *Night Probe*, and Ryan will process a second order for one copy of *Night Probe* and one copy of *The Stranger*. Suppose also that Elena has locked the row for *The Stranger* and is attempting to lock the row for *Night Probe*. However, Ryan has already locked the row for *Night Probe*, so Elena must wait for him to unlock it. Before Ryan unlocks *Night Probe*, though, he needs to update, and thus lock, the row for *The Stranger*, which is currently locked by Elena. Elena is waiting for Ryan to act (release the lock for *Night Probe*), while Ryan, on the other hand, is waiting for Elena to act (release the lock for *The Stranger*). Without the aid of some outside intervention, this dilemma could go on forever. Terms used to describe such situations are deadlock and deadly embrace. Obviously, some strategy is necessary to either prevent or handle deadlock.

Locking on PC-Based DBMSs

Mainframe DBMSs typically offer sophisticated schemes for locking as well as for detecting and handling deadlocks. PC-based DBMSs provide facilities for the same purposes, but they are usually much more limited than the facilities provided by mainframe DBMSs. These limitations, in turn, put an additional burden on the programmers who write the programs that allow several users to update the same database simultaneously.

Although the exact features for handling these problems vary from one PC-based DBMS to another, the following list is fairly typical of the types of facilities provided:

1. Programs can lock an entire table or an individual row within a table, but only one or the other. As long as one program has a row or table locked, no other program may access that row or table.

2. Programs can release any or all of the locks they currently hold.

3. Programs can inquire whether a given row or table is locked.

This list, although it is short, comprises the complete set of facilities provided by many systems. Consequently, the following guidelines have been devised for writing programs for a shared-update environment:

1. If more than one row in the same table must be locked during an update, the whole table must be locked.

2. When a program attempts to read a row that is locked, it may wait a short period of time and then try to read the row again. This process could continue until the row becomes unlocked. It usually is preferable, however, to impose a limit on the number of times a program may attempt to read the row. In this case, reading is done in a loop, which proceeds until either (a) the read is successful, or (b) the maximum number of times that the program can repeat the operation is reached. Programs vary in terms of what action is taken should the loop be terminated without the read being successful. One possibility is to notify the user of the problem and let him or her decide whether to try the same update again or move on to something else.

3. Because there is no facility to detect *and* handle deadlocks, you must try to prevent them. A common approach to this problem is for every program in the system to attempt to lock all the rows and/or tables it needs before beginning an update. Assuming it is successful in this attempt, each program can then perform the required updates. If any row or table that the program needs is already locked, it should immediately release all the locks that it currently holds, wait some specified period of time, and then try the entire process again. In some cases, it may be better to notify the user of the problem and see whether the user wants to try again. In effect, this means that any program that encounters a problem will immediately get out of the way of all the other programs, rather than be involved in a deadlock situation.

4. Because locks prevent other users from accessing a portion of the database, it is important that no user keep rows or tables locked any longer than necessary. This is especially significant for online update programs. Suppose, for example, that a user is using some online update program to update books. Suppose further that once the user enters the book code of the book to be updated, the book row is locked and remains locked until the user has entered all the new data and the update has taken place. What if the user is interrupted by a phone call before he or she has completed filling in the new data? What if the user goes to lunch? The row might remain locked for an extended period of time. If the update involves several rows, all of which must be locked, the problem becomes that much worse. In fact, in many DBMSs, if more than one row from the same table must be locked, the whole table must be locked, which means that whole tables may be locked for extended periods of time. Clearly, this must not be permitted to occur.

A solution is for programs to read the information they need at the beginning of the update and then immediately release all locks. After the user enters all the new data, the update takes place as described earlier—that is, the program attempts to lock all required rows, and then proceeds with the update if successful, or releases all locks if unsuccessful. This does pose a problem, however. Suppose the program reads the data for *The Stranger* and then releases its lock on this book while Ryan is filling in new data on the screen. What if Elena updates *The Stranger* in the meantime and the update is completed before Ryan finishes filling in the new data? If Ryan then finishes filling in the new data and the program blindly proceeds to update the row for *The Stranger* with this new data, Elena's update is lost, that is, overwritten with Ryan's data. So, the program should take a further precautionary step. Before blindly updating the database with Ryan's data, the program should make sure that nobody else has updated the data in the meantime. If someone has, the program cannot update the database with Ryan's data; instead, Ryan must be informed of the situation and permitted to decide whether he wants to redo the update or move on to something else.

How will your program know whether some other user has updated the row for *The Stranger*? Several methods can be used to provide the answer. One is to include an additional field in each record, perhaps a number called Update Counter. Every time any program updates a row in any way, it should also update the value in this field by adding 1 to it. Assuming that every program in the system were to adhere to this approach, you could utilize the following logic:

1. Read all the data from the row for *The Stranger*, including the value of Update Counter. (Let's assume for the purposes of this example that the value is 478.) Unlock the row.

2. Let Ryan enter all the new data.

3. When it is time to do the update, Ryan locks the row for *The Stranger*, reads the current data, and examines the value of Update Counter. If it is still the same (in this case, 478), the row has not been updated and he can finish the update. If it is different (479 or 480, for example), he knows that at least one other program has updated the data in the meantime and he cannot complete the update. In this latter case, he must redo the update from the start.

4. If Ryan has to lock multiple rows, the same procedure is followed for each row. When it is time to do the update, he locks all the rows, reads each row's Update Counter, and compares it with the count he has stored. If the counts all agree, he can perform the update. If one or more counts don't agree, the update cannot take place, and he must redo the update from the start.

Two crucial points arise from the preceding discussion. First, the logic to support shared update certainly adds a fair amount of complexity to each of the programs in the system. Second, cooperation among programs is essential. Every program must do its job. If one program doesn't update the Update Counter field, for example, another program might assume that a row has not been updated when, in fact, it has been. If a program doesn't release all its locks when it encounters a row or table it needs that is locked by some other program, the possibility of deadlock arises. If a program does not release its locks while its user is entering data on the screen, the performance of the whole system may suffer.

Timestamping

An alternative to two-phase locking is timestamping. With timestamping, the DBMS assigns to each database update the unique time when the update started; this time is called a timestamp. In addition, every database row includes the timestamp associated with the last update to the row. The DBMS processes updates to the database in timestamp order. If two users try to change the same row at the same time, the DBMS processes the change with the earlier timestamp. The other transaction is restarted and assigned a new timestamp value.

Timestamping avoids the need to lock rows in the database and eliminates the processing time needed to apply and release locks and to detect and resolve deadlocks. On the other hand, additional disk and memory space are required to store the timestamp values; and the DBMS uses extra processing time to update the timestamp values.

One might naturally ask at this point, is the ability to have several users simultaneously updating the database worth the complexity that it adds to every program in the system? In some cases, the answer will be no. Shared update may be far from a necessity. In most cases, however, shared update will be necessary to the productivity of the users of the system. In these cases, implementation of either of the ideas discussed or of some similar scheme is essential to the proper performance of the system.

■ Backup and Recovery

A DBMS must provide a mechanism for recovering the database in the event that the database is damaged in any way.

A database can be damaged or destroyed in a number of ways. Users can enter data that are incorrect; programs that are updating the database can end abnormally during an update; a hardware problem can occur; and so on. After any such event has occurred, the database may contain invalid data. It may even be totally destroyed.

Obviously, a situation in which data have been damaged or destroyed must not be allowed to go uncorrected. The database must be returned to a correct state. This process is called recovery; that is, you say that you recover the database. In situations where indexes or other physical structures in the database have been damaged but the data have not, many DBMSs provide a feature that you can use to repair the database automatically to recover it.

If the data in a database have been damaged, the simplest approach to recovery involves periodically making a copy of the database (called a backup or a save). If a problem occurs, the database is recovered by copying this backup copy over it. In effect, the damage is undone by returning the database to the state it was in when the last backup was made.

Unfortunately, other activity besides that which caused the destruction also is undone. Suppose the database is backed up at 10:00 P.M. and users begin updating it at 8:00 the next morning. Then suppose that at 11:30 A.M., something happens that destroys the database. If the previous night's backup is used to recover the database, the entire database is returned to the state it was in at 10:00 the previous night. All updates made in the morning are lost, not just the update or updates that were in progress at the time the problem occurred. This means that during the final part of the recovery process, users would have to redo all the work they had done between 8:00 A.M. and 11:30 A.M.

As you might expect, large, expensive DBMSs provide sophisticated facilities to avoid the costly and time-consuming process of having users redo their work. These facilities maintain a record, which is called a journal or log, of all updates to the database.

Such features generally are not available at this time on PC-based DBMSs. Most of them only provide users with a simple way to make backup copies and to recover the database later by copying the backup over the database.

Given this state of affairs, how should you handle backup and recovery in any application system you develop with a PC-based DBMS? You could simply use the features of the DBMS to periodically make backup copies, and use the most recent backup if a recovery were necessary. The more crucial it is to avoid redoing work, the more often you would make backup copies. For example, if a backup were made every eight hours, you might have to redo up to eight hours of work. If one were made every two hours, on the other hand, at most two hours of work would have to be redone.

In many situations, this approach, although not particularly desirable, is acceptable. For systems with a large number of updates made to the database between backups, however, this approach is not acceptable. In such cases, the necessary recovery features that are not supplied by the DBMS must be included in the application programs. Each of the programs that update the database could, for example, also write a record to a separate file—the journal—indicating the update that had taken place. A separate program could be written that would look at this file and recreate all the updates indicated by the records in the file. The recovery process would then consist of first copying the backup over the actual database, and then running this special program.

While this approach does simplify the recovery process for the users of the system, it also causes some problems. First, each of the programs in the system becomes more complicated because of the extra logic involved in adding records to the special file. Second, a separate program to update the database with the information in this file must be written. Finally, every time a user completes an update, the system now has extra work to do, and this additional processing may slow down the system to an unacceptable pace. Thus, in any application, you must determine whether the ease of recovery provided by this approach is worth the price you may have to pay for it. The answer will vary from one system to another.

Security

As mentioned in Chapter 4, a DBMS must provide a mechanism that restricts access to the database to authorized users.

The term security refers to the protection of the database against unauthorized (or even illegal) access, either intentional or accidental. The most common features used by PC-based DBMSs to provide for security are passwords and encryption.

Passwords

Most DBMSs include sophisticated schemes whereby system administrators can assign passwords. Each password may be associated with a list of actions that the user who uses it is permitted to take. A user who enters the password XY1JE, for example, might be allowed to view and alter any book sales data. Another user who enters the password GS36Y might be permitted to view and alter a book's name, view but not alter a book's number on hand, and not even view a branch's data.

Encryption

Encryption refers to the storing of the data in the database in an encrypted, or encoded, format. Any time a user stores or modifies data in the database, the DBMS encrypts the data before actually updating the database. Before a legitimate user retrieves the data via the DBMS, the data are decrypted, or decoded. The whole encryption process is transparent to a legitimate user; that is, he or she is not even aware it is happening. If an unauthorized user attempts to bypass all the controls of the DBMS and get to the database directly, however, he or she will be able to see only the encrypted version of the data.

Views

Recall from Chapter 4 that a view is a snapshot of certain data in the database at a given moment in time. If a DBMS provides a facility that allows various users to have their own views of a database, this facility can be used for security purposes. Tables or fields to which the user does not have access in his or her view effectively do not exist for that user.

Integrity

A DBMS must provide a mechanism to ensure that both the data in the database and changes in the data follow certain rules, as discussed in Chapter 4.

In any database, there are conditions, called integrity constraints, that must be satisfied by the data within the database. The types of constraints that may be present fall into the following four categories:

1. ***Data type.*** The data entered for any field should be consistent with the data type for that field. For a numeric field, only numbers should be allowed to be entered. If the field is a date, only a legitimate date should be permitted. For instance, February 30, 2001, would be an illegitimate date that should be rejected by the DBMS.

2. ***Legal values.*** It may be that for certain fields, not every possible value that is of the right data type is legitimate. For example, even though Credit Limit is a numeric field, only the values 750, 1000, 1500, and 2000 may be valid. It may be that only numbers between 2.00 and 800.00 are legal values for Price.

3. ***Format.*** It may be that certain fields have a special format that must be followed. Even though the Part Number field is a character field, for example, only specially formatted strings of characters may be acceptable. Legitimate part numbers may have to consist of two letters followed by a hyphen, followed by a three-digit number. This is an example of a format constraint.

4. ***Key constraints.*** There are two types of key constraints: primary key constraints and foreign key constraints. Primary key constraints enforce the uniqueness of the primary key. For example, forbidding the addition of a sales rep whose number matches the number of a sales rep already in the database is a primary key constraint. Foreign key constraints enforce the fact that a value for a foreign key must match the value of the primary key for some row in another table. Forbidding the addition of a customer whose sales rep is not already in the database is an example of a foreign key constraint.

An integrity constraint can be treated in one of four ways:

1. The constraint can be ignored, in which case no attempt is made to enforce the constraint.

2. The burden of enforcing the constraint can be placed on the users of the system. This means that users must be careful that any changes they make in the database do not violate the constraint.

3. The burden can be placed on programmers. Logic to enforce the constraint is then built into programs. Users must update the database only by means of these programs and not through any of the built-in entry facilities provided by the DBMS, because these would allow violation of the constraint. The programs are designed to reject any attempt on the part of the user to update the database in such a way that the constraint is violated.

4. The burden can be placed on the DBMS. The constraint is specified to the DBMS, which then rejects any attempt to update the database in such a way that the constraint is violated.

Which of these approaches is best?

The fourth approach is best. Here is why.

The first approach is undesirable, because it can lead to invalid data in the database—two customers with the same number, part numbers with an invalid format, illegal credit limits, and so on.

The second approach is a little better, because at least an attempt is made to enforce the constraints. However, it puts the burden of enforcement on the user. Not only does this mean extra work for the user, but any mistake on the part of a single user, no matter how innocent, can lead to invalid data in the database.

The third approach removes the burden of enforcement from the user and places it on the programmers. This is better still, because it means that users will be unable to violate the constraints. The disadvantage is that all of the update programs in the system are made more complex. This complexity makes the programmers less productive and makes the programs more difficult to create and to modify. It also makes changing an integrity constraint more difficult, because this may mean changing all the programs that update the database. Furthermore, if the logic in any of the programs used to enforce the constraints is faulty, the program could permit some constraint to be violated, and you might not realize that this had happened until a problem occurs at a later time. Finally, you must guard carefully against a user bypassing the programs in the system in order to enter data directly into the database—for example, by using some built-in facility of the DBMS. If this happens, all the controls that were so diligently placed into the programs would be helpless to prevent a violation of the constraints.

The best approach is the one in which you put the burden of integrity enforcement on the DBMS. You specify any constraints to the DBMS and the DBMS ensures that they are never violated.

Most popular DBMSs today include most of the necessary capabilities to enforce the various types of integrity constraints. Consequently, you let the DBMS enforce all the constraints that it is capable of enforcing; then any other constraints are enforced by application programs. You also might create a special program whose sole purpose would be to examine the data in the database to determine whether any constraints had been violated. This program would be run periodically. Corrective action could be taken to remedy any violations that were discovered by means of this program.

Current PC-Based DBMSs and Integrity

Current DBMSs are able to enforce four types of constraints. All DBMSs do an excellent job of enforcing data-type constraints. At a minimum, they typically allow data types of numeric, character, and date. Users are prevented from entering nonnumeric data into numeric fields or invalid dates into date fields.

Most DBMSs provide direct support for enforcing constraints that involve legal values. For example, most DBMSs enforce constraints for a range of numbers (price must be between 2.00 and 800.00) and for selected numbers (credit limit must be 750, 1000, 1500, or 2000), as shown in Figure 7.5. Of the few systems that don't provide direct support, some will supply support if users update the data through custom-generated forms; in other words, the constraints can be specified during the description of a form and the constraints will be enforced for any user who uses that form to update the data in the database. However, if the database is updated in some other way, these constraints will not be enforced.

Most PC-based DBMSs also provide direct support for enforcing a substantial number of format constraints, and these constraints are enforced no matter how the data are entered into the database.

FIGURE 7.5
· · · · · · · · · · · · · · · · · · · ·
Integrity constaints
in a DBMS

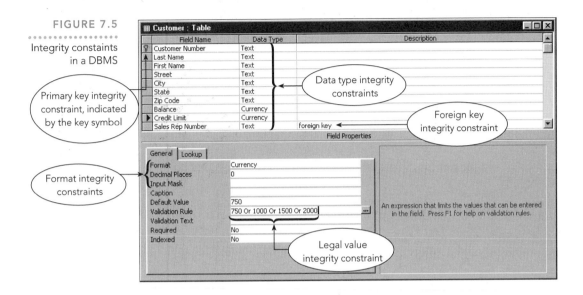

Finally, most PC-based DBMSs support key constraints. They allow a primary key to be specified and build a unique index automatically for the designated primary key. Most systems also support foreign key constraints.

■ Data Independence

A DBMS must include facilities that allow programs to be independent of the structure of the database.

You may have written or worked with application systems that accessed a collection of files. Were any changes ever required in the types of data stored in the files? Did users ever propose any further requirements that necessitated the addition of fields? What about changing the characteristics of a field; for example, expanding the number of characters in the Part Description field from 25 to 30 or the number of digits in a Zip Code field from 5 to 9? What about additional processing requirements—for example, a new requirement to rapidly access a customer's record on the basis of his or her name?

If any of these scenarios sounds familiar, you know that even the simplest of database structure changes can be painful. Adding a new field or changing the characteristics of an existing field, for example, usually entails writing a program that will read each record from the existing file and will write a corresponding record with the new layout to a new file. In addition, each of the programs in the existing system must be changed to reflect the new layout, and these changes must be tested.

One of the advantages of working with a DBMS is data independence—that is, the property that allows changes to be made in the structure of a database without application programs necessarily being affected. You will now examine how the various types of changes that can be made in the structure of the database can affect programs that access the database.

Addition of a Field

No program should need to be changed except, of course, those programs that will utilize the new field. Some programs may need to be changed, however. If, for example, a program uses something like the SQL "SELECT * FROM …" to select all the fields from a given table, the user suddenly is presented with an extra field. To prevent this from happening, the output of the program must be restricted to only the desired fields. To avoid the imposition of this extra work, it is a good idea to list specific fields in an SQL SELECT command instead of using the *.

Changing the Length of a Field

In general, programs should not have to change because the length of a field has been changed. For the most part, the DBMS will handle all the details concerning this change in length. If, however, a program is designed to set aside a certain portion of the screen or a report for the field and the length of the field has increased to the point where the previously allocated space is inadequate, the program will need to be changed.

Creating a New Index

Typically, a simple command is all that is required to create a new index. Most DBMSs will use the new index automatically for all updates and queries. For some DBMSs, you might need to make minor changes in already existing programs to use the new index.

Adding or Changing a Relationship

This change is the trickiest of all and is best illustrated with an example. Suppose that Premiere Products now has the following requirements:

1. Customers are assigned to territories.

2. Each territory is assigned to a single sales rep.

3. A sales rep can have more than one territory.

4. A customer is represented by the sales rep who covers the territory to which the customer is assigned.

To implement these changes, you might choose to restructure the database as follows:

```
Sales Rep (Sales Rep Number, Last Name, First Name, Street, City, State,
      Zip Code, Commission, Rate)
Territory (Territory Number, Territory Description, Sales Rep Number)
Customer (Customer Number, Last Name, First Name, Street, City, State,
      Zip Code, Balance, Credit Limit, Territory Number)
```

Now suppose that a user is accessing the database via the following view, named Sales Cust:

```
CREATE VIEW Sales Cust (Snum, SLast, SFirst, Cnum, CLast, CFirst) AS
    SELECT Sales Rep.Sales Rep Number, Sales Rep.Last Name,
        Sales Rep.First Name, Customer.Customer Number,
        Customer.Last Name, Customer.First Name
        FROM Sales Rep, Customer
        WHERE Sales Rep.Sales Rep Number = Customer.Sales Rep Number
```

The defining query is no longer legitimate, because there is no Sales Rep Number field in the Customer table. A relationship still exists between sales reps and customers, however. The difference is that you now must go through the Territory table to relate the two. If users have been accessing the tables directly to form the relationship, their programs will have to change. If they are using the Sales Cust view, then only the definition of the view will have to change. The new definition will be as follows:

```
CREATE VIEW Sales Cust (Snum, SLast, SFirst, CNum, CLast, CFirst) AS
    SELECT Sales Rep.Sales Rep Number, Sales Rep.Last Name,
        Sales Rep.First Name, Customer.Customer Number,
        Customer.Last Name, Customer.First Name
        FROM Sales Rep, Territory, Customer
        WHERE Sales Rep.Sales Rep Number = Territory.Sales Rep Number
            AND Territory.Territory Number = Customer.Territory Number
```

The defining query is now more complicated than it was before, but this does not affect users of the view. They continue to access the database in exactly the same way they did before, and their programs do not need to change.

You've now seen how the use of views can allow changes to be made in the logical structure of the database without application programs being affected. As helpful as this is, however, all is not quite as positive as it might seem. For one thing, this entire discussion is not relevant to the many DBMSs that do not permit the use of views. Second, even those DBMSs that support views often limit the types of updates that can be accomplished through a view. In particular, if the view involves a join, often little or no updating is allowed to take place. So the benefits that can be derived from the use of views very well may be unavailable to the user who needs to update the database. This problem is the focus of a great deal of current research and should be resolved in the near future.

Replication

A DBMS must provide a facility to manage copies of the same data at multiple locations.

Sometimes data should be duplicated—technically called replicated—at more than one physical location, for performance or other reasons. For example, accessing data at a local site is much more efficient than accessing data remotely; because it does not involve data communication and network time delays, it avoids competing for data with other users, and it keeps data available to local users at times when the data might not be available at other sites. If certain information needs to be accessed frequently from all sites, a company might choose to store the information at all of its locations. At other times, users on the road, for example, sales reps meeting at their customers' sites, might need access to data but would not have this access unless the data were stored on their laptops.

Replication lets users at different sites use and modify copies of a database and then share their changes with the other users. Replication is a two-step process. First, the DBMS creates copies, called replicas, of the database at one or more sites (Figure 7.6a). The master database and all replicas form a replica set. Users then update their individual replicas, just as if they were updating the master database. Periodically, the DBMS exchanges all updated data between two databases in a replica set in a process called synchronization (Figure 7.6b).

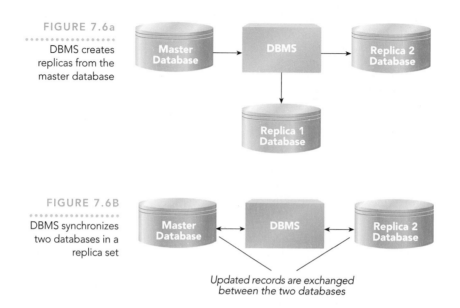

FIGURE 7.6a
....
DBMS creates replicas from the master database

FIGURE 7.6B
....
DBMS synchronizes two databases in a replica set

Updated records are exchanged between the two databases

Ideally, the DBMS should handle all the issues associated with replication. Any work to keep the various copies of data consistent should be done behind the scenes; users should not be aware of it. You will learn more about replication in Chapter 9.

Utilities

In addition to the services already discussed, a DBMS can provide a number of utility services that assist in the general maintenance of the database. Following is a list of such services that might be provided by a PC-based DBMS:

1. Services that permit changes to be made in the database structure—adding new tables or fields, deleting existing tables or fields, changing the name or characteristics of a field, etc.

2. Services that permit the addition of new indexes and the deletion of indexes that are no longer needed.

3. Access to DOS, Windows, Linux, and other operating system services from within the DBMS.

4. Services that provide export to and import from other software products; for example, these services allow data to be transferred in a relatively easy fashion between the DBMS and a spreadsheet, word processing, or graphics program, or even another DBMS.

5. Support for easy-to-use edit and query capabilities, screen generators, report generators, etc.

6. Access to both procedural and nonprocedural languages. With a procedural language, the computer must be told precisely how a given task is to be accomplished. BASIC, C++, and COBOL are examples of procedural languages. With a nonprocedural language, the task is merely described to the computer, which then determines how to accomplish it. SQL is an example of a nonprocedural language.

7. An easy-to-use menu-driven or switchboard-driven interface that allows users to tap into the power of the DBMS without having to resort to a complicated set of commands.

◼ SUMMARY

- A DBMS must provide users with the ability to store, retrieve, and update the data that are in the database.

- A DBMS must provide a catalog in which descriptions of the structure of a database are stored and that can be queried by users.

- A DBMS must provide support for shared update, allowing more than one user to update the database at the same time.

  - If care is not taken, incorrect results can be produced in the database.

  - Locking is one approach that ensures correct results. As long as a portion of the database is locked by one user, other users cannot gain access to it. Two-phase locking includes a growing phase, in which more and more rows are locked but none of the locks are released, followed by a shrinking phase, in which all locks are released and no new ones are added.

  - Deadlock and deadly embrace are terms used to describe the situation in which two or more users are each waiting for the other to release a lock before they can proceed. Mainframe

DBMSs have sophisticated facilities for detecting and handling deadlock. Most PC-based DBMSs do not have such facilities, which means that programs that access the database must be written in such a way that deadlocks are avoided.

  - An alternative to two-phase locking is timestamping, in which the DBMS processes updates to a database in timestamp order.

- A DBMS must provide facilities for recovering the database in the event that it is damaged or destroyed. Most DBMSs provide facilities for periodically making a backup copy of the database. To recover the database when it is damaged or destroyed, the backup is copied over the database.

- A DBMS must provide security facilities; that is, features that prevent unauthorized access to the database. Such facilities typically include passwords, encryption (the storing of data in an encoded form), and views (which limit users to accessing only the tables and fields included in the view).

- An integrity constraint is a rule that data in the database must follow. A DBMS should include features that prevent integrity constraints from being violated.

- A DBMS must include facilities that promote data independence, which is the property that the database structure can change without application programs necessarily being affected.

- A DBMS must provide a facility to handle replication by managing copies of a database at multiple locations.

- The DBMS must provide a set of utility services.

■ KEY TERMS

backup
batch processing
data dictionary
data independence
deadlock
deadly embrace
encryption
growing phase
integrity constraint
journal
locking
log
nonprocedural language
password

procedural language
recovery
replicas
replication
save
security
shared update
shrinking phase
synchronization
timestamp
timestamping
two-phase locking
utility services

■ REVIEW QUESTIONS

1. What do you mean when you say that a DBMS should provide facilities for storage, retrieval, and update?

2. What is the purpose of the catalog? What types of information are usually found in the catalogs that accompany PC-based DBMSs? What additional types of information are often found in the catalogs that accompany mainframe DBMSs?

3. What is meant by shared update?

4. Describe a situation (other than the one used in the text) in which an uncontrolled shared update would produce incorrect results.

5. What is meant by locking?

6. Describe two-phase locking.

7. What is deadlock? How does it occur?

8. Are most PC-based systems capable of detecting and breaking deadlocks?

9. Assuming that you are using a DBMS that provides the locking facilities described in the text, how should programs be written to (a) avoid deadlock, (b) guarantee correct results, and (c) keep any individual user from tying up portions of the database for extended periods of time?

10. What is meant by recovery? What facilities are typically provided by PC-based DBMSs to handle backup and recovery? What main feature is lacking in such facilities? What problems can this cause for users? What is timestamping?

11. What is meant by security?

12. How are passwords used by DBMSs to promote security?

13. What is encryption? How does it relate to security?

14. How do views relate to security?

15. What is meant by integrity? What is an integrity constraint? Describe four different ways of handling integrity constraints. Which approach is the most desirable?

16. What is meant by data independence? What benefit does it provide?

17. Describe a situation, other than the ones given in the text, when replication would be useful to an organization.

18. Name some utility services that a DBMS should provide.

19. How well does your school's DBMS fulfill the functions of a DBMS described in this chapter? Which functions are fully supported, which are partially supported, and which are not supported at all?

20. Many computer magazines and a number of Web sites present comparisons of several DBMSs. Find one such DBMS comparison and compare the functions in this chapter to the listed features and functions in the comparison. Which functions from this chapter are included in the comparison, which functions are missing from the comparison, and what additional functions are included in the comparison?

CHAPTER 8

Database Administration

OBJECTIVES

- Discuss the need for database administration (DBA).

- Explain the role of DBA in formulating and implementing database policies.

- Discuss the role of DBA with regard to the data dictionary, user training, and the selection and support of a DBMS.

- Discuss the role of DBA in the database design process.

Introduction

Henry has learned from his consultant about the many benefits of the database approach. At the same time, the consultant has pointed out that the use of a DBMS involves potential hazards, especially when the database serves more than one user. For example, as you learned in Chapter 7, problems are associated with shared update and with security: Who is allowed to access various parts of the database, and in what way? How do you prevent unauthorized accesses? Just managing the database involves fundamental difficulties. Users must be made aware of the database structure, or, at least, that portion of the database that they are allowed to access so that they can use the database effectively. Any changes that are made in the structure must be communicated to all users, along with information about how the changes will affect them. Backup and recovery must be carefully coordinated, much more so than in a single-user environment, and this presents another complication.

In order to resolve these problems, the consultant recommends that Henry use the services of a resource, commonly referred to as **database administration (DBA)**, that is responsible for supervising both the database and the use of the DBMS. DBA is usually a group rather than an individual, although sometimes the term DBA is used to refer to the database administrator — the individual who is in charge of this group. Usually the context makes clear which meaning is intended.

In this chapter, you will learn about the role and responsibilities of DBA, which are summarized in Figure 8.1. You'll be focusing on the role of DBA in a PC environment similar to Henry's bookstore operation. In the next section, DBA's role in formulating and implementing important policies with respect to the database and its use will be discussed. Then you will examine DBA's role in the use of the data dictionary and the crucial role of DBA in training various users. After that, you'll learn about DBA's role in the selection and support of the DBMS. Finally, the role DBA plays in the extremely important process of database design will be discussed.

FIGURE 8.1

Responsibilities of DBA

```
1. Policy Formulation and Implementation
   a.   Access privileges
   b.   Security
   c.   Disaster planning
   d.   Archives
2. Data Dictionary Management
3. Training
4. DBMS Support
   a.   DBMS evaluation and selection
   b.   DBMS responsibility
5. Database Design
```

Policy Formulation and Implementation

DBA formulates database policies and communicates these policies to users. DBA is also charged with the implementation of these policies. Among these policies are those covering access privileges, security, disaster planning, and archives.

Access Privileges

Access to every table and field in the database is not a necessity for every user. For example, Sam is an employee at Premiere Products; his main responsibility is the inventory. While he may very well need access to the entire Part table, does he also need access to the Sales Rep table? It is unlikely. He should probably be able to print inventory reports, but should he be able to change the layout of these reports? Probably not. Figure 8.2 illustrates the permitted and denied access privileges for Sam.

FIGURE 8.2

Permitted and denied access for Sam

Sales Rep

Sales Rep Number	Last Name	First Name	Street	City	State	Zip Code	Commission	Rate
03	Jones	Mary	123 Main	Grant	MI	49219	2150.00	.05
06	Smith	William	102 Raymond	Ada	MI	49441	4912.50	.07
12	Diaz	Miguel	419 Harper	Lansing	MI	49224	2150.00	.05

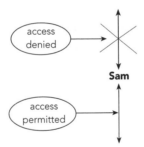

Part

Part Number	Part Description	On Hand	Class	Warehouse	Price
AX12	Iron	104	HW	3	$24.95
AZ52	Dartboard	20	SG	2	$12.95
BA74	Basketball	40	SG	1	$29.95
BH22	Cornpopper	95	HW	3	$24.95
BT04	Gas Grill	11	AP	2	$149.99
BZ66	Washer	52	AP	3	$399.99
CA14	Griddle	78	HW	3	$39.99
CB03	Bike	44	SG	1	$299.99
CX11	Blender	112	HW	3	$22.95
CZ81	Treadmill	68	SG	2	$349.95

Betty, whose responsibility is customer mailings, clearly requires access to customers' names and addresses, but what about their balances or credit limits? Should she be able to change an address? Figure 8.3 illustrates the permitted and denied access privileges for Betty.

FIGURE 8.3

Permitted and denied access for Betty

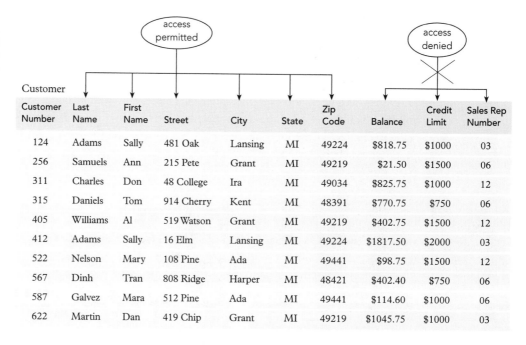

While sales rep 03 (Mary Jones) should be able to obtain some of the information about her own customers, should she be able to obtain the same information about other customers? Figure 8.4 illustrates the permitted and denied access privileges for Mary Jones.

FIGURE 8.4

Permitted and denied access for Betty

Customer

Customer Number	Last Name	First Name	Balance	Credit Limit	Sales Rep Number
124	Adams	Sally	$818.75	$1000	03
256	Samuels	Ann	$21.50	$1500	06
311	Charles	Don	$825.75	$1000	12
315	Daniels	Tom	$770.75	$750	06
405	Williams	Al	$402.75	$1500	12
412	Adams	Sally	$1817.50	$2000	03
522	Nelson	Mary	$98.75	$1500	12
567	Dinh	Tran	$402.40	$750	06
587	Galvez	Mara	$114.60	$1000	06
622	Martin	Dan	$1045.75	$1000	03

DBA must answer questions like these and take steps to ensure that users access the database only in ways to which they are entitled. Policies concerning such access should be clearly documented by DBA, approved by top-level management, and communicated to all concerned parties.

Security

As you learned earlier, the term security refers to the prevention of unauthorized access to the database. Of course, this includes access by someone who has no right to access the database at all; for example, someone who is not connected with Premiere Products. It can also include users who have legitimate access to some portion of the database but who are attempting to access a portion for which they are not authorized. Figures 8.5a and 8.5b illustrate both types of security violation.

FIGURE 8.5a

Attempted security violation. John is not an authorized user.

FIGURE 8.5b

Attempted security violation. Although Betty is an authorized user, she is not authorized to access customers' balances.

Customer

Customer Number	Last Name	First Name	Balance	Credit Limit	Sales Rep Number
124	Adams	Sally	$818.75	$1000	03
256	Samuels	Ann	$21.50	$1500	06
311	Charles	Don	$825.75	$1000	12
315	Daniels	Tom	$770.75	$750	06
405	Williams	Al	$402.75	$1500	12
412	Adams	Sally	$1817.50	$2000	03
522	Nelson	Mary	$98.75	$1500	12
567	Dinh	Tran	$402.40	$750	06
587	Galvez	Mara	$114.60	$1000	06
622	Martin	Dan	$1045.75	$1000	03

DBA must take steps to ensure that the database is secure. Once access privileges have been specified and security features are in place, DBA draws up policies to explain the security privileges and then distributes these policies to authorized users.

Security features that are present in the DBMS, such as passwords, encryption, and views, are utilized by DBA to implement these policies. Any necessary features that the DBMS lacks are added by DBA through the use of special programs. Figures 8.6a and 8.6b show security features of the DBMS both with and without DBA enhancement.

FIGURE 8.6a

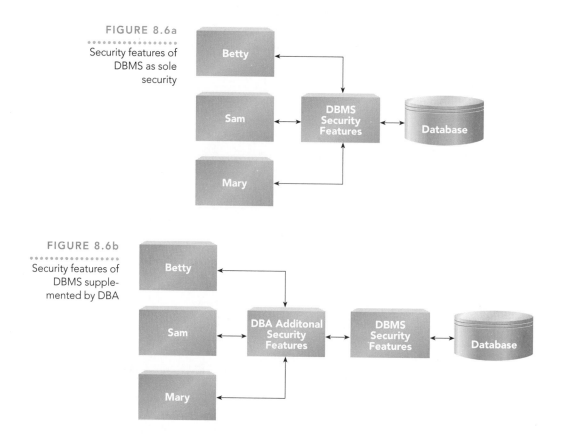

Security features of DBMS as sole security

FIGURE 8.6b

Security features of DBMS supplemented by DBA

One security feature that we have mentioned, passwords, deserves further attention. Sometimes people think that simply establishing a password scheme will ensure security. After all, Tim can't get access to Pam's data if he doesn't know her password — assuming, of course, that Tim doesn't have a password of his own that allows access to the same data.

But what if Tim observes Pam typing in her password? What if he guesses her password? You might think this sort of occurrence is so unlikely that it is nothing to worry about. In fact, it is not so unlikely. Many people often choose passwords that they can remember easily. A very common choice, for example, is the name of a family member. So if Pam is a typical user, Tim might very well be able to obtain her password just by trying names of her family members. Other users choose unusual passwords or have such passwords assigned to them, but in order to remember them, they often have these passwords written down somewhere. Without giving it much thought, such users are often careless about storing the paper on which a password is written, giving people like Tim still another vehicle for unauthorized access. Figure 8.7 illustrates the careless use of passwords.

FIGURE 8.7
. . . .
Careless use of
passwords. Tim is
trying to look over
Pam's shoulder to
see the paper on
which her pass-
word is written.

It is up to DBA to educate users on the use of passwords. The pitfalls just discussed should be stressed, as should precautionary measures, including the need for frequent changes of passwords. Whenever security is violated or whenever an attempt at a security breach is made, DBA must determine who breached security and how the violation was achieved.

Planning for Disaster

The type of security discussed so far concerns harm done by unauthorized users. A database can be harmed in another way as well, and that is through some physical occurrence such as an abnormally terminated program, a disk problem, a power outage, a computer malfunction, a flood, a tornado, or other natural disasters. This issue was discussed in Chapter 7 in the material on recovery, but it is included here as well because it is DBA's responsibility to establish and implement backup and recovery procedures. In the event that damage does occur, procedures for recovery must be part of a disaster recovery plan. Because of its management and control responsibilities for the database, DBA must take an active role in the formulation of this plan. For example, some companies need to keep their computers functioning no matter what problems occur. Credit card companies, for instance, can switch quickly to duplicate backup computers in the event of a malfunction in the main computers. Other companies contract with firms using hardware and software similar to their own so that in the event of a catastrophe, they can temporarily use these other facilities. As in other cases, DBA will use the built-in disaster and recovery features of the DBMS wherever possible and will supplement them where they are lacking.

For example, many PC-based DBMSs lack facilities to maintain a journal of changes in the database. Thus, recovery is usually limited to copying the most recent backup over the live database. This means, as you already have seen, that any changes made since this backup have to be redone by the users. If this presents a major problem, DBA may decide to supplement the DBMS facilities. A typical solution is to have each program that updates the database also make appropriate entries in a journal (Figure 8.8a) and then make use of this journal in the recovery process (Figure 8.8b). The database is first recovered by copying the backup version over the live database; then it is brought up to date through a special DBA-created program that updates the database with changes recorded in the journal.

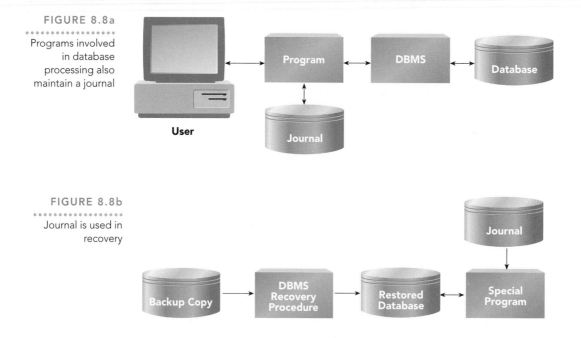

FIGURE 8.8a
....
Programs involved
in database
processing also
maintain a journal

User

Program

DBMS

Database

Journal

FIGURE 8.8b
....
Journal is used in
recovery

Journal

Backup Copy

DBMS Recovery Procedure

Restored Database

Special Program

Archives

Often, data need to be kept in the database for only a limited time. An order that has been filled, has appeared on some statement, and has been paid is in one sense no longer important. Should the order be left in the database? If data are always left in the database as a matter of policy, the database will continually grow. The disk space that is occupied by the database expands, and the performance of programs that access the database may deteriorate. Both of these situations can lead to problems. This is a good reason to remove an already filled order and all of its associated order lines from the database.

On the other hand, it may be necessary to retain such data for future reference. Reasons for keeping the data could include customer inquiries, government regulations, and auditing requirements. If this is the case, you now have a conflict on your hands: You should remove the old data from the database, yet you need to have access to it.

The solution is to use what is known as a data archive. In ordinary usage, an archive (technically archives) is a place where records and documents are kept. A data archive is similar. It is a place where a record of certain corporate data is kept. In fact, a data archive simply is referred to as an archive. In the case of the previously mentioned order, you would remove it from the database and place it in the archive, thus storing it for future reference (Figure 8.9).

FIGURE 8.9

Movement of order
12498 from live
database to
archive

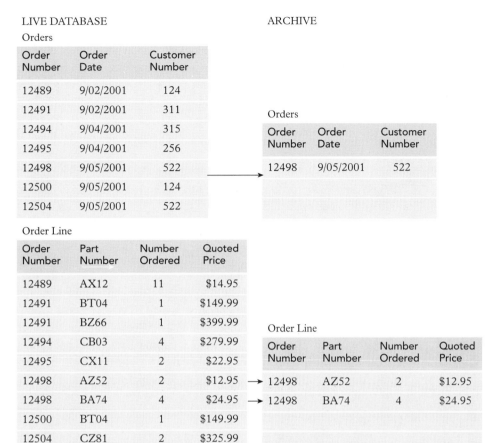

Typically, the archive is kept on some mass-storage device — for example, a disk, a tape, a CD, or a DVD. Whichever medium is used, it is important that copies of archives *and* backups be kept off-site, so that recovery can take place even if a company's buildings and contents are destroyed. Once again, it is up to DBA to establish and implement procedures for the use, maintenance, and storage of the archive.

Data Dictionary Management

In addition to administering the database, DBA also manages the data dictionary. The data dictionary is essentially the catalog mentioned in Chapter 7, but it often contains a wider range of information, including at the very least, information on tables, fields, indexes, and programs.

DBA establishes naming conventions for tables, fields, indexes, and so on. It creates the data definitions for all tables as well as any data integrity rules. It is also charged with the update of the contents of the data dictionary. The creation and distribution of appropriate reports from the data dictionary is another of DBA's responsibilities.

▮ Training

DBA provides training in the use of the DBMS and in how to access the database. It also coordinates the training of users. In cases where training is provided by the vendor of software the organization has purchased, DBA handles the scheduling in order to make sure that users receive the training they require.

▮ DBMS Support

DBA is responsible for all aspects of a DBMS within an organization, including the selection and maintenance of the system.

DBMS Evaluation and Selection

DBA is responsible for the evaluation and selection of the DBMS. In order to oversee this responsibility, it sets up a checklist like the one shown in Figure 8.10. (This checklist applies specifically to a relational system, because most DBMSs are, at least in part, relational. If we had not already selected a data model, such as the relational model, for the focus of this text, a category called "Choice of Data Model" would have to be added to the list.) DBA must evaluate each prospective purchase of a DBMS in terms of all the categories shown in the figure. An explanation of the various categories follows.

FIGURE 8.10

. . . .

DBMX evaluation
checklist

```
1. Data Definition
   a.    Data types
             (1) Numeric
             (2) Character
             (3) Date
             (4) Logical (T/F)
             (5) Memo
             (6) Currency
             (7) Binary object (pictures, drawings, sounds, and so on)
             (8) Link to an Internet, Web, or other address
             (9) User-defined data types
             (10) Other
   b.    Support for nulls
   c.    Support for primary keys
   d.    Support for foreign keys
   e.    Unique indexes
   f.    Views

2. Data Restructuring
   a.    Possible restructuring
             (1) Add new tables
             (2) Delete old tables
             (3) Add new columns
             (4) Change layout of existing columns
             (5) Delete columns
             (6) Add new indexes
             (7) Delete old indexes
   b.    Ease of restructuring

3. Nonprocedural Languages
   a.    Nonprocedural languages supported
             (1) SQL
             (2) QBE
             (3) Natural language
             (4) Own language. Award points on the basis of ease of use as well as the types of operations
                 (joining, sorting, grouping, calculating various statistics, and so on) that are available in the
                 language. SQL can be used as a standard against which such a language can be judged.
   b.    Optimization done by one of the following:
             (1) User, in formulating the query
             (2) DBMS (through built-in optimizer)
             (3) No optimization possible; system will do only sequential searches
```

continued

FIGURE 8.10
....
DBMX evaluation
checklist

continued

4. Procedural Languages
   a. Procedural languages supported
       (1) Own language. Award points on the basis of the quality of this language both in terms
           of the types of statements and control structures available and the database manipulation
           statements included in the language.
       (2) C or C++
       (3) GUI language such as PowerBuilder or Visual Basic
       (4) COBOL
       (5) Other
   b. Can nonprocedural language be used in conjunction with the procedural language
       (e.g., could SQL be embedded in COBOL programs)?

5. Data Dictionary
   a. Type of entities
       (1) Tables
       (2) Columns
       (3) Indexes
       (4) Relationships
       (5) Programs
       (6) Other
   b. Integration of data dictionary with other components of the system

6. Shared Update
   a. Level of locking
       (1) Column
       (2) Row
       (3) Page
       (4) Table
   b. Type of locking
       (1) Shared
       (2) Exclusive
       (3) Both
   c. Responsibility for handling deadlock
       (1) Programs
       (2) DBMS (automatic rollback of transaction causing deadlock)

7. Backup and Recovery Services
   a. Backup facilities
   b. Journaling facilities
   c. Recovery facilities
       (1) Recover from backup copy only
       (2) Recover using backup copy and journal
   d. Rollback of individual transactions
   e. Incremental backup

8. Security
   a. Passwords
       (1) Access to database only
       (2) Read or write access to any column or combination of columns
   b. Encryption
   c. View
   d. Difficulty in bypassing security controls

9. Integrity
   a. Support for entity integrity
   b. Support for referential integrity
   c. Support for data-type integrity
   d. Support for other types of integrity constraints

10. Replication and Distributed Databases
    a. Partial replicas
    b. Handling of duplicate updates in replicas
    c. Data distribution
    d. Procedure support
        (1) Language used
        (2) Procedures stored in database
        (3) Support for remote stored procedures
        (4) Trigger support

11. Limitations
    a. Number of tables
    b. Number of columns
    c. Length of individual column
    d. Total length of all columns in a table
    e. Number of rows per table
    f. Number of files that can be open at the same time
    g. Sizes of database, tables, and other objects
    h. Types of hardware supported
    i. Types of LANs supported
    j. Other

continued

FIGURE 8.10
....
DBMS evaluation
checklist

continued

```
12. Documentation and Training
    a.    Clearly written manuals
    b.    Tutorial
          (1) Printed
          (2) Online
    c.    Online help available
          (1) General help
          (2) Context-sensitive help
    d.    Training
          (1) Vendor or other company
          (2) Location
          (3) Types (DBA, programmers, users, others)
          (4) Cost

13. Vendor Support
    a.    Type of support available
    b.    Quality of support available
    c.    Cost of support
    d.    Reputation of support

14. Performance
    a.    External benchmarking done by various organizations
    b.    Internal benchmarking
    c.    Includes a performance monitor

15. Portability
    a.    Operating systems
          (1) Unix
          (2) Microsoft Windows
          (3) Microsoft Windows NT
          (4) NetWare
          (5) OS/2
          (6) Other
    b.    Import/export/linking file support
          (1) Other databases
          (2) Other applications (e.g., spreadsheets and graphics)
    c.    Internet and intranet support

16. Cost
    a.    Cost of basic DBMS
    b.    Cost of any additional components
    c.    Cost of any additional hardware that is required
    d.    Cost of network version (if required)
    e.    Cost and types of support

17. Future Plans
    a.    What does the vendor plan for the future of the system?
    b.    What is the history of the vendor in terms of keeping the system up to date?
    c.    When changes are made in the system, what is involved in converting to the new version?
          (1) How easy is the conversion?
          (2) What will it cost?

18. Other Considerations (Fill in your own special requirements.)
    a.    Special purpose reports
    b.    ?
    c.    ?
    d.    ?
```

1. ***Data definition*** What types of data are supported? Is support for nulls provided? What about primary and foreign keys? The DBMS undoubtedly will provide indexes, but is it possible to specify that an index is unique and then have the system enforce the uniqueness? Is support for views provided?

2. ***Data restructuring*** What type of database restructuring is possible? How easy is it to do this restructuring? Will the system do most of the work or will the DBA have to create special programs for this purpose?

3. ***Nonprocedural languages*** What types of nonprocedural language are supported? The possibilities are SQL, QBE, natural language, or a DBMS built-in language. If one of the standard languages is supported, how good is the version provided by the DBMS? If the DBMS provides its own language, how good is it? How does its functionality compare to that of SQL? How does the DBMS achieve

optimization of queries? Either the DBMS itself optimizes each query—the user must do so by the manner in which he or she states the query—or no optimization occurs. Most desirable, of course, is the first option.

4. ***Procedural languages*** What types of procedural languages are supported? Are they common languages, such as C or C++, COBOL, or a GUI language, or does the DBMS come with its own language? In the latter case, how complete is the language? Does it contain all the required types of statements and control structures? What facilities are provided for accessing the database? Is it possible to make use of the nonprocedural language while using the procedural language?

5. ***Data dictionary*** What kind of data dictionary support is available? Is it a simple catalog, or can it contain more content, such as information about programs and the various data items these programs access? How well is the data dictionary integrated with other components of the system — for example, the nonprocedural language?

6. ***Shared update*** Is support provided for shared update? What is the unit that may be locked (field, row, page, or table)? Are exclusive locks the only ones permitted, or are shared locks also allowed? (A shared lock permits other users to read the data; with an exclusive lock, no other user may access the data in any way.) How is deadlock handled? Will the DBMS take care of the deadlock, or is it the responsibility of programs to ensure that it is handled correctly?

7. ***Backup and recovery services*** What type of backup and recovery facilities are provided? Can the DBMS maintain a journal of changes in the database and use the journal during the recovery process? If a transaction has aborted, is the DBMS capable of rolling it back, that is, undoing the updates of the transaction? Can the DBMS perform an incremental backup of just the data that have changed?

8. ***Security*** What type of security features does the system make available? Are passwords supported? Do passwords simply regulate whether a user may access the database, or is it possible to associate read or write access to a combination of fields with a password? Is encryption supported? Does the system have some type of view mechanism that can be used for security? How difficult is it to bypass the security controls?

9. ***Integrity*** What type of integrity constraints are supported? Is there support for entity integrity (the fact that the primary key cannot be null)? What about referential integrity (the property that states that values in foreign keys must match values already in the database)? Does the DBMS support data-type integrity (which prohibits values that do not match the data type for the field into which they are being entered from being allowed to occur in the database)? Is there support for any other types of constraints?

10. ***Replication and distributed databases*** Does the DBMS support replication? If so, does it allow partial replicas (copies of selected rows and fields from tables in a database), and how does it handle updates to the same data from two or more replicas? Can a database be distributed, that is, stored on more than one computer? If so, what types of distribution are allowed and what types of procedure support exist?

11. ***Limitations*** What limitations exist with respect to the number of tables, fields, and rows per table? How many files can be open at the same time? (For some databases, each table and each index is in a separate file. Thus, a single table with three indexes,

all in use at the same time, would account for *four* files. Problems may arise if the number of files that can be open is relatively small and many indexes are in use.) On what types of operating system and hardware is the DBMS supported? What types of local area networks can be used?

(A local area network [LAN] is a configuration of several computers all hooked together, thereby allowing users to share a variety of resources. One of these resources is the database. In a local area network, support for shared update is very important, because many users may be updating the database at the same time. The relevant question here, however, is not how well the DBMS supports shared update, but which LANs can be used in conjunction with this DBMS?)

12. ***Documentation and training*** How good are the manuals? Are they easy to use? Is there a good index? Is a tutorial, in either printed or online form, available to assist users in getting started with the system? Is online help available? If so, is it general help or context-sensitive? (Context-sensitive help means that if a user is having trouble and asks for help, the DBMS will provide assistance for the particular feature being used at the time the user asks for it.) Does the vendor provide training classes; do other companies offer training? Are the classes on-site or off-site? Are there classes for DBA and separate classes for programmers and for users and for others? What is the cost for each type of training?

13. ***Vendor support*** What type of support is provided by the DBMS vendor, and how good is it? What is the cost? What is the vendor's reputation for support among current users?

14. ***Performance*** How well does the system perform? This is a tough one to answer. One way to determine relative performance is to look into benchmark tests that have been performed on several DBMSs by various organizations. Benchmarking is typically done in areas such as sorting, indexing, reading all rows, and changing data values in all rows. For example, the Transaction Processing Performance Council (www.tpc.org) provides the results of database benchmark tests to its membership. Beyond this, if an organization has some specialized needs, it may have to set up its own benchmark tests. Does the DBMS provide a performance monitor, which measures different types of performance while the DBMS is operational?

15. ***Portability*** On what types of operating systems is the DBMS supported? What types of files can be imported or exported? Can the DBMS link to other data sources, such as files and other types of DBMSs? Does the DBMS provide Internet and intranet support? (An intranet is a company's internal network that uses software tools typically used on the Internet and the World Wide Web.)

16. ***Cost*** What is the cost of the DBMS and of any additional components the organization is planning to purchase? Is additional hardware required and, if so, what is the associated cost? If the organization requires a special version of the DBMS for a network, what is the additional cost? What is the cost of vendor support, and what types of support plans are available?

17. ***Future plans*** What plans has the vendor made for the future of the system? This information is often difficult to obtain, but you can get an idea by looking at the performance of the vendor with respect to how it has kept the existing system up to date. How easy has it been for users to convert to new versions of the system?

18. ***Other considerations*** This is a final, catch-all category that contains any special requirements not covered in the other categories.

Once each DBMS has been examined with respect to all the preceding categories, the results can be compared. Unfortunately, this process can be difficult, because of the number of categories and their generally subjective nature. To make the process more objective, DBA can assign a numerical ranking to each DBMS for its performance in each category (for example, a number between zero and 10, where zero is poor and 10 is excellent). Furthermore, the categories can be assigned weights. This allows an organization to signify which categories are more critical to it than others. Then each of the numbers being used in the numerical ranking can be multiplied by the appropriate weight. The results are added up, producing a weighted total. The weighted totals for each DBMS then can be compared, producing the final evaluation.

How does DBA arrive at the numbers to assign each DBMS in the various categories? Several methods are used. It can request feedback from other organizations that are currently using the DBMS in question. It can read journal reviews of the various DBMSs. Sometimes a trial version of the DBMS can be obtained, in which case members of the staff can give it a hands-on test. In practice, all three methods are sometimes combined. Whichever method is used, however, it is crucial that the checklist and weights be carefully thought out; otherwise, the findings may be inadvertently slanted in a particular direction.

Responsibility for DBMS

Once the DBMS has been selected, DBA continues to have primary responsibility for it. DBA installs the DBMS in a way that is suitable for the organization. If the DBMS configuration needs to be changed, DBA makes the changes.

When a new version of the DBMS is released, DBA reviews it and determines whether the organization should upgrade to it. If the decision is made to convert to the new version or perhaps to a new DBMS, DBA coordinates the conversion. Any fixes to problems in the DBMS that are sent by the vendor are also handled by DBA.

■ Database Design

DBA is responsible for carrying out the process of database design. It must ensure that a sound methodology for database design, such as the one discussed in Chapter 6, is established and is followed by all personnel who are involved in the process. It also must ensure that all pertinent information is obtained from the appropriate users.

DBA is responsible for the implementation of the final information-level design; in other words, it is responsible for the physical-level design process. If performance problems surface, it is up to DBA to make the changes that will improve the system's performance. This is called tuning the design.

DBA also is responsible for establishing standards for documentation of all the steps in the database design process. It also has to make sure that these standards are followed, that the documentation is kept up to date, and that the appropriate personnel have access to the documentation they need.

Requirements don't remain stable over time; they are constantly changing. DBA must review such changes and determine whether a change in the database design is warranted. If so, it must make such changes in the design and in the data in the database. It then also must make sure that all programs affected by the change are modified in any way necessary and that the corresponding documentation is also modified.

SUMMARY

- Database administration (DBA) is the person or group that is assigned responsibility for supervising the database and the use of the DBMS.
- DBA formulates and implements policies concerning the following:
  - those users who can access the database; which portions of the database these persons may access, and in what manner;
  - security, that is, the prevention of unauthorized access to the database;
  - recovery of the database in the event that it is damaged; and
  - management of an archive for data that are no longer needed in the database but must be retained for reference purposes.
- DBA is in charge of maintaining the data dictionary.
- DBA is in charge of training with respect to the use of the database and the DBMS. Training that is provided by an outside vendor is scheduled by DBA, which ensures that users receive the training they need.
- DBA is in charge of supporting the DBMS. This responsibility has two facets:
  - The evaluation and selection of a new DBMS; DBA develops a checklist of desirable features for a DBMS and evaluates each prospective purchase of a DBMS against this list.
  - The responsibility for installing and maintaining the DBMS after it has been selected and procured.
- DBA is in charge of database design at both the information level and the physical level. It is also in charge of evaluating changes in requirements to determine whether a change in the database design is warranted. If so, DBA makes the change and reports it to affected users.

KEY TERMS

data archive
database administration (DBA)

local area network (LAN)
tuning

1. What is DBA? Why is it necessary?

2. What is DBA's role in regard to access privileges?

3. What is DBA's role in regard to security? What problems can arise in the use of passwords? How should these problems be handled?

4. Suppose a typical DBMS is being used by your company. Suppose also that in the event the database is damaged in some way, it is essential that it be recovered without the users having to redo any work. What action should DBA take?

5. What are data archives? What purpose do they serve? What is the relationship between databases and data archives?

6. What is DBA's responsibility with regard to the data dictionary?

7. Who trains computer users within an organization? What is DBA's role in this training?

8. Describe the method that should be used to select a new DBMS.

9. Describe the relevance of the following categories on a DBMS checklist:

    a. data definition
    b. data restructuring
    c. nonprocedural languages
    d. procedural languages
    e. data dictionary
    f. shared update

    g. backup and recovery services
    h. security
    i. integrity
    j. replication and distributed databases
    k. limitations
    l. documentation and training
    m. vendor support
    n. performance
    o. portability
    p. cost
    q. future plans
    r. other considerations

10. How does DBA obtain the necessary information to award points for the various categories on the checklist?

11. What is DBA's role regarding the DBMS once it has been selected?

12. What is DBA's role in database design?

13. Many computer magazines and a number of Web sites present comparisons of several DBMSs using an evaluation checklist. Find one such DBMS evaluation checklist for PC-based DBMSs and compare it with the checklist in this chapter. What items appear on one checklist but not the other? If a DBMS is recommended in your selected comparison, why was it recommended?

CHAPTER 9

Advanced Topics

OBJECTIVES

- Describe distributed database management systems.

- Discuss client/server systems.

- Define data warehouses and explain their uses.

- Discuss the general concepts of object-oriented database management systems.

- Summarize the impact of the Internet and intranets on database management systems.

Introduction

Previous chapters of this text have focused on relational database management systems, which dominate the database market today. In this chapter, you will examine several advanced database topics, most of which are applicable to relational systems.

The centralized approach to processing data, wherein users access a central computer through terminals and workstations, was dominant from the late 1960s through the mid-1980s, because there was no alternative approach to compete with it. The advent of reasonably priced personal computers during the 1980s, however, facilitated the placement of computers at various locations within an organization, which meant that users could use the database directly at those various locations. These computers were connected through some type of network that allowed users to access data not only in their local computer but anywhere along the entire network. Thus, distributed processing was born. In the next section, you will study the issues involved in distributed databases—the database component of distributed processing.

It has long been common practice to use smaller computers to off-load communications functions from a central computer. Similarly, it is now common to use client/server systems for off-loading database access functions from workstations and a central computer. These client/server systems are the subject of the second section of this chapter. The following section covers special database systems that focus on the rapid, timely, and accurate retrieval of data; these systems are called data warehouses. Then you will study object-oriented systems, which treat data as objects, complete with the actions that can occur to the objects. The final section briefly reviews the impact of the Internet and intranets on database systems.

Distributed Databases

Premiere Products has several sites around the country. Each location has its own sales reps and customer base, and each location maintains its own inventory. Instead of using a single, centralized mainframe computer accessed by all the separate locations, Premiere Products is considering installing a computer at each site. If it does so, each site would maintain its own data concerning its sales reps, customers, parts, and orders. However, occasionally an order at one site might involve parts from another site. Also, customers from one site might place orders at another site. Thus, the computer at each site would have to be able to communicate with the computers at all the other sites. The computers would have to be connected in some kind of communications network, as illustrated in Figure 9.1.

FIGURE 9.1
....
Communications
network

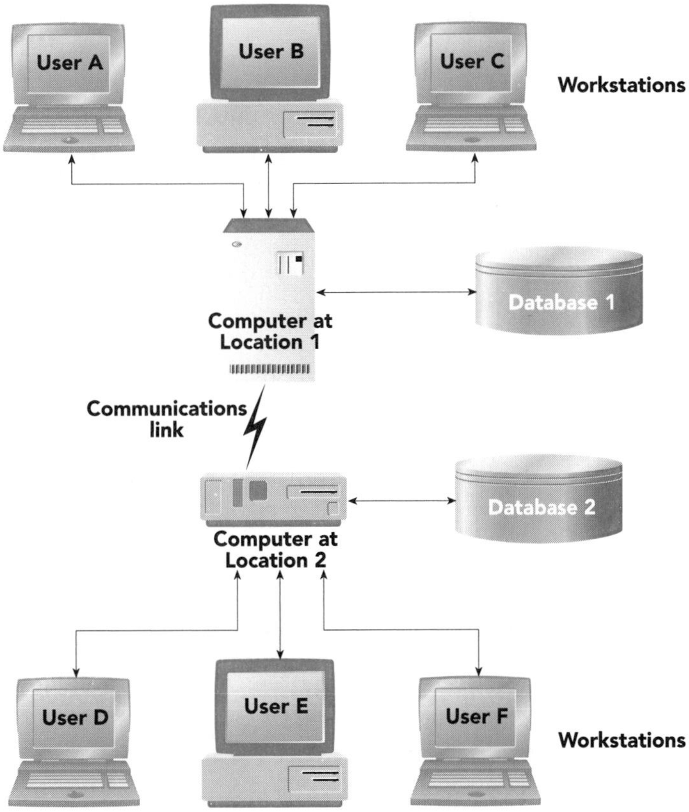

Additionally, Premiere Products would need to divide its existing database and distribute to each site the data needed at that site. In doing so, Premiere Products would be creating a distributed database. A distributed database is a single logical database that is physically distributed to computers at several sites of a computer network. To make such a distributed database work properly, Premiere Products needs to purchase a distributed database management system. A distributed database management system (DDBMS) is a DBMS capable of supporting and manipulating distributed databases.

Communication between computers in the network is achieved through messages; that is, one computer sends a message to another. The word "message" is used in a fairly broad way here. It could mean a request for data. It could also be used to indicate a problem. For example, one computer could send a message to another computer indicating that the requested data are not available. Finally, a message could be the actual data.

Accessing data using messages over a network is substantially slower than accessing data on a disk. To access data rapidly in a centralized system, design decisions are made to minimize disk accesses, but, in general, to access data rapidly in a distributed system, it is more important to minimize the number of messages. Although the mechanics of sending a message are not discussed in this book, it is important to realize that the length of time required to send one message depends on the length of the message and the characteristics of the network. There is a fixed amount of time, sometimes called the access delay, required for every message. In addition, the time for each message must include the time it takes to transmit all the characters. The formula for message transmission time is as follows:

```
Communication time = access delay + ( data volume / transmission rate)
```

As an example, suppose you have an access delay of 2 seconds and a transmission rate of 30,000 bits per second. Assuming that a message consists of 1,000 records, each of which is 800 bits long (the total of which is equivalent to approximately 25 pages of single-spaced text), the communication time would be as follows:

```
Communication time = 2 + ((1,000 * 800) / 30,000)
                   = 2 + (800,000 / 30,000)
                   = 2 + 26.67
                   = 28.67 seconds
```

To transmit a message that is 100 bits long would take:

```
Communication time = 2 + (100 / 30,000)
                   = 2 + .003
                   = 2.003 seconds or, for practical purposes
                   = 2 seconds
```

As you can see, in short messages, the access delay can become the dominant feature. Thus, in general, a small number of lengthy messages is preferable to a large number of short messages.

Characteristics of Distributed Database Management Systems

Because a distributed database management system effectively contains a local DBMS at each site, an important property of such systems is that they are either homogeneous or heterogeneous. A homogeneous DDBMS is one that has the same local DBMS at each site. A heterogeneous DDBMS is one that does not; there are at least two sites at which the local DBMSs are different. Heterogeneous systems are more complex than homogeneous systems and, consequently, have more problems and are more difficult to manage.

All DDBMSs share several important characteristics. Among them are location transparency, replication transparency, and fragmentation transparency.

Location Transparency

The definition of a distributed database says nothing about the *ease* with which users access data that are stored at another site. Systems that support distributed databases should enable a user to access data at a remote site—a site other than the one at which the user is located—just as easily as he or she accesses data from the local site—or the site where the user is located. Response times for accessing data stored at a remote site might be much slower, but, except for this difference, it should feel to a user as though the entire database is stored at his or her location. This property is called location transparency and is one of the major objectives of distributed systems.

Replication Transparency

As described in Chapter 7, replication lets users at different sites use and modify copies of a database and then share their changes with the other users. While this replication of data can improve the efficiency of certain types of processing, it creates update problems and causes associated problems with data consistency. If you update the record of a single part at Premiere

Products, the update must be made at each of the locations at which data concerning this part are stored. Not only does this make the update process more cumbersome, but, should one of the copies of data for this part be overlooked, there would be inconsistent data in the database. Ideally, the DDBMS should handle this problem. Any work to keep the various copies of data consistent should be done behind the scenes by the DDBMS; the user should not be aware of it. This property is called replication transparency.

Fragmentation Transparency

When you store data at each Premiere Products site for the customers served by that site, you have what is termed data fragmentation. A system supports data fragmentation if a logical object, such as the collection of all records of a given type, can be divided among the various locations. The main purpose of data fragmentation is to place data at the site where they are most often accessed.

Fragmentation can occur in a variety of ways. Assume, for example, Premiere Products has three sites named Site1, Site2, and Site3. Also assume that an additional field in the Customer table, named Site Number, identifies the primary site with which a customer is associated.

Using a SQL-like language, you could define the following fragments:

```
DEFINE FRAGMENT F1 AS
    SELECT Customer Number, Last Name, First Name, Street,
           City, State, Zip Code, Balance, Credit Limit,
           Sales Rep Number, Site Number
        FROM Customer
        WHERE Site Number = 'Site1'


DEFINE FRAGMENT F2 AS
    SELECT Customer Number, Last Name, First Name, Street,
           City, State, Zip Code, Balance, Credit Limit,
           Sales Rep Number, Site Number
        FROM Customer
        WHERE Site Number = 'Site2'


DEFINE FRAGMENT F3 AS
    SELECT Customer Number, Last Name, First Name, Street,
           City, State, Zip Code, Balance, Credit Limit,
           Sales Rep Number, Site Number
        FROM Customer
        WHERE Site Number = 'Site3'
```

Each of these fragment definitions indicates what data are selected from the Customer table and included in the fragment. Note that the Customer table does not actually exist in any one place. Rather, parts of it exist in three pieces. These pieces, or fragments, are assigned to locations. Here, fragment F1 is assigned to site Site1, fragment F2 is assigned to site Site2, and fragment F3 is assigned to site Site3. The effect of this assignment is that data about each customer are stored at the site at which he or she is a customer.

The Premiere Products data shown in Figure 9.2 are used as the basis for the fragmentation illustrated in Figure 9.3. Creation of the complete Customer table entails taking the union of these three fragments.

Customer

Customer Number	Last Name	First Name	Street	City	State	Zip Code	Balance	Credit Limit	Sales Rep Number	Site Number
124	Adams	Sally	481 Oak	Lansing	MI	49224	$818.75	$1000	03	Site1
256	Samuels	Ann	215 Pete	Grant	MI	49219	$21.50	$1500	06	Site2
311	Charles	Don	48 College	Ira	MI	49034	$825.75	$1000	12	Site3
315	Daniels	Tom	914 Cherry	Kent	MI	48391	$770.75	$750	06	Site2
405	Williams	Al	519 Watson	Grant	MI	49219	$402.75	$1500	12	Site2
412	Adams	Sally	16 Elm	Lansing	MI	49224	$1817.50	$2000	03	Site1
522	Nelson	Mary	108 Pine	Ada	MI	49441	$98.75	$1500	12	Site2
567	Dinh	Tran	808 Ridge	Harper	MI	48421	$402.40	$750	06	Site3
587	Galvez	Mara	512 Pine	Ada	MI	49441	$114.60	$1000	06	Site2
622	Martin	Dan	419 Chip	Grant	MI	49219	$1045.75	$1000	03	Site2

FIGURE 9.2

Premiere Products customer data, including Site Number

Fragment F1

Customer

Customer Number	Last Name	First Name	Street	City	State	Zip Code	Balance	Credit Limit	Sales Rep Number	Site Number
124	Adams	Sally	481 Oak	Lansing	MI	49224	$818.75	$1000	03	Site1
412	Adams	Sally	16 Elm	Lansing	MI	49224	$1817.50	$2000	03	Site1

Fragment F2

Customer

Customer Number	Last Name	First Name	Street	City	State	Zip Code	Balance	Credit Limit	Sales Rep Number	Site Number
256	Samuels	Ann	215 Pete	Grant	MI	49219	$21.50	$1500	06	Site2
315	Daniels	Tom	914 Cherry	Kent	MI	48391	$770.75	$750	06	Site2
405	Williams	Al	519 Watson	Grant	MI	49219	$402.75	$1500	12	Site2
522	Nelson	Mary	108 Pine	Ada	MI	49441	$98.75	$1500	12	Site2
587	Galvez	Mara	512 Pine	Ada	MI	49441	$114.60	$1000	06	Site2
622	Martin	Dan	419 Chip	Grant	MI	49219	$1045.75	$1000	03	Site2

Fragment F3

Customer

Customer Number	Last Name	First Name	Street	City	State	Zip Code	Balance	Credit Limit	Sales Rep Number	Site Number
311	Charles	Don	48 College	Ira	MI	49034	$825.75	$1000	12	Site3
567	Dinh	Tran	808 Ridge	Harper	MI	48421	$402.40	$750	06	Site3

FIGURE 9.3

Fragmentation of customer data by site

Again, users should not be aware of the underlying activity, in this case the fragmentation. They should feel as if they are using a single central database. If users are unaware of fragmentation, the system has **fragmentation transparency**.

Advantages of Distributed Databases

As compared with a single centralized database, distributed databases offer some advantages. They are listed in Figure 9.4 and are discussed below.

FIGURE 9.4

Advantages of
distributed
databases

1. Local control of data
2. Increasing database capacity
3. System availability
4. Added efficiency

1. ***Local control of data*** Because each location retains its own data, it can exercise greater control over that data. With a single centralized database, on the other hand, the central data processing center that maintains the database will usually not be aware of all the local issues at the various sites served by the database.

2. ***Increasing database capacity*** In a properly designed and installed distributed database, the process of increasing system capacity is often simpler than in a centralized system. If the size of the database at a single site becomes inadequate, potentially only the local database at that site needs to be changed. Furthermore, the capacity of the database as a whole can be increased by merely adding a new site.

3. ***System availability*** When a centralized database becomes unavailable for any reason, *no* users are able to continue processing. In contrast, if one of the local databases in a distributed database becomes unavailable, only users who need data in that particular database are affected; other users can continue normal processing. In addition, if the data have been replicated (another copy of it exists in other local databases), potentially all users can continue processing. However, processing for users at the site of the unavailable database will be much less efficient, because data that were formerly obtained locally must now be obtained through communication with a remote site.

4. ***Added efficiency*** As you saw earlier, the fact that data are available locally means the speed with which those data can be retrieved is much greater than with a remote centralized system.

Disadvantages of Distributed Databases

Distributed databases also have some disadvantages. They are listed in Figure 9.5 and are discussed following the figure.

FIGURE 9.5

....

Disadvantages of
distributed
databases

1. Update of replicated data
2. More complex query processing
3. More complex treatment of shared update
4. More complex recovery measures
5. More difficult management of data dictionary
6. More complex database design

1. ***Update of replicated data*** It often is desirable to replicate data, both for the sake of performance and to ensure that the overall system will remain available even when the database at one site is not available. Replication can cause severe update problems, most obviously in terms of the extra time needed to update all the copies. Instead of updating a single copy of the data, several copies must be updated. Because most of these copies are at sites other than the site initiating the update, time to communicate all the update messages over the network must be added to the time needed to update each copy.

   There is another, slightly more serious problem, however. Let's assume that data at five sites must be updated, and that the fifth site is currently unavailable. If all updates must be made or none at all, the whole update fails. Thus, data are unavailable for update at all sites if even one of the sites that is the target of the update is not available. This certainly contradicts earlier remarks about additional availability. On the other hand, if you do not require all updates to be made, the data will be inconsistent.

   Often a compromise strategy is used. One copy of the data is designated as the primary copy. As long as the primary copy is updated, the update is deemed complete. It is the responsibility of the primary copy under the control of the DDBMS to ensure that all the other copies are in sync. The site holding the primary copy sends update transactions to all other sites to accomplish the update and notes whether any sites are currently unavailable. If it discovers an unavailable site, the primary site must try to send the update again at some later time and continue trying until it succeeds. This strategy overcomes the basic problem, but it obviously uses more time. Furthermore, if the primary site itself is unavailable, the problem remains unresolved.

2. ***More complex query processing*** The issues involved in processing queries can be much more complex in a distributed environment. The problem stems from the difference between the time it takes to send messages between sites and the time it takes to access a disk. As you saw earlier, minimizing message traffic is extremely important.

   To illustrate the problems involved with query processing, consider the following query for Premiere Products: List all parts in item class SG and whose price is more than $100.00.

   For this query, assume that (1) the Part table contains 1000 rows and is stored at a remote site; (2) there is no special structure, such as an index, that would be helpful in processing this query faster; and (3) only 10 of the 1000 rows in the Part table satisfy the conditions. How would you process this query?

   One solution involves retrieving each row from the remote site and examining the item class and price to determine whether the row should be included in the result. For each row, this solution requires two messages: a message from the local site to the remote site requesting a row, followed by a message from the remote site to the local site containing either the data or, ultimately, an indication that there are no more data, because you have retrieved every row in the table. Thus, in addition to the database accesses themselves, this strategy requires 2000 messages.

A second solution involves sending a single message from the local site to the remote site requesting the complete answer to the query. The remote site examines each row in the table and finds the 10 rows that satisfy the query. The remote site then sends a single message back to the local site containing all the rows in the answer. Although the second message might be quite lengthy, especially where many rows satisfied the conditions, this solution is still a vast improvement over the first one. A small number of lengthy messages is preferable to a large number of short messages.

The net result is that systems that are only record-at-a-time oriented can create severe performance problems in distributed systems. If the only choice is to transmit every record from one site to another as a message and then examine it at the other site, the communication time required can become unacceptably high. Systems that permit a request for a set of records, as opposed to an individual record, will inherently outperform record-at-a-time systems.

3. ***More complex treatment of shared update*** Shared update in a distributed system is treated in basically the same way as it is treated in nondistributed systems: locks are acquired; locking is two-phase (locks are acquired in a growing phase, during which no locks are released, and then all locks are released in the shrinking phase); deadlocks must be detected and broken; and offending updates must be rolled back or undone. The primary distinction lies not in the kinds of activities that take place, but in the additional level of complexity created by the very nature of a distributed database.

If all the records to be updated by a particular transaction occur at one site, the problem is essentially the same as in a nondistributed database. However, the records might be stored at a number of different sites, and, if the data are replicated, each occurrence might be stored at several sites, each requiring the same update to be performed. Assuming each record occurrence has replicas at three different sites, an update that would affect five record occurrences in a nondistributed system might affect 20 different occurrences in a distributed system (each occurrence together with its three replicas). Furthermore, these 20 different occurrences could conceivably be stored at 20 different sites.

Having more occurrences to update is only part of the problem. Assuming each site keeps its own locks, several messages must be sent for each record to be updated: a request for a lock; a message indicating that either the record is already locked by another user or that the lock has been granted; a message indicating the update to be performed; an acknowledgment of the update; and, finally, a message indicating that the record is to be unlocked. Because all these messages must be sent for each record and the number of records can be much larger than in a nondistributed system, the total time for an update can be substantially longer in a distributed environment.

There is a partial solution to this problem. It involves the use of the primary copy mentioned earlier. Recall that one of the replicas of a given record occurrence was designated as the primary copy. If this is done, then merely locking the primary copy rather than all copies will suffice. This cuts down on the number of messages concerned with the process of locking and unlocking records. The number of messages might still be large, however, and the unavailability of the primary copy can cause an entire transaction to fail. Thus, even this partial solution presents problems.

As in a nondistributed system, deadlock is a possibility. In a distributed system, however, deadlock is more complicated, because two types of deadlock, local deadlock and global deadlock, are possible. Local deadlock can be detected at one site. If two transactions are each waiting for a record held by the other at the same site, the local DBMS can detect and resolve the deadlock with a minimum number of messages needed to communicate the situation to the other databases in the distributed system. On the other hand, global deadlock involves one transaction that requires a record held by another transaction at one site, while the second transaction requires a record held by the first at a different site. In this case, neither site has information on its own to allow this deadlock to be detected; this is a global deadlock, and it can be detected and resolved only by sending a large number of messages between the databases at the two sites.

The various factors involved in supporting shared update greatly add to the communications time in a distributed system.

4. ***More complex recovery measures*** While the basic recovery process is the same for a distributed database as the one described in Chapter 7, there is an additional potential problem. To make sure the database remains consistent, each database update should be either made permanent or aborted and undone, in which case *none* of its changes will be made. In a distributed environment, with several local databases being updated by an individual transaction, it is possible—due to problems affecting individual sites—that the updates might be committed at some sites and rolled back at others, thereby creating an inconsistent state in the global database. This *must not* be allowed to happen.

This possibility is usually prevented through the use of the two-phase commit. The basic idea of the two-phase commit is that one site, often the site initiating the update, will act as coordinator. In the first phase, the coordinator sends messages to all other sites requesting they prepare to update the database; in other words, they acquire all necessary locks. They do not update at this point, however, but send a message to the coordinator that they are ready to update. If for any reason they cannot secure the necessary locks, or if the update must be aborted at their site, they send a message to the coordinator that they must abort. The coordinator waits for replies from all sites involved before determining whether to commit the update. If all replies are positive, the coordinator sends a message to each site to commit the update. At this point, each site *must* proceed with the commit process. If any reply is negative, the coordinator sends a message to each site to abort the update and each site *must* follow this instruction. In this way, consistency is guaranteed.

While a process similar to the two-phase commit is essential to the consistency of the database, there are two problems associated with it. For one thing, as you may have noticed, many messages are sent in the process. For another, during the second phase, each site must follow the instructions from the coordinator; otherwise, the process will not accomplish its intended result. This means the sites are not as independent as they seem.

5. ***More difficult management of data dictionary*** The distributed environment introduces further complexity to the management of the data dictionary or catalog. Where should the data dictionary entries be stored? There are several possibilities:

   a. Choose one site and store the complete data dictionary at this site and this site alone.
   b. Store a complete copy of the data dictionary at each site.
   c. Distribute (possibly with replication) the dictionary entries among the various sites.

   While storing the complete dictionary at a single site is a relatively simple approach to administer, retrieval of information in the dictionary from any other site will suffer because of the communication involved. Storing a complete copy at every site solves the retrieval problem, because any retrieval can be satisfied completely locally. Because this approach involves total replication (every occurrence is replicated at every site), it suffers from severe update problems. If the dictionary is updated with any frequency, the length of update time probably will be unacceptable. Thus, some intermediate strategy usually is implemented.

   One fairly obvious partitioning of the dictionary involves storing dictionary entries at the site at which the data they describe are located. Interestingly, this approach also suffers from a problem. If a user is querying the dictionary in an attempt to access an entry not stored at the site, the system has no way of knowing where the data are. Satisfying this user's query may well involve sending a message to every other site, which involves a considerable amount of time.

6. ***More complex database design*** The distributed environment adds another level of complexity to database design. The information-level phase of design is unaffected by the fact that the system is distributed, but, during the physical-level phase of design, an additional factor must be considered, and that is communication. In a nondistributed environment, one of the principal concerns during the physical design is disk activity; both numbers of disk accesses and volumes of data to be transported must be considered. While this is also a factor in the distributed environment, you must also consider another important factor: communication activity. Because transmitting data from one site to another is much slower than transferring data to and from disk, in many situations communication activity will be the most important factor of all.

   In addition to the standard issues encountered for nondistributed systems, possible fragmentation and/or replication must be considered during the physical level of database design. The process of analyzing and choosing among alternative designs must include any message traffic necessitated by each alternative.

Rules for Distributed Systems

C. J. Date (C. J. Date, "Twelve Rules for a Distributed Database," *ComputerWorld*, 21.23 June 8, 1987.) formulated 12 rules that distributed systems should follow. The basic goal of these systems is that a distributed system should feel like a nondistributed system to the user; that is, the user need not be aware that the system is distributed. The 12 rules are as follows:

1. ***Sites should be autonomous*** No site should depend on another site to function.

2. ***No master site*** There should not be reliance on a single site, often called a master site, to control specific types of operations. For example, a system in which one site is in charge of update management would violate this rule.

3. **No need for planned shutdowns** Performing functions, such as adding sites, changing versions of DBMSs, and modifying hardware, should not require planned shutdowns of the entire distributed system.

4. **Location transparency** Users should not need to be concerned with the location of any specific data in the network. It should feel to users as though the entire database is stored at their location.

5. **Fragmentation transparency** Users should not be aware of any fragmentation that has taken place. They should feel as if they are using a single central database.

6. **Replication transparency** Users should not be aware of any replication that has taken place. Any work to keep the various copies of data consistent should be done behind the scenes by the DDBMS; the user should not be aware of it.

7. **Query processing** You have already learned about the complexities of query processing in a distributed environment. It is critical that the DDBMS be able to process these queries efficiently.

8. **Update management** You have already learned about the complexities of update management and the need for the two-phase commit protocol. It is essential that the DDBMS effectively manage this activity.

9. **Not dependent on specific hardware** Because installations typically have a number of different types of hardware, it is desirable that the distributed system is able to integrate these various types. Without this feature, users would be restricted to only the data stored on similar computers.

10. **Not dependent on a specific operating system** Even though the hardware in use may be the same, there may be different operating systems in use. For the same reasons that it is desirable for a distributed system to support various types of hardware, it is also advantageous for it to support various operating systems.

11. **Not dependent on a specific network** Because different sites within an organization may employ different communications networks, it is desirable for a distributed system to support the various types of networks within the organization and not to be restricted to a single type.

12. **Not dependent on a specific DBMS** Another way of stating this requirement is that the DDBMS should be heterogeneous; that is, capable of supporting local DBMSs that are different. This is a difficult task. In practice, the way it will be accomplished is for each of the local DBMSs to be capable of "speaking" a common language. This common language most likely will be SQL.

▨ Client/Server Systems

Until recently, it was common for a local area network (LAN) to contain a file server, as shown in Figure 9.6. The server contained the files required by the individual workstations on the network. When a workstation required a particular file or files, the workstation sent a request to the server. The server then sent the requested file or files to the workstation. While this approach worked, it generated a large amount of traffic on the network. As users' networks grew in the number of workstations and the amount of data processed, this approach caused severe performance problems.

FIGURE 9.6

File server architecture

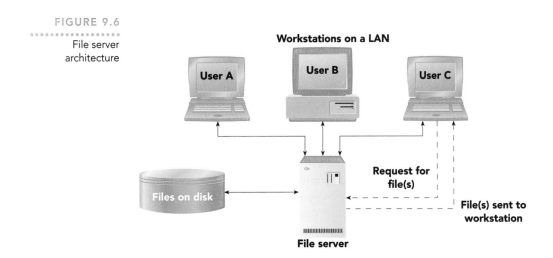

The alternative, which is called client/server, is illustrated in Figure 9.7. In client/server terminology, the "server" is the computer providing data to the "clients," who are the users accessing the data through their workstations. With this alternative, a DBMS runs on the file server. Users send requests, not for entire *files*, but only for specific *data*. The DBMS on the server processes the request and then extracts the requested data, which are then sent back to the workstation.

FIGURE 9.7

Client/server architecture

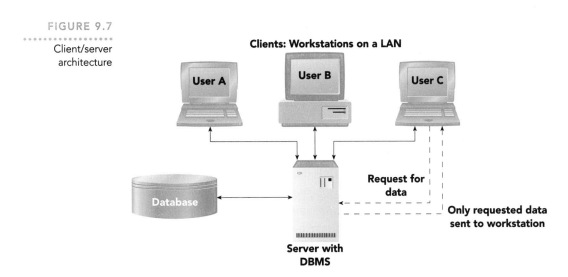

In order for a workstation to take advantage of this approach, the software running on the workstation has to be capable of communicating with the DBMS running on the server.

Currently there are several DBMSs that can be used on servers. The common language that they use is, as you might expect, SQL. There are also many software products that have been modified to be able to communicate with one or more of these DBMSs.

It should be emphasized that the changes to these software products do not affect the way the users interact with them. The screens still look the same. The options still work the same way they always did. The users don't even need to be aware that the data they are accessing reside on the server rather than on their own PCs. Note that a client/server system stores the database on a single server, and the DBMS resides and processes on that server. Only in a distributed database management system is the database itself distributed.

Advantages of Client/Server Systems

There are several advantages to the client/server approach.

1. It is more efficient than the file server system. Only the necessary data, rather than the entire file, are transmitted across the network.

2. It provides for the possibility of distributing work among several processors.

3. The workstations do not necessarily need to be as powerful as they would in a file server environment, because the server will handle more of the work.

4. As far as a user is concerned, the software runs on the workstations just as it does on a standalone system. The user does not need to learn any special commands or techniques to work in the client/server environment.

5. Because client/server systems use SQL as a common language, it is easier for users to access data from a variety of sources. A single operation can access data from multiple networks and multiple platforms. Without a common language, this would be a very difficult process.

6. Client/server systems provide a greater level of security than do file server systems.

7. Client/server systems have proven to be powerful enough that users have replaced, at a considerable savings, mainframe applications and mainframe databases with PC applications and databases managed by client/server systems.

Triggers and Stored Procedures

One special aspect of the support client/server systems provide for integrity is the use of triggers. A trigger is an action that automatically occurs when an associated database operation takes place. Triggers are created with special SQL statements similar to the following:

```
CREATE AddOrder TRIGGER ON Orders
    FOR INSERT, UPDATE AS
    IF NOT EXISTS
        (SELECT Customer Number
            FROM Inserted
            WHERE Customer Number IN
                (SELECT Customer Number
                    FROM Customer))
    BEGIN
        Print("Invalid Customer Number")
    END
```

This trigger, which is named AddOrder, ensures that the customer number entered for an order matches a customer in the Customer table. It will be applied on both INSERT and UPDATE actions on a row in the Orders table. The row to be changed is in the special temporary table called Inserted. If the customer number in the new row is not in the collection of customer numbers in the Customer table, then the update does not take place. Instead the system displays the message "Invalid Customer Number."

Another important aspect of client/server systems relates to performance. If the same collection of SQL statements will be executed repeatedly, the statements can be placed in a special file, called a **stored procedure**. The statements in a stored procedure are compiled and optimized. From that point on, whenever users execute the collection of statements, they execute the compiled, optimized code in the stored procedure.

Data Warehouses

Among the objectives that organizations have when they use relational database management systems (RDBMSs) are data integrity, high performance, and ample availability. The leading RDBMSs are able to satisfy these requirements. Typically, when users interact with an RDBMS, they use transactions, such as add a new order and change a customer's sales rep. These types of systems thus are called **on-line transaction processing (OLTP)** systems. For each transaction, OLTP typically deals with a small number of rows from the tables in a database in a highly structured, repetitive, and predetermined way. If you need to know the status of specific customers, parts, and orders, or if you need to update data for specific customers, parts, and orders, an RDBMS and OLTP are the ideal tools to use.

When you need to analyze data from a database, however, an RDBMS and OLTP often suffer from severe performance problems. For example, finding total sales by region and by month requires the joining of all the rows in many tables; such processing takes a considerable number of database accesses and considerable time to accomplish. Consequently, many organizations continue to use RDBMSs and OLTP for their normal, day-to-day processing, or for *operational purposes*, but have turned to data warehouses for the *analysis* of their data. The following definition for a data warehouse is credited to W.H. Inmon (W.H. Inmon, *Building the Data Warehouse*, QED, 1990.), who originally coined the phrase:

Definition: A **data warehouse** is a subject-oriented, integrated, time-variant, nonvolatile collection of data in support of management's decision-making process.

Subject-oriented means that data are organized by entity rather than by the application that uses the data. For example, Figure 9.8 shows the databases for typical operational applications such as inventory, order entry, production, and accounts payable. When the data from these operational databases are loaded into a data warehouse, they are transformed into subjects such as product, customer, vendor, and financial. Data about products appear once in the warehouse, even though they might appear in many files and databases in the operational environment.

FIGURE 9.8
· · · · · · · · · · · · · · · · · · ·
Data warehouse
architecture

Note: The operational applications in this example use a variety of DBMSs and file-processing systems because they've been developed over the past 30 years. This is a typical situation for many organizations.

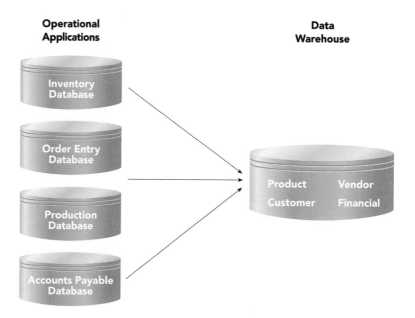

Integrated means that data are stored in one place in the data warehouse, even though the data originate from everywhere in the organization and from a variety of external sources. The data can come from recently developed applications or from legacy systems developed many years ago.

Time-variant means that data in a data warehouse represent snapshots of data at various points in time in the past, such as the ends of each month, unlike an operational application whose data are accurate as of the moment. Data warehouses also retain historical data for long periods of time, summarized to specific time periods such as daily, weekly, monthly, and annual.

Nonvolatile means that data are read-only. Data are loaded into a data warehouse periodically, but users cannot update a data warehouse directly.

In summary, a data warehouse contains read-only snapshots of highly consolidated and summarized data from multiple internal and external sources that are refreshed periodically, usually on a daily or weekly basis. Companies use data warehouses in support of their decision-making processing, which typically consists of unstructured and nonrepetitive requests for exactly the type of information contained in a data warehouse.

Data Warehouse Structure

A typical data warehouse structure is shown in Figure 9.9. The central Sales Fact table is called a fact table. A fact table consists of many rows that contain consolidated and summarized data. The fact table contains a multipart primary key, each part of which is a foreign key to the surrounding dimension tables. Each dimension table contains a single-part primary key that serves as an index into the fact table and also contains other fields associated with the primary key value. The overall structure shown in Figure 9.9 is generically called a multidimensional database because of its structure, and the specific type of multidimensional database shown is called a star join schema because of its conceptual shape.

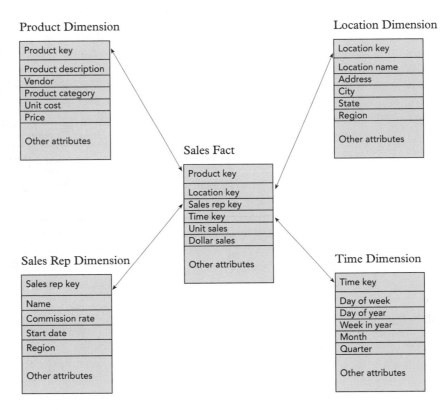

FIGURE 9.9

A star join schema with four dimension tables and a central fact table

Access to a multidimensional database is accomplished through the use of on-line analytical processing (OLAP) software. OLAP software is optimized to work efficiently with multidimensional databases in a data warehouse environment.

Rules for OLAP Systems

E.F. Codd (E.F. Codd, S.B. Codd, and C.T. Salley, "Providing OLAP [On-line Analytical Processing] to User-Analysts: An IT Mandate," Arbor Software, August 1993) formulated 12 rules that OLAP systems should follow. The rules are as follows:

1. *Multidimensional conceptual view* Users must be able to view data in a multidimensional way, matching the way data appear naturally in an organization.

2. *Transparency* Users should not have to know the physical location of the OLAP software.

3. *Accessibility* Users should perceive data as a single user view, even though the data may be located physically in several heterogeneous locations.

4. *Consistent reporting performance* Retrieval performance should not degrade as the number of dimensions and the size of the warehouse grows.

5. *Client/server architecture* The server component of OLAP software must be intelligent enough so that a variety of clients can be connected with minimal effort.

6. *Generic dimensionality* Every dimension table must be equivalent in both its structural and operational capabilities. For example, you should be able to obtain information about products as easily as you obtain information about sales reps.

7. *Dynamic sparse matrix handling* Missing data should be handled correctly and efficiently.

8. *Multiuser support* OLAP software must provide secure, concurrent access. Because you don't update a data warehouse when you're using it, shared update is not an issue, so problems of security and access are less difficult than in an OLTP environment.

9. *Unrestricted, cross-dimensional operations* Users must be able to perform the same operations across any number of dimensions. For example, you should be able to ask for statistics based on the dimensions of time, location, and product just as easily as you ask for statistics based on the single dimension of location.

10. *Intuitive data manipulation* Users should be able to act directly on individual data values without needing to use menus or other interfaces. Of course, these other interfaces can be used, but they should not be the required method of processing.

11. *Flexible reporting* Users should be able to report data results any way they want.

12. *Unlimited dimensions and aggregation levels* OLAP software should allow at least 15 data dimensions and an unlimited number of aggregation (summary) levels.

■ Object-Oriented Database Management Systems

In the past, people used databases to store data consisting only of text and numbers. Today, people also store graphics, drawings, photographs, video, sound, voice mail, spreadsheets, and other complex objects in their databases. Relational database management systems store these complex objects using special data types, generically called binary large objects (BLOBs). Some applications, such as computer-aided design and manufacturing (CAD/CAM) and geographic information systems (GIS), have as their primary focus the storage and management of complex objects. For these systems, many companies use object-oriented database management systems.

What is an Object-Oriented Database Management System?

The relational model, which has a strong theoretical foundation, is the basic standard for relational database management systems. Although object-oriented database management systems do not have a corresponding standard, they all exhibit several common characteristics. The concept of an object is at the core of all such systems. An object is some unit of data along with the actions that can take place on that object. A customer object, for example, would consist of the data relevant to customers (number, name, balance, and so on) together with the actions that can take place on customer data (add customer, change credit limit, delete customer, and so on).

The primary emphasis in object-oriented systems is on the data rather than on the actions. The actions are defined as part of the data definition. They can then be used whenever they are required. In contrast, in the more traditional, nonobject-oriented systems, the actions are created as part of data manipulation (in the programs that update the database), rather than data definition. In an object-oriented system, the data and actions are actually encapsulated, which means that they are hidden from the end user. In other words, you don't need to know the details of how the actions act on the data in order to use the actions or access the data. These ideas lead to the following definition:

Definition: An object-oriented database management system (OODBMS) is one in which data and the methods that operate on data are encapsulated into objects.

To become familiar with OODBMSs, you should have a general understanding of the following five key concepts: objects, classes, methods, messages, and inheritance.

Objects and Classes

Objects and classes are illustrated by examining an object-oriented representation of the Premiere Products database (Figure 9.10). Actually, there is a slight variation to the Premiere Products database. There is a extra field, Allocated, in the Part table that represents the number of units of a given part that are currently on order (allocated). Figure 9.11 shows a representation of this database as a collection of objects.

Sales Rep

Sales Rep Number	Last Name	First Name	Street	City	State	Zip Code	Commission	Rate
03	Jones	Mary	123 Main	Grant	MI	49219	2150.00	.05
06	Smith	William	102 Raymond	Ada	MI	49441	4912.50	.07
12	Diaz	Miguel	419 Harper	Lansing	MI	49224	2150.00	.05

Customer

Customer Number	Last Name	First Name	Street	City	State	Zip Code	Balance	Credit Limit	Sales Rep Number
124	Adams	Sally	481 Oak	Lansing	MI	49224	$818.75	$1000	03
256	Samuels	Ann	215 Pete	Grant	MI	49219	$21.50	$1500	06
311	Charles	Don	48 College	Ira	MI	49034	$825.75	$1000	12
315	Daniels	Tom	914 Cherry	Kent	MI	48391	$770.75	$750	06
405	Williams	Al	519 Watson	Grant	MI	49219	$402.75	$1500	12
412	Adams	Sally	16 Elm	Lansing	MI	49224	$1817.50	$2000	03
522	Nelson	Mary	108 Pine	Ada	MI	49441	$98.75	$1500	12
567	Dinh	Tran	808 Ridge	Harper	MI	48421	$402.40	$750	06
587	Galvez	Mara	512 Pine	Ada	MI	49441	$114.60	$1000	06
622	Martin	Dan	419 Chip	Grant	MI	49219	$1045.75	$1000	03

Orders

Order Number	Order Date	Customer Number
12489	9/02/2001	124
12491	9/02/2001	311
12494	9/04/2001	315
12495	9/04/2001	256
12498	9/05/2001	522
12500	9/05/2001	124
12504	9/05/2001	522

Order Line

Order Number	Part Number	Number Ordered	Quoted Price
12489	AX12	11	$14.95
12491	BT04	1	$149.99
12491	BZ66	1	$399.99
12494	CB03	4	$279.99
12495	CX11	2	$22.95
12498	AZ52	2	$12.95
12498	BA74	4	$24.95
12500	BT04	1	$149.99
12504	CZ81	2	$325.99

Part

Part Number	Part Description	On Hand	Class	Warehouse	Price	Allocated
AX12	Iron	104	HW	3	$24.95	11
AZ52	Dartboard	20	SG	2	$12.95	2
BA74	Basketball	40	SG	1	$29.95	4
BH22	Cornpopper	95	HW	3	$24.95	0
BT04	Gas Grill	11	AP	2	$149.99	2
BZ66	Washer	52	AP	3	$399.99	1
CA14	Griddle	78	HW	3	$39.99	0
CB03	Bike	44	SG	1	$299.99	4
CX11	Blender	112	HW	3	$22.95	2
CZ81	Treadmill	68	SG	2	$349.95	2

FIGURE 9.10

Premiere Products sample data

FIGURE 9.11
....
Object-oriented
representation of
the Premiere
Products database

```
Sales Rep OBJECT
Sales Rep Number:        Sales Rep Numbers
Last Name:               Names
First Name:              Names
Street:                  Addresses
City:                    Cities
State:                   States
Zip Code:                Zip Codes
Commission:              Commissions
Rate:                    Commission Rates
Customer:                Customer OBJECT; MV


Customer OBJECT
Customer Number:         Customer Numbers
Last Name:               Names
First Name:              Names
Street:                  Addresses
City:                    Cities
State:                   States
Zip Code:                Zip Codes
Balance:                 Balances
Credit Limit:            Credit Limits
Sales Rep:               Sales Rep OBJECT; SUBSET[Sales Rep Number,
                             Last Name, First Name]


Part OBJECT
Part Number:             Part Numbers
Part Description:        Part Descriptions
On Hand:                 Units
Class:                   Item Classes
Warehouse:               Warehouse Numbers
Price:                   Prices
Allocated:               Units
Order Line:              Order LIne OBJECT; MV


Orders OBJECT
Order Number:            Order Numbers
Order Date:              Dates
Customer:                Customer OBJECT; SUBSET[Customer Number, Last Name,
                             First Name, Sales Rep Number]
Order Line:              Order Line OBJECT; MV


Order Line OBJECT
Order Number:            Order Numbers
Part Number:             Part Numbers
Number Ordered:          Units
Quoted Price:            Prices
```

Note: Figure 9.11 shows just one approach to representing objects. There are many different ways of doing so. They all represent the same general features, however.

At first glance, the collection of objects in Figure 9.11 doesn't look much different from the relational model representation you are used to working with (Figure 9.12).

Sales Rep (<u>Sales Rep Number</u>, Last Name, First Name, Street, City, State, Zip Code, Commission, Rate)

Customer (<u>Customer Number</u>, Last Name, First Name, Street, City, State, Zip Code, Balance, Credit Limit, Sales Rep Number)

Part (<u>Part Number</u>, Part Description, On Hand, Class, Warehouse, Price, Allocated)

Orders (<u>Order Number</u>, Order Date, Customer Number)

Order Line (<u>Order Number</u>, <u>Part Number</u>, Number Ordered, Quoted Price)

If you look closer, however, you'll see some differences. In Figure 9.11:

1. For each entity (Sales Rep, Customer, and so on) there is an *object* rather than a relation.

2. The properties (attributes) are listed vertically under the object names. In addition, each property is followed by the set of values with which the property is associated.

3. Objects can contain other objects. For example, the Sales Rep object contains the Customer object as one of its properties. The letters *MV* following the Customer object indicate it is multivalued. In other words, a single occurrence of the Sales Rep object can contain multiple occurrences of the Customer object. Roughly speaking, this is analogous to a relation containing a repeating group.

4. An object can contain just a portion of another object. For example, the Customer object contains the Sales Rep object. The word *SUBSET* indicates, however, that Customer only contains a subset of the Sales Rep object. In this case, it only contains three of the properties: Sales Rep Number, Last Name, and First Name.

Notice that two objects can each appear to contain the other. The Sales Rep object contains the Customer object, and the Customer object contains the Sales Rep object (or at least a subset of it). The important thing to keep in mind here is that users deal with *objects*. If the users of the Customer object require the sales rep's number and name, the Sales Rep number and name will be part of the Customer object. If the users of the Sales Rep object require data about all the customers of the sales rep, the Customer object will be viewed as part of the Sales Rep object. This is not to imply that the data will be physically stored in this fashion, but this is the way it appears as far as users are concerned.

Objects can contain more than one other object. Consider the Orders object. It contains the Customer object and the Order Line object, with the Order Line object being multivalued. Nevertheless, to users of this object, Orders is a single unit.

Technically, what are defined here are not objects, but classes. The term **class** refers to the general structure. The term object really refers to a specific occurrence of a class. Thus, Sales Rep is a class, whereas the data for sales rep 12 would be an object. Often, however, you don't need to bother with this distinction and you can use the words almost interchangeably.

Methods and Messages

The actions defined for an object (class) are called **methods**. Figure 9.13 shows two methods associated with the Orders object. The first method, Add Order, is used to add an order. Data entered by the user are placed temporarily in W-Orders, which consists of user-entered values for the order number in W-Order Number, for the order date in W-Order Date, and so on.

FIGURE 9.13

Two methods for the Premiere Products object-oriented database

```
Add Order (W-Orders)
      Add row to Orders table
            Order Number            = W-Order Number
            Order Date              = W-Order Date
            Customer Number         = W-Customer Number
      For each order line record in W-Orders DO
            Add row to Order Line table
                  Order Number            = W-Order Number
                  Part Number             = W-Part Number
                  Number Ordered          = W-Number Ordered
                  Quoted Price            = W-Quoted Price
            Update Part table (WHERE Part Number = W-Part Number)
                  Allocated               = Allocated + W-Number Ordered
Delete Order (W-Order Number)
      Delete row from Orders table (WHERE Order Number = W-Order Number)
      For each Order Line record (WHERE Order Number = W-Order Number) DO
            Delete row from Order Line table
            Update Part table (WHERE Part.Part Number = Order Line.Part Number)
                  Allocated  = Allocated — Number Ordered
```

QUESTION   Describe the steps in the Add Order method.

ANSWER   The steps accomplish the following:

1. Add an appropriate row to the Orders table.
2. For each order line record associated with the order, add an appropriate row to the Order Line table.
3. Also for each order line record, update the Allocated value for the appropriate part.

The other method, Delete Order, is used to delete an order. The number of the order to be deleted, which is placed temporarily in W-Order Number, is the only data required as input to this method.

QUESTION   Describe the steps in the Delete Order method.

ANSWER   The steps accomplish the following:

1. Delete the order with the indicated number from the Orders table.
2. For each Order Line record on which the order number matches the indicated number, delete the record.

3. Also for each such Order Line record, add the Number Ordered value to the Allocated value for the corresponding part. (With this record deleted, the parts are no longer allocated.)

Note: The methods illustrated here are fairly complicated, each involving many separate updates. Many methods are much simpler.

These methods are defined during the data definition process. To actually execute the steps indicated in a method, the user would send a message to the object. A message is a request to execute the method. As part of sending the message, you must send the required data (for example, full order data for Add Order; only the order number for Delete Order). The whole process is similar to the process of calling a subroutine in a standard programming language.

Inheritance

One of the key features of object-oriented systems is inheritance. For any class, you can define a subclass. Every occurrence of the subclass is also considered to be an occurrence of the class. The subclass *inherits* the structure of the class as well as the methods. In addition, you can define additional properties and methods for the subclass.

As an example, suppose Premiere Products has a special type of order that has all the characteristics of other orders. In addition, it contains a freight amount and a discount that are calculated in a special way. Rather than create a new class for this type of order, it will be a subclass of Orders. In that way, the special type of order automatically has all the properties of Orders. It has all the same methods, including the appropriate updating of Allocated whenever orders are added or deleted. The only thing you would have to add would be those properties and methods that are specific to this new type of order, greatly simplifying the entire process.

Rules for Object-Oriented Systems

Just as there are rules indicating desired characteristics for DDBMSs and OLAP, there is a similar set of rules for object-oriented systems. They are as follows:

1. ***Complex objects***   The DBMS supports the creation of complex objects from simple objects such as integers, characters, and so on.

2. ***Object identity***   The DBMS must provide a way to identify objects; that is, there must be a way to distinguish between one object and another.

3. ***Encapsulation***   The data and the procedures that act on data should be stored as part of the database. Details concerning the way the data are stored and the actual implementation of the procedures are hidden from the users of the database.

4. ***Types or classes***   You are already familiar with the idea of a class. Types are very similar to classes and correspond to abstract data types in programming languages. The differences between the two are subtle and will not be explored here. It is important that an object-oriented DBMS supports either abstract types or classes (it doesn't matter which).

5. **Inheritance** You already learned about the important concept of inheritance and the benefits that it provides. An object-oriented DBMS should support inheritance.

6. **Late Binding** Binding, in this case, refers to the association of operations to actual program code. With late binding, this association does not happen until runtime, that is, until some user actually invokes the operation. Late binding allows the use of the same name for different operations. For example, an operation to display an object on the screen will require different program code if the object is a picture than if the object is text. With late binding, you could use the same name for both operations. At the time a user invokes this "display" operation, the system will determine the object being displayed and then bind the operation to the appropriate program code.

7. **Computational completeness** Functions for performing various computations can be expressed in the language of the DBMS.

8. **Extensibility** Any DBMS, object-oriented or not, comes with a set of predefined data types, such as Numeric and Character. An OODBMS should be **extensible**, meaning that it is possible to define new data types. Furthermore, there should be no distinction between the data types provided by the system and these new data types.

9. **Persistence** In object-oriented programming, **persistence** refers to the ability to have a program *remember* its data from one execution to the next. Although this is unusual in programming languages, it is common in all database systems. After all, one of the fundamental capabilities of any DBMS is the ability to store data for later use.

10. **Performance** An OODBMS should have sufficient performance capabilities to effectively manage very large databases.

11. **Shared update support** An OODBMS should support shared update. (This concept was discussed in Chapter 7.)

12. **Recovery support** An OODBMS should provide recovery services. (This concept was discussed in Chapter 7.)

13. **Query facility** An OODBMS should provide some type of query facility. (Query facilities such as QBE and SQL were discussed in Chapter 2 and Chapter 3.)

The Internet and Intranets

Over the past few years, the Internet and the closely related World Wide Web (Web) have shown phenomenal growth, both in numbers of users and the availability of software tools. In particular, many database vendors now allow their products to connect to the Web; this is clearing the way for electronic commerce (**e-commerce**) using an organization's databases. Internally, organizations are constructing **intranets** (internal Internets) to do their internal processing, using a combination of Web browsers, RDBMSs, DDBMSs, OODBMSs, client/server systems, and data warehouses. Figure 9.14 shows a typical use of Web browsers through the Internet and on an intranet to access and update a company's database.

FIGURE 9.14
· ·
Using Web
browsers on the
Internet and on an
intranet to access
and update a
company's
database

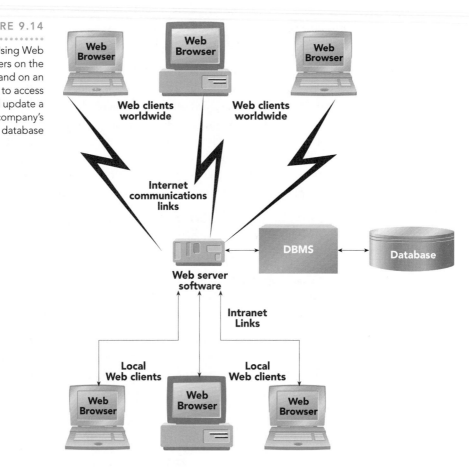

Externally, companies benefit in two ways from using the Web for database processing. First, they can export and link data from their databases to suppliers, customers, and others outside the company; this provides current information in a timely way to those needing the information. Second, companies can allow customers, for example, to place orders that directly update the organization's database and trigger the processing required to fulfill the order.

Over the next few years, more and more database processing will be handled through the Internet and the Web. This will allow organizations to be more efficient and effective in the way they carry out their business functions.

▪ SUMMARY

- A distributed database is a database stored on several computers connected through some kind of network. A user at any site can access data at any other site. A distributed database management system (DDBMS) is a DBMS capable of supporting and manipulating distributed databases.

- A homogenous DDBMS is one that has the same local DBMS at each site, whereas a heterogeneous DDBMS is one that does not.

- Location transparency, replication transparency, and fragmentation transparency are characteristics of DDBMSs.

- DDBMSs permit local control of data, increased capacity, improved system availability, and increased efficiency.

- DDBMSs are more complicated in the areas of the update of replicated data, the processing of queries, the treatment of shared updates, the measures for recovery, the management of the data dictionary, and the design of databases.

- C.J. Date cited 12 rules that a DDBMS should follow.

- In a client/server system, a DBMS runs on a file server, handling requests for data from the individual workstations, or clients.

- A trigger is an action that will take place automatically when an associated database operation takes place in a client/server system.

- On-line transaction processing (OLAP) is used with relational database management systems,

and on-line analytical processing (OLAP) is used with data warehouses.

- A data warehouse is a subject-oriented, integrated, time-variant, nonvolatile collection of data in support of management's decision-making process.

- The typical data warehouse data structure is a multidimensional database, consisting of a central fact table, surrounded by dimension tables.

- E.F. Codd cited 12 rules that an OLAP system should follow.

- Object-oriented systems deal with data as objects. Each of the properties of an object is associated with a class. The key concept is that the actions that manipulate an object are defined as part of the definition of the object. These actions are called methods. To cause a particular method to be executed, you send a message to the object. Users can define subclasses that inherit both the structure and methods of another class.

- Thirteen rules describe the desired characteristics for object-oriented systems.

- The Internet and the Web are playing an increasingly important role in organizations' database processing in an electronic commerce (e-commerce) environment. Web browsers can be used to access and update databases both through the Internet and through internal networks (intranets).

▪ KEY TERMS

binary large object (BLOB)
binding
class
client/server system
communications network
coordinator

data warehouse
dimension table
distributed database
distributed database management system
  (DDBMS)
e-commerce

encapsulated
extensible
fact table
file server
fragmentation transparency
global deadlock
heterogeneous DDBMS
homogeneous DDBMS
inheritance
intranet
local deadlock
local site
location transparency
lock
message
method
multidimensional database

object
object-oriented database management system
  (OODBMS)
on-line analytical processing (OLAP)
on-line transaction processing (OLTP)
persistence
primary copy
remote site
replication
replication transparency
roll back
shared update
star join schema
stored procedure
trigger
two-phase commit

■ REVIEW QUESTIONS

1. What is a distributed database? What is a distributed database management system (DDBMS)?

2. How does a homogeneous DDBMS differ from a heterogeneous DDBMS? Which is more complex?

3. What is meant by a local site? By a remote site?

4. What is location transparency?

5. What is replication? Why is it used? What benefit is derived from using it? What are the biggest potential problems?

6. What is replication transparency?

7. What is data fragmentation? What purpose does it serve?

8. What is fragmentation transparency?

9. Explain why each of the following features of distributed systems is advantageous:
   a. Local control of data
   b. Ability to increase system capacity
   c. System availability
   d. Increased efficiency

10. Why is query processing more complex in a distributed environment?

11. What is meant by local deadlock? By global deadlock?

12. Describe the principle of two-phase commit. How does it work? Why is it necessary?

13. Describe the various possible approaches to storing data dictionary entries in a distributed system.

14. What additional factors must be considered during the information-level design process if the design is for a distributed database?

15. What additional factors must be considered during the physical-level design process if the design is for a distributed database?

16. List and briefly describe the 12 rules that a distributed system should follow.

17. What is the difference between a file server and a client/server system?

18. List the advantages to the client/server approach.

19. What are triggers? What purpose do they serve?

20. What language is usually used to create triggers?

21. What are stored procedures? What purpose do they serve?

22. What are the characteristics of on-line transaction processing (OLTP) systems?

23. What is a data warehouse?

24. What does it mean that a data warehouse is nonvolatile?

25. What are the names of the different tables in a multidimensional database?

26. When is on-line analytical processing (OLAP) used?

27. List and briefly describe the 12 rules that an OLAP system should follow.

28. What is an object? What is a class? How do classes relate to objects?

29. What is the meaning of encapsulation in an object-oriented system?

30. What is a method? What is a message? How do messages relate to methods?

31. What is inheritance? What are the benefits to inheritance?

32. List and briefly describe the 13 rules that an object-oriented system should follow.

33. How are organizations employing their databases on the Internet and the Web?

34. If your school is using the Internet and/or an intranet to manipulate data stored in a database, investigate how this is being accomplished (which software and database entities are used). If not, what are your school's plans in this arena?

35. If your school is using a data warehouse, investigate the data warehouse and write a report that describes its structure and features.

■ ANSWERS TO ODD-NUMBERED QUESTIONS

Chapter 1 — Introduction To Database Management

1. A file is a structure that is used to store data about a single entity; it can be viewed as a table. A record is a row in the table. A field is a column.

3. A relationship is an association between entities.

5. A database is a structure that can store information about several types of entities, the attributes of these entities, and the relationships among them.

7. All data being stored in a single database, instead of being stored in dozens of separate files, makes the process of obtaining information quicker, easier, and even possible in certain situations.

9. Database Administration (DBA) is the central person or group in an organization in charge of the database and the DBMS that runs the database. DBA attempts to balance the needs of individuals and the overall needs of the organization.

11. When you control redundancy, you eliminate duplicate copies of attribute values and, thus, eliminate the possibility that two copies of an attribute value can have different values.

13. Security is the prevention of access to a database by unauthorized users. A DBMS has a number of features that help to ensure the enforcement of security measures.

15. The large size of a DBMS requires many megabytes of disk storage space and a substantial amount of internal memory.

17. Because several users are sharing the same database, a failure on the part of any one user that damages the database in some way affects all the other users.

19. IBM's Data Language/I (DL/I) was the first product offered to the public in 1966.

Chapter 2 — The Relational Model 1: Introduction, QBE, and the Relational Algebra

1. a. Ann Samuels; Al Williams; Sally Adams; Mary Nelson

   b. 12500

   c. BT04, Gas Grill, $1,649.89; BZ66, Washer, $20,799.48

   d. 522, Mary Nelson

   e. 4

   f. $1327.25

   g. 12489, 9/02/2001, 124, Sally Adams; 12491, 9/02/2001, 311, Don Charles; 12494, 9/04/2001, 315, Tom Daniels; 12495, 9/04/2001, 256, Ann Samuels; 12498, 9/05/2001, 522, Mary Nelson; 12500, 9/05/2001, 124, Sally Adams; 12504, 9/05/2001, 522, Mary Nelson

   h. 12498, 522, Mary Nelson; 12500, 124, Sally Adams; 12504, 522, Mary Nelson

   i. 03, Mary Jones; 06, William Smith; 12, Miguel Diaz

j. 12489, 9/02/2001, 124, Sally Adams, 03, Mary Jones; 12491, 9/02/2001, 311, Don Charles, 12, Miguel Diaz; 12494, 9/04/2001, 315, Tom Daniels, 06, William Smith; 12495, 9/04/2001, 256, Ann Samuels, 06, William Smith; 12498, 9/05/2001, 522, Mary Nelson, 12, Miguel Diaz; 12500, 9/05/2001, 124, Sally Adams, 03, Mary Jones; 12504, 9/05/2001, 522, Mary Nelson, 12, Miguel Diaz

3. A relation is a two-dimensional table in which (1) the entries in the table are single-valued; (2) each column has a distinct name; (3) all of the values in a column are values of the same attribute; (4) the order of the columns is irrelevant; (5) each row is distinct; and (6) the order of the rows is irrelevant.

5. An unnormalized relation is a structure that satisfies all the properties of a relation except the restriction that entries must be single-valued. It is not a relation.

7. In the shorthand representation, each table is listed, and after each table, all the columns of the table are listed in parentheses. Primary keys are underlined.

Branch (<u>Branch Number</u>, Branch Name, Branch Location, Number of Employees)

Publisher (<u>Publisher Code</u>, Publisher Name, Publisher City)

Author (<u>Author Number</u>, Author Name)

Book (<u>Book Code</u>, Book Title, Publisher Code, Book Type, Book Price, Paperback)

Wrote (<u>Book Code</u>, <u>Author Number</u>, Sequence Number)

Invent (<u>Book Code</u>, <u>Branch Number</u>, On Hand)

9. The primary key is the column or collection of columns that uniquely identifies a given row. The primary key of the Branch table is Branch Number. The primary key of the Publisher table is Publisher Code. The primary key of the Author table is Author Number. The primary key of the Book table is Book Code. The primary key of the Wrote table is the concatenation (combination) of Book Code and Author Number. The primary key of the Invent table is the concatenation of Book Code and Branch Number.

11. Place the asterisk in the Design grid. Do not enter any criteria.

13. Place the Customer Number, Last Name, First Name, Credit Limit, and Sales Rep Number fields in the Design grid. Type 03 in the Sales Rep Number column and 1000 in the Credit Limit column. Clear the check marks from the Show check boxes in the Credit Limit and Sales Rep Number columns.

15. Field lists for both the Orders table and the Customer table must be on the screen. Place the Order Number, Order Date, Customer Number, and Last Name fields in the Design grid.

17. Place the Customer Number and Credit Limit fields in the Design grid. Include the Totals row. Place Count in the Totals row in the Customer Number column. Place Where in the Totals row for the Credit Limit column and type 1000 in the Criteria row for the Credit Limit column.

19. Place the Part Number and Part Description fields in the Design grid. Right-click the next column and click Zoom. Type the computation for the On-Hand Value ([On Hand]*[Price]) and click the OK button.

21. SELECT [Part] WHERE [Part Number] = 'BT04' GIVING ANSWER

23. JOIN [Orders] [Customer] WHERE [Orders].[Customer Number] = [Customer].[Customer Number] GIVING [Temp1]
    JOIN [Temp1] [Sales Rep] WHERE [Temp1].[Sales Rep Number] = [Sales Rep].[Sales Rep Number] GIVING [Temp2]

    SELECT [Temp2] WHERE [Sales Rep].[Last Name] = 'Jones' GIVING [Temp3]

    PROJECT [Temp3] OVER ([Order Number], [Order Date], [Customer Number], [Last Name], [First Name]) GIVING [Answer]

25. JOIN [Orders] [Customer] WHERE [Orders].[Customer Number] = [Customer].[Customer Number] GIVING [Temp1]

    SELECT [Temp1] WHERE [Credit Limit] = 1000 AND [Order Date]='9/02/2001' GIVING [Temp2]

    PROJECT [Temp2] OVER ([Order Number], [Order Date]) GIVING [Answer]

Chapter 3 — The Relational Model 2: SQL

1. To create a table in SQL, use a CREATE TABLE command that gives the name of the table followed by the names and data types of the columns that comprise the table. INTEGER allows the field to contain integers. SMALLINT allows the field to contain "small" integers (integers less than 32,767). DECIMAL allows the field to contain numbers that have a decimal point. CHAR allows the field to contain character strings. DATE allows the field to contain dates.

3. Compound conditions are formed by connecting simple conditions using AND, OR, or NOT. A compound condition using AND is true only if all the simple conditions contained in it are true. A compound condition using OR is true if one (or more) of the simple conditions contained in it are true. Preceding a condition, simple or compound, by NOT reverses the truth or falsity of the original condition. You enter compound conditions in SQL in the WHERE clause just as you enter simple conditions.

5. Use a SQL built-in function (COUNT, SUM, AVG, MAX, and MIN) by including it in the SELECT clause followed by the name of the field to which it applies.

7. To join tables in SQL, use a SELECT command that lists two or more tables to be joined in the FROM clause, and then specifies the columns to be matched in the WHERE clause.

9. The update commands in SQL are INSERT, which allows you to insert new rows in a table; UPDATE, which allows you to make changes to all the rows that satisfy some condition; and DELETE, which allows you to delete all the rows that satisfy a condition.

11. SELECT*
    FROM Sales Rep

13. SELECT [Order Number]
    FROM Orders
    WHERE [Customer Number] = 124
    AND [Order Date] = '9/05/2001'

15. SELECT [Customer Number], [Last Name], [First Name]
    FROM Customer
    WHERE [Last Name] = 'Nelson'

17. SELECT COUNT(Customer Number)
    FROM Customer
    WHERE [Credit Limit] = 1000

19. SELECT [Order Number], [Order Date],
    Customer.[Customer Number], [Last Name], [First Name]
    FROM Orders, Customer
    WHERE Orders.[Customer Number] =
    Customer.[Customer Number]

21. SELECT [Sales Rep].[Sales Rep Number], [Sales Rep].[Last Name],
    [Sales Rep].[First Name]
    FROM [Sales Rep], Customer
    WHERE [Sales Rep].[Sales Rep Number] =
    Customer.[Sales Rep Number]
    AND [Credit Limit] = 1000

23. UPDATE Part
    SET [Part Description] = 'Gas Stove'
    WHERE [Part Number] = 'BT04'

25. DELETE FROM Customer
    WHERE Balance < 100.00
    AND [Sales Rep Number] = '12'

Chapter 4 — The Relational Model 3: Advanced Topics

1. A view is an individual user's picture of the database. It is defined through a defining query. The data in the view never actually exist in the form described in the view. Rather, when a user accesses the view, his or her query is merged with the defining query of the view to form a query that pertains to the whole database.

3. a. CREATE VIEW Cust Order AS
   SELECT Customer.[Customer Number], [Last Name], [First Name],
   Balance, [Order Number], Date
   FROM Customer, Orders
   WHERE Customer.[Customer Number] = Orders.[Customer Number]

   b. SELECT [Customer Number], [Last Name], [First Name], [Order Number],
   Date
   FROM Cust Order
   WHERE Balance > 100

   c. SELECT Customer.[Customer Number], [Last Name], [First Name],
   [Order Number], Date
   FROM Customer, Orders
   WHERE Customer.[Customer Number] = Orders.[Customer Number]
   AND Balance > 100

5. The GRANT mechanism is used to assign privileges to users of a database. It relates to security, since a user who has not been granted the privilege of accessing a certain portion of a database cannot access the data in that portion. The privileges that can be assigned include the privilege of selecting rows from a table, inserting new rows, and updating existing rows. The REVOKE command is used to revoke privileges.

7. If the DBMS updates the catalog automatically, the information in the catalog is guaranteed to match the actual database structure. If users update the catalog themselves, they can make mistakes, in which case the information in the catalog might not match the actual structure.

9. Entity integrity is the rule that the primary key cannot contain null values. This ensures that one entity can be distinguished from another. Referential integrity is the rule that if a foreign key is not null, it must contain a legitimate value of the primary key it is required to match, that is, a value that currently exists in the database. With referential integrity, (1) relationships are explicit and (2) a row in the table containing the foreign key cannot exist without being related to a row in the other table.

11. The structure of a table can be changed in SQL through the ALTER command. Columns can be added (ALTER TABLE table-name ADD column-name); columns can be deleted (ALTER TABLE table-name DELETE column-name); and columns can be changed (ALTER TABLE table-name CHANGE column-name TO new description). Tables can be deleted (DROP TABLE table-name).

Chapter 5 — Database Design 1: Normalization

1. Column B is functionally dependent on column A if a value for A determines a unique value for B at any time.

3. The primary key of a table is the column or collection of columns that determines all other columns in the table and for which there is no subcollection that also determines all other columns.

5. A table is in first normal form if it does not contain a repeating group.

7. A table is in third normal form if it is in second normal form and if the only determinants it contains are candidate keys. If a table is not in 3NF, redundant data will cause wasted space and update problems. Inconsistent data might also be a problem.

9. Student Number → Student Name, Major Department, Advisor Number, Advisor Name, Advisor Office Number, Advisor Phone Number, Number Credits, Class Standing

Advisor Number → Advisor Name, Advisor Office Number, Advisor Phone Number, Major Department

Number Credits → Class Standing

Assumptions:
Student has one advisor.
Student's advisor must be in the department in which the student is majoring.
Advisor only has one office.
Class Standing is determined by the number of credits a student has earned.

Note: Other answers are possible.

11. Patient (<u>Patient</u> <u>Number</u>, Household Number, Patient Name)
Household (<u>Household</u> <u>Number</u>, Household Name, Household Street, Household City, Household State, Household Zip, Household Balance)

Service (<u>Service</u> <u>Code</u>, Service Description, Service Fee)

13. Student Number → Student Name, Number Credits, Advisor Number, Advisor Name, Department Number, Department Name
Advisor Number → Advisor Name
Department Number → Advisor Name
Student Number, Course Number → Course Description, Course Term, Grade
Course Number → Course Description

Student (<u>Student</u> <u>Number</u>, Student Name, Number Credits, Advisor Number, Department Number)
Advisor (<u>Advisor</u> <u>Number</u>, Advisor Name)
Department (<u>Department</u> <u>Number</u>, Department Name)
Course (<u>Course</u> <u>Number</u>, Course Description)
Student Course (<u>Student</u> <u>Number</u>, <u>Course</u> <u>Number</u>, Course Term, Grade)

15. Convert to 1NF:
Course (<u>Course</u> <u>Number</u>, Course Description, Number Credits)
Course Textbook (<u>Course</u> <u>Number</u>, <u>Textbook</u>)
Course Instructor (<u>Course</u> <u>Number</u>, <u>Instructor</u> <u>Number</u>, Instructor Name)

These are in 2NF. Convert to 3NF:
Course (<u>Course</u> <u>Number</u>, Course Description, Number Credits)
Course Textbook (<u>Course</u> <u>Number</u>, <u>Textbook</u>)
Course Instructor (<u>Course</u> <u>Number</u>, <u>Instructor</u> <u>Number</u>)
Instructor (<u>Instructor</u> <u>Number</u>, Instructor Name)

These are also in 4NF. You did not encounter the table from the previous problem. This difficulty was avoided by the manner in which you converted to 1NF.

Chapter 6 — Database Design 2: Design Methodology

1. A user view is the view of data that is necessary to support the operations of a particular user. By considering individual user views rather than the complete design problem, you greatly simplify the database design process.

3. If the design problem is extremely simple, the overall design might not have to be broken down into a consideration of individual user views.

5. The primary key is the column or columns that uniquely identify a given row and that provide the main mechanism for directly accessing a row in the table. An alternate key is a column or combination of columns that could have functioned as the primary key but was not chosen to do so. A secondary key is a column or combination of columns that is not any other type of key but is of interest for purposes of retrieval. A foreign key is a column or combination of columns in one table whose values are required to match the primary key in another table. Foreign keys provide the mechanism through which relationships are made explicit.

7. a. Include the project number as a foreign key in the employee table.

   b. Include the employee number as a foreign key in the project table.

   c. Create a new table whose primary key is the concatenation of employee number and project number.

9. Instead of the advisor number being included as a foreign key in the student table, there would be an additional table whose primary key is the concatenation of student number and advisor number.

11. Branch (<u>Branch Number</u>, Branch Name, Branch Location,
       Number of Employees)
       Secondary key: Branch Name
       Branch Number must be unique
   Publisher (<u>Publisher Code</u>, Publisher Name, Publisher City)
       Publisher Code must be unique
   Author (<u>Author Number</u>, Author Name)
       Author Number must be unique
   Book (<u>Book Code</u>, Book Title, Publisher Code, Book Type,
       Book Price, Paperback)
       Foreign key: Publisher Code; matches Publisher
       Book Code must be unique
   Wrote (<u>Book Code</u>, <u>Author Number</u>, Sequence Number)
       Foreign key: Book Code; matches Book
       Foreign key: Author Number; matches Author
       The combination of Book Code and Author Number must be unique
       Book Code must match the code of a book in the Book table
       Author Number must match the number of an author in the Author table
   Invent (<u>Book Code</u>, <u>Branch Number</u>, On Hand)
       Foreign key Book Code matches Book
       Foreign key Branch Number matches Branch
       The combination of Book Code and Branch Number must be unique
       Book Code must match the code of a book in the Book table
       Branch Number must match the number of a branch in the Branch table

13. a. Remove Faculty Number as a column in the Section table. Create a separate table whose primary key is the concatenation of Semester Code, Schedule Code, and Faculty Number. This new table will have no other columns.

   b. One solution is to include Major Number and Major Description as columns in the Department table and delete the Major table from the design. In the Advises table, replace Major Number with Department Number. A second solution is to make Department Number an alternate key within the Major table and leave everything else as is.

   c. Either of the solutions to Question 6 will also work here. In addition, however, Major Number should be removed from the Advises table and the primary key changed to the concatenation of Student Number and Faculty Number.

   d. Either of the solutions to Question 6 will also work here. In addition, however, the number of the faculty member who advises the student will be included in the Student table and the Advises table will be deleted.

e. Student Name is designated as a secondary key within the Student table.

f. Office Number is removed from the Faculty table and a new table is created whose primary key is the concatenation of Office Number and Faculty Number.

g. Credits Earned (and Grade Points) should be removed from the Student Grade table. (The Credits Earned for a course is obtained by finding the Number Credits in the Course table for the given course provided the grade is a passing grade.)

h. Course Code replaces Course Number in all tables. Department Code can be removed from any table in which Course Code appears other than the Course table itself. Although Department Code still appears in the Course table, it is no longer part of the primary key. It is still a foreign key identifying the Department table, however.

i. A new table should be created whose primary key is the concatenation of Student Number, Primary Code, Semester Code, and Alternate Code. Alternate Code should be removed as a column in Registration Request.

Chapter 7 — Functions of a Database Management System

1. The DBMS must provide a mechanism for storing data and for enabling users to retrieve data from the database and to update data in the database. This mechanism should not require the users to be aware of the details with respect to how the data are actually stored.

3. Shared update refers to two or more users updating data in a database at the same time.

5. Locking is the process whereby only one user is allowed to access a specific portion of a database at a time. When a user is accessing a portion of the database, it is locked, meaning that it is unavailable to any other user.

7. Deadlock is the circumstance in which user A is waiting for resources that have been locked by user B, and user B is waiting for resources that have been locked by user A; unless action to the contrary is taken, the two could wait for each other forever. Deadlock occurs when each of the two users is attempting to access data that are held by the other.

9. a. Each user must attempt to lock all the resources he or she needs before beginning any updates. If any of the resources are already locked by another user, all locks must be released and the process must begin all over again.

b. Before updating a record, user A should make sure that the record has not been updated by user B since the time user A first read it. To understand why this is necessary, read part c of this answer.

c. After reading a record, a user should immediately release the lock on it.

11. Security is the prevention of unauthorized access to the database.

13. Encryption is the process whereby data are transformed into another form (encoded) before being stored in the database. Data are returned to their original form when they are retrieved by a legitimate user. This process prevents a person who bypasses the DBMS and accesses the database directly from seeing the relevant data.

15. A database has integrity when the data in it follow certain established rules, called integrity constraints. Integrity constraints can be handled in four ways: (1) They can be ignored. (2) The responsibility for enforcing them can be assigned to the user (that is, it would be up to the user not to enter invalid data). (3) They can be enforced by programs. (4) They can be enforced by the DBMS. Of these four, the last is the most desirable. When the DBMS enforces the integrity constraints, users don't have to constantly guard against entering incorrect data, and programmers are spared having to build the logic to enforce these constraints into the programs they write.

17. Many examples are possible, such as auditors might need their own replicas to review the status of data at the end of a reporting period, and an executive might need a replica as part of a presentation to other executives.

19. The answer depends on the particular DBMS being used at your school.

Chapter 8 — Database Administration

1. DBA is database administration, the person or group responsible for the database. The responsibilities of DBA are crucial to success in the database environment, especially if the database is to be shared among many users. These responsibilities include determining access privileges, establishing and enforcing security procedures, determining and enforcing policies with respect to the use of a data dictionary, and so on.

3. DBA determines access privileges, uses the DBMS security facilities such as passwords, encryption, and views, and supplements these features, where necessary, with special programs.

   Users often choose passwords that are easy for others to guess, such as the names of family members. Users can also be careless with the paper on which passwords are written. To prevent others from guessing their passwords, users should guard against doing either of these things and should also change their passwords frequently.

5. Certain corporate data, though no longer required in the active database, must be kept for future reference. A data archive is a place for storing this type of data. The use of data archives allows an organization to keep records indefinitely, without causing the database to become unnecessarily large. Data can be removed from the database and placed in the data archive, instead of just being deleted.

7. DBA does some of the training of computer users. Other training, such as that which is provided by a software vendor, is coordinated by DBA.

9. a. What facilities are provided by the system for defining a new database? What data types are supported?

   b. What facilities are present to assist in the restructuring of a database?

   c. What nonprocedural language (a language in which you tell the computer what the task is rather than how to do it) is provided by the system? How does its functionality compare with that of SQL?

d. What procedural language (a language in which you tell the computer how to do the task) is provided by the system? How complete is it? How is the integration between the procedural language and the nonprocedural language accomplished?

e. What data dictionary is included? What types of information can be held in the dictionary? How well is it integrated with the other parts of the system?

f. What support does the system provide for shared update? What type of locking is used? Can the system handle deadlock?

g. What services does the system provide for backup and recovery? Does recovery consist only of copying a backup over the live database, or does the system support the use of a journal in the recovery process?

h. What security features are provided by the system? Does it support passwords, encryption, and/or views? How easy is it for a user to bypass the security controls of the DBMS?

i. What type of integrity support is present? What kinds of integrity constraints can be enforced?

j. What types of support does it provide for replication and for distributing data?

k. What are the system limitations with respect to the number of tables, columns, rows, and the number of files that can be open at the same time? What hardware limitations exist?

l. How good are the manuals? How good is the online help facility, if there is one?

m. What reputation does the vendor have for support of its products?

n. How well does the system perform under different benchmarking situations?

o. How portable is the DBMS? That is, what are the different types of operating systems and hardware systems that can be used with the DBMS?

p. What is the cost of the DBMS, of additional hardware, and of support?

q. What plans does the vendor have for further development of the system?

r. This category includes any special requirements an organization might have that do not fit into any of the previous categories.

11. DBA has primary responsibility for the DBMS once it has been selected. DBA installs the DBMS, makes any changes to its configuration when they are required, determines whether it is appropriate to install a new version of the DBMS when it becomes available, and, if a decision is made to install a new DBMS, coordinates the installation.

13. The answer depends on the DBMS you selected.

Chapter 9 — Advanced Topics

1. A distributed database is one in which the data are physically stored at more than one site. A distributed database management system is a database management system capable of managing a distributed database.

3. The local site is the one at which the user is currently working. A remote site is any other site in the network.

5. Replication is the storing of the same data item at more than one site in the network. It is done to speed access to the data. The benefit is that users at each of the sites where the replicated data are stored can access the data more efficiently than they could if the data were stored only at some remote site. The main problem concerns update: when replicated data are updated, all copies of the data around the network must be updated.

7. Data fragmentation is the dividing of a logical object, like the collection of all records of a given type, among the various locations in a network. Its main purpose is to place data at the site where they are most often accessed.

9. a. Because each location can keep its own data, greater local control can be exercised over it.

   b. In a well-designed distributed system, capacity can often be increased at only one site rather than for the whole database. Capacity can be further increased through the addition of new sites to the network.

   c. Other users can continue their processing even though a site on the network is unavailable. In a centralized system, no users can continue processing if the database is unavailable.

   d. Data available locally can be retrieved much more efficiently than data stored on a remote, centralized system.

11. Local deadlock means two users at the same site are in deadlock. Global deadlock means two users at different sites are in deadlock.

13. The complete data dictionary may be stored at a single site. A complete copy of the data dictionary may be stored at every site. The entries in the dictionary may be distributed among the sites in the network (possibly with replication).

15. In the physical-level design process, in addition to all the usual factors, communication time must be considered in the choice of an optimum design.

17. A file server returns entire files to workstations on a network, whereas in a client/server system, the server only returns the necessary data.

19. A trigger is an action that occurs automatically when an associated database operation takes place. Triggers assist in providing data integrity.

21. Stored procedures are special files containing a collection of SQL statements that are executed frequently. The statements in a stored procedure are compiled and optimized, enabling the stored procedure to execute as efficiently and as rapidly as possible.

23. A data warehouse is a subject-oriented, time-variant, nonvolatile collection of data in support of management's decision-making process.

25. A multidimensional database contains a central fact table, which consists of many rows containing consolidated and summarized data, and several dimension tables, each of which contains a single-part primary key that serves as an index into the fact table and contains other fields associated with that primary key value. The fact table has a multipart primary key, each part of which is a foreign key to the surrounding dimension tables.

27. OLAP systems should follow the following 12 rules: (1) users should be able to view data in a multidimensional way; (2) the location of OLAP software should be transparent to users; (3) the location of data should be transparent to users; (4) the size and complexity of the warehouse should not affect performance; (5) the server portion of the OLAP software should allow the use of different types of clients; (6) each data dimension should have the same structural and operational capabilities; (7) nulls should be handled correctly and efficiently; (8) OLAP should provide secure, concurrent access; (9) users should be able to perform the same operations across any number of dimensions; (10) users should not need to use special interfaces to make their requests; (11) users should be able to report data results any way they want; (12) OLAP software should allow at least 15 data dimensions and an unlimited number of summary levels.

29. In an object-oriented system, encapsulation is the characteristic that the details about the data and its procedures are hidden from the users of a database without affecting their ability to access the data and use the procedures.

31. When one class is a subclass of another, it inherits the structure of the class as well as the methods that apply to the class. The benefit to this is that you only need to define the structure or methods that were not inherited from the class.

33. Organizations are using the Internet and the Web increasingly to provide information from their databases to customers, suppliers, and others. At the same time, customers and other external entities use the Internet and the Web to directly update an organization's internal databases.

35. The answer depends on the data warehouse investigated.

GLOSSARY

Aggregate function   A function to calculate the number of entries, the sum or average of all the entries in a given column, or the largest or smallest of the entries in a given column; also called a *built-in function*.

Alias   An alternate name for a table; can be used within a query.

Alternate key   A candidate key that was not chosen to be the primary key.

Archive   See *data archive*.

Attribute   A property of an entity.

Background   The permanent part of a screen form, that is, the part that does not change from one transaction to the next. Also see *foreground*.

Backup   A copy of a database; used to recover the database when it has been damaged or destroyed.

Batch processing   Processing of a transaction file, which contains a *batch* of records, to update a database or another file.

Binary large object (BLOB)   A generic term for a special data type used by relational database management systems to store complex objects.

Binding   The association of operations to actual program code in an object-oriented system.

Built-in function   A function to calculate the number of entries, the sum or average of all the entries in a given column, or the largest or smallest of the entries in a given column; also called an *aggregate function*.

Candidate key   A minimal collection of columns (attributes) in a table on which all columns are functionally dependent but that has not necessarily been chosen as the *primary key*.

Calculated field   A field whose value may be computed from other fields in the database; also called a *computed field*.

Cardinality   The number of items that must be included in a relationship.

Catalog   A source of information on the types of entities, attributes, and relationships in a database.

Class   The general structure of an object in an object-oriented system.

Client/server system   A networked system in which a special site on the network, called the *server*, provides services to the other sites, called the *clients*. Clients send requests for the specific services they need. Software, often including a DBMS, running on the server then processes the request and sends only the appropriate data and other results back to the client.

CODASYL   The COnference on DAta SYstems Languages.

Command   An instruction by the user that directs the database to perform a certain function.

Communications network   A group of computers connected in such a way that data can be sent from any one computer in the network to any other.

Comparison operator   An operator used to compare values. Valid operators are =, <, >, <=, >=, <>, and !=. Also called a *relational operator*.

Composite entity   An entity in the Entity-Relationship model used to implement a many-to-many relationship.

Compound condition   Two simple conditions combined with AND or OR.

Compound criteria   Two simple criteria combined with AND or OR.

Computed field   A field whose value may be computed from other fields in the database; also called a *calculated field*.

Concatenation   The combination of columns. To say a primary key is a concatenation of two columns means that a combination of values of both columns is required to uniquely identify a given row.

Concurrent update   Several updates taking place to the same file or database at almost the same time; also called *shared update*.

Condition   A statement that can be either true or false. In queries, only records for which the statement is true will be included; also called *criterion*.

Coordinator   In a distributed network, the site that directs the update process. Often, it is the site that initiates the transaction.

Criterion   A statement that can be either true or false. In queries, only records for which the statement is true will be included; also called *condition*.

Data archive   A place where historical corporate data are kept. Data that are no longer needed in the corporate database but must be retained for future reference are removed from the database and placed in the archive.

Data definition language   A language that is used to communicate the structure of a database to the database management system.

Data dictionary   A tool that is used to store descriptions of the entities, attributes, relationships, programs, and so on that are associated with an organization's database.

Data file   A file used to store data.

Data fragmentation   The process of dividing a logical object, such as the collection of records of a certain type, among various locations in a distributed database.

Data independence   The property that allows the structure of the database to change without requiring changes in programs.

Data Language/I   An early DBMS product developed by IBM.

Data model   The format of data within a DBMS; it characterizes the DBMS. A data model has two components: *structure* and *operations*.

Data warehouse   A subject-oriented, integrated, time-variant, nonvolatile collection of data in support of management's decision-making process.

Database   A structure that can store information about various types of entities and about the relationships among the entities.

Database administration (DBA)   The individual or group that is responsible for the database.

Database administrator   The individual who is responsible for the database, or the head of database administration.

Database design   The process of determining the content and arrangement of data in a database in order to support some activity on behalf of a user or group of users.

Database Design Language (DBDL)   A relational-like language that is used to represent the result of the database design process.

Database management system (DBMS)   A software package that is designed to manipulate the data in a database on behalf of a user.

Database navigation   The procedure used to manipulate a network-structured database.

Database processing   The type of processing in which the data are stored in a *database* and manipulated by a *DBMS*.

DBA   See *database administration*. (Sometimes the acronym stands for database administrator.)

DBDL   See *Database Design Language*.

DBMS   See *database management system*.

DDBMS   See *distributed database management system*.

Deadlock   A state in which two or more users are each waiting to use resources that are held by the other(s).

Deadly embrace   Another name for *deadlock*.

Defining query   The query that is used to define the structure of a view.

Dependency diagram   A diagram that indicates the dependencies among the columns in a table.

Dependent entity   An entity that requires a relationship to another entity for identification.

Design grid   The portion of the Query Design screen in Microsoft Access where you enter fields, criteria, sort order, etc.

Determinant   A column (attribute) that determines at least one other column.

Difference   When comparing tables, the set of all rows that are in the first table but that are not in the second.

Dimension table   A table in a data warehouse that contains a single-part primary key, serving as an index into the central fact table and other fields associated with the primary key value.

Distributed database   A database that is stored on computers at several sites of a computer network and from which users can access data at any site on the network.

Distributed database management system (DDBMS)   A database management system that is capable of manipulating distributed databases.

E-commerce   Electronic commerce on the World Wide Web (Web).

Encapsulated   The binding together of data and actions in an object-oriented system so that they are hidden from the user's view.

Encryption   The transformation, or encoding, of data into another form, for the purpose of security, before being stored in the database. The data are returned to their original form for any legitimate user who accesses the database.

Entity   An object (person, place, or thing) of interest.

Entity integrity   The rule that no column (attribute) that is part of the primary key may accept null values.

Entity-Relationship (E-R) diagram   A graphic model for database design in which entities are represented as rectangles and relationships are represented as either arrows or diamonds connected to the entities they relate.

Equijoin   A form of join in which the join column appears twice.

Example   In Query-by-Example, an entry that represents a possible value in a field. Matching examples are used to join tables.

Extensible   The capability of defining new data types in an object-oriented database management system.

Fact table   The central table in a data warehouse that consists of many rows that contain consolidated and summarized data.

Field   The smallest unit of data to which a name can be assigned; it can be thought of as a column in a table. For example, in a table for customers, the fields (columns) would include such things as the customer's number, the customer's name and address, etc.

File   A collection of bytes (characters) on a disk; a file could be data, a program, a document created with a word processor, etc. Often refers to a data file, which is a structure used to store data about some entity. Such a file can be thought of as a table. The rows in such a table are called records, and the columns are called fields.

File server   A networked system in which a special site on the network stores files for users at other sites. When a user needs a file, the file server sends the entire file to the user.

First Normal Form (1NF)   A table is in first normal form if it does not contain repeating groups. (This is part of the definition of a table.)

Foreground   The portion of a screen form that changes from one transaction to the next, that is, the portion of the form into which the user enters data and/or data are displayed. Also see *background*.

Foreign key   A column (attribute) or collection of columns in a table whose value is required either to match the value of a primary key in another table or to be null.

Form   A screen object used to maintain, view, and print records from a database.

Fourth Normal Form (4NF)   A table is in fourth normal form (4NF) if it is in 3NF and there are no multivalued dependencies.

Fragmentation transparency   The property that states that users do not need to be aware of any data fragmentation (splitting of data) that has taken place in a distributed database.

Functionally dependent   Column B is functionally dependent on column A (or on a collection of columns) if a value for A determines a single value for B at any one time.

Functionally determine   Column A functionally determines column B if B is *functionally dependent* on A.

Generalized Update Access Method (GUAM)   An early database system capable of handling vast amounts of data. Produced in 1964 for use in the moon launch program.

Global deadlock   Deadlock in a distributed database that cannot be detected solely at any individual site.

Grouping   Creating collections of records that share some common characteristic.

Growing phase   A phase during an update in which new locks are acquired but no locks are released.

Help facility   A facility through which users can receive online assistance.

Heterogeneous DDBMS   A distributed DBMS in which at least two of the local DBMSs are different from each other.

Hierarchy   A network with an added restriction that each record type cannot be related on the "many" side in more than one one-to-many relationship.

Hierarchical model   A database model that is perceived by the user as a collection of hierarchies, or trees.

Homogeneous DDBMS   A distributed DBMS in which all the local DBMSs are the same.

Identifying relationship   A relationship that is necessary for identification of an entity.

Independent entity   An entity that does not require a relationship to another entity for identification.

Index   A file that relates key values to records that contain those key values.

Information-level design   The step during *database design* in which the goal is to create a clean, DBMS-independent design that will support user requirements.

Information Management System (IMS)   An early, dominant DBMS developed by IBM and still in use in some legacy systems.

Inheritance   The property that states that a subclass inherits the structure of the class as well as the methods.

Integrated Data Store (I-D-S)   An early DBMS developed by a team at General Electric.

Integrity   A database has integrity if all *integrity constraints* that have been established for it are currently met.

Integrity constraint   A condition that data within a database must satisfy; also, a condition that indicates the types of processing that may or may not take place.

Integrity Enhancement Feature   The component of SQL that provides support for integrity.

Integrity rules   See *entity integrity* and *referential integrity*.

Intersection   When comparing tables, an intersection is the new table containing all rows that are in both original tables.

Intranet   The use of Internet and Web software tools on an internal network.

Join   In the *relational algebra*, the operation in which two tables are connected on the basis of common data.

Join column   The column on which two tables are joined. See *join*.

Journal   A record of all changes in the database; also called a *log*. Used to recover a database that has been damaged or destroyed.

Key   A field that is used for sorting. Key types are primary, foreign, candidate, alternate, and secondary.

LAN   See *local area network*.

Local Area Network (LAN)   A configuration of several computers that are all connected within a limited geographic area; allows users to share a variety of resources.

Local deadlock   Deadlock that occurs at a single site in a distributed system.

Local site   From a user's perspective, the site in a distributed system at which the user is working.

Location transparency   The property that states that users do not need to be aware of the location of data in a distributed database.

Lock   A device that prevents other users from accessing a portion of a database.

Locking   The process of placing a lock on a portion of a database, which prevents other users from accessing that portion.

Log   A record of all changes in the database; also called a *journal*. Used to recover a database that has been damaged or destroyed.

Major sort key   When sorting on two fields, the more important field; also called a *primary sort key*.

Many-to-many relationship   A relationship between two entities in which each occurrence of each entity is related to many occurrences of the other entity.

Menu-driven   A style of program in which the user selects an action from a list (called a menu) of available options that are displayed on the screen.

Message   A request to execute a method.

Method   An action defined for an object (class).

Minor sort key   When sorting on two fields, the less important field; also called a *secondary sort key*.

Multidimensional database   The overall structure of the tables in a data warehouse.

Multivalued dependency   In a table with columns A, B, and C, there is a multivalued dependence of column B on column A (also read as "B is multidependent on A" or "A multidetermines B") if each value for A is associated with a specific collection of values for B and, furthermore, this collection is independent of any values for C.

Natural join   The most common form of join. A form in which the join column only appears once.

Natural language   A language in which users communicate with the computer through the use of standard English questions and commands.

Network   The logical structure of records and relationships for a network model database.

Network model   A database model that is perceived by a user as a collection of record types and relationships between these record types.

Nonidentifying relationship   A relationship that is not necessary for identification.

Nonkey attribute   An attribute (column) that is not part of the primary key.

Nonprocedural language   A language in which the user specifies the task that is to be accomplished rather than the steps that are required to accomplish it.

Normal form   See *first normal form, second normal form, third normal form,* and *fourth normal form.*

Normalization   The process of removing repeating groups to produce a *first normal form* table. Sometimes refers to the process of creating a *third normal form* table.

Null   A data value meaning "unknown" or "not applicable."

Object   A unit of data and the actions that can take place on those data.

Object-oriented database management system (OODBMS)   A DBMS in which data and the methods that operate on those data are encapsulated into objects.

OLAP   See *on-line analytical processing*.

OLTP   See *on-line transactional processing*.

On-line analytical processing (OLAP)   Software that is optimized to work efficiently with multidimensional databases in a data warehouse environment.

On-line transaction processing (OLTP)   A system that processes a transaction by dealing with a small number of rows in a relational database in a highly structured, repetitive, and predetermined way.

One-to-many relationship A relationship between two entities in which each occurrence of the first entity is related to many occurrences of the second entity, but each occurrence of the second entity is related to only one occurrence of the first entity.

One-to-one relationship A relationship between two entities in which each occurrence of the first entity is related to one occurrence of the second entity and each occurrence of the second entity is related to one occurrence of the first entity.

OODBMS See *object-oriented database management system*.

Operations One of the two components of a *data model;* the facilities provided to users of the DBMS to manipulate data within the database.

Optimizer The DBMS component that selects the best way to satisfy a query.

Outer join Form of join in which all records appear, even if they don't match.

Partial dependency A dependency of a column on only a portion of the primary key.

Password A word that must be entered before a user can access certain computer resources. Used as a security mechanism.

Persistence The ability to have a program "remember" its data from one execution to the next.

Physical-level design The step during *database design* in which a design for a given DBMS is produced from the final information-level design.

Primary copy In a distributed database with replicated data, the copy of the database that must be updated in order for the update to be deemed complete.

Primary sort key When sorting on two fields, the more important field; also called a *major sort key*.

Primary key A minimal collection of columns (attributes) in a table on which all columns are functionally dependent and that is chosen as the main direct-access vehicle to individual rows. Also see *candidate key*.

Procedural language A language in which the user must specify the steps that are required for accomplishing a task instead of merely specifying the task itself.

QBE See *Query-by-Example*.

Qualify To indicate the table (relation) of which a given column (attribute) is a part by preceding the column name with the table name. For example, *Customer.Address* indicates the column named *Address* within the table named *Customer*.

Query A question, the answer to which is found in the database; also used to refer to a command in a *nonprocedural language* such as SQL that is used to obtain the answer to such a question.

Query-By-Example (QBE) A *data manipulation language* for relational databases in which users indicate the action to be taken by filling in portions of blank tables on the screen.

Query facility A facility that enables users to obtain information easily from the database.

Query language A language that is designed to permit users to obtain information easily from the database.

Record A collection of related fields; can be thought of as a row in a table.

Recovery The process of restoring a database that has been damaged or destroyed.

Redundancy Duplication of data.

Referential integrity The rule that if a table A contains a *foreign key* that matches the primary key of table B, then the value of this foreign key must either match the value of the primary key for some row in table B or be null.

Relation A two-dimensional table-style collection of data in which all entries are single-valued; each column has a distinct name; all the values in a column are values of the attribute that is identified by the column name, the order of columns is irrelevant; each row is distinct; and the order of rows is irrelevant.

Relational algebra A relational data manipulation language in which new tables are created from existing tables through the use of a set of operations.

Relational database A collection of relations (tables).

Relational model A *data model* in which the structure is the *table* or *relation*.

Relational operator An operator used to compare values. Valid operators are =, <, >, <=, >=, <>, and !=. Also called a *comparison operator*.

Relationship An association between entities.

Remote site From a user's perspective, any site other than the one at which the user is working.

Repeating group Several entries at a single location in a table.

Replicas Duplicate versions of data that are stored at more than one site in a distributed database.

Replication Duplicating data at more than one site in a distributed database.

Replication transparency The property that states that users do not need to be aware of any replication that has taken place in a distributed database.

Roll back The process of undoing changes that have been made to a database.

Save   A backup copy.

Second Normal Form (2NF)   A table is in second normal form if it is in first normal form and no nonkey attribute is dependent on only a portion of the primary key.

Secondary sort key   When sorting on two fields, the less important field; also called a *minor sort key*.

Secondary key   A column (attribute) or collection of columns that is of interest for retrieval purposes (and that is not already designated as some other type of key).

Security   The protection of the database against unauthorized access.

Shared update   Several updates taking place to the same file or database at almost the same time; also called *concurrent update*.

Shrinking phase   A phase during an update in which all locks are released and no new locks are acquired.

Simple condition   A condition that involves only a single field and a single value.

Sort key   The field on which data are sorted.

SQL   See *Structured Query Language*.

Star join schema   A multidimensional database whose conceptual shape resembles a star.

Statistics   Mathematical functions supported by Microsoft Access; they include Count, Sum, Avg (average), Max (largest value), Min (smallest value), StDev (standard deviation), Var (variance), First, and Last.

Stored procedure   A file containing a collection of SQL statements that are available for future use.

Structure   One of the two components of a *data model*: the manner in which the system structures data or, at least, the manner in which the users perceive that the data are structured.

Structured Query Language (SQL)   A very popular relational data definition and manipulation language that is used in many relational DBMSs.

Subquery   In SQL, a query that is contained within another query.

Switchboard   A form used to provide controlled access to the data, forms, reports, and other content of a database.

Synchronization   The periodic exchange by a DBMS of all updated data between two databases in a replica set.

Table   In the database environment, another name for a *relation*.

Tabular   A type of DBMS in which users perceive data as tables but that does not provide any of the other characteristics of a relational DBMS.

Third Normal Form (3NF)   A table is in third normal form if it is in second normal form and if the only determinants it contains are candidate keys.

Timestamp   The unique time when an update is started.

Timestamping   The practice of using timestamps to avoid the need to lock rows in the database and eliminate processing time needed to apply and release locks and to detect and resolve deadlocks.

Trigger   An action that takes place automatically when an associated database operation occurs.

Tuning   The process of altering a database design in order to improve performance.

Tuple   A formal name for a row in a table.

Two-phase commit   An approach to the commit process in distributed systems in which there are two phases. In the first phase, each site is instructed to prepare to commit and must indicate whether the commit will be possible. After each site has responded, the second phase begins: If every site has replied in the affirmative, all sites must commit. If any site has replied in the negative, all sites must abort the transaction.

Two-phase locking   An approach to locking in which there are two phases: a growing phase, in which new locks are acquired but no locks are released, and a shrinking phase, in which all locks are released and no new locks are acquired.

Union   A combination of two tables consisting of all records that are in either table.

Union-compatible   Two tables are union-compatible if they have the same number of fields and if their corresponding fields have identical data types.

Unnormalized relation   A structure that satisfies the properties required to be a relation (table) with one exception: repeating groups are allowed; that is, the entries in the table do not have to be single-valued.

Update anomaly   An update problem that can occur in a database as a result of a faulty design.

User view   The view of data that is necessary to support the operations of a particular user.

Utility services   DBMS-supplied functions that assist in the maintenance of the database.

View   An application program's or an individual user's picture of the database.

Wild card   A symbol that can be used in place of an unknown character or group of characters in a query.

I N D E X

DL/I (Data Language/I), 20, 21

documentation, 230

DROP TABLE command, 95–96

duplication of data, 14

electronic commerce (e-commerce), 259

encryption, 207, 222

entities, 2

    attributes, 11

    dependent, 147

    independent, 147

    integrity, 90, 91

    Marvel College, 163

    relationships, 2, 12

E-R (Entity-Relationship) diagrams, 137–139

    alternatives, 154–156

    attributes, 154

    relationships, 154

fact table, 251

fields, 3

    adding, 210

    changing length, 211

file-oriented system, 2

files, 3, 12, 210

file server, 246

1NF (first normal form), 104, 109–110

FOREIGN KEY clause, 99

foreign key constraints, 208

foreign keys, 91–92, 99, 136, 138, 152

format constraints, 208, 209

forms, 8

    switchboard system, 10

4NF (fourth normal form), 104, 122

fragmentation transparency, 239–241

FROM clause, 73

functional dependencies, 105–106, 124

    splitting across two tables, 119

functionally depends, 106

functionally determines, 106

future plans, 230

Gemstone, 20

General Electric, 20

global deadlock, 244

GRANT command, 90

greater than (>) comparison operator, 38

GROUP BY clause, 71

grouping, 42

    SQL (Structured Query Language), 71–72

growing phase, 202

GUAM (Generalized Update Access Method), 19, 21

HAVING clause, 72

heterogeneous DDBMS, 238

hierarchical model databases, 20–22

hierarchy, 22

homogeneous DDBMS, 238

Housewares view, 85

Publisher file, 3–4

publishers entity, 148

QBE (Query-By-Example), 34

    calculating statistics, 41–42

    compound criteria, 38–39

    computed fields, 40–41

    grouping, 42

    joining table, 43–44

    simple criteria, 36–38

    simple queries, 35–36

queries, 34–35

    Access, 34

    defining, 83

    nesting, 68–70

    simple, 35–36

    SQL (Structured Query Language), 58

RDBMSs (relational database management systems), 249

records, 3

    identity of, 91

    numbers, 87–88

recovery, 205–206, 223

redundancy, 17

referential integrity, 90, 91–94

    cascading delete, 93

    cascading update, 93

    violating, 94

referential model and changing relational database structure, 94–96

relational algebra

    join operation, 47–49

    normal set operations, 49

    PROJECT command, 46

    qualifying fields, 73

    SELECT command, 45–46

relational databases

    changing structure, 94–6

    information about tables, 98

relational model, 20, 82

    catalog, 96–98

    entity integrity, 90, 91

    foreign keys, 91–92

    indexes, 87–90

    integrity rules, 90–96

    referential integrity, 90, 91–94

    security, 90

    views, 82–87

relational operators, 38

relationships, 11, 12

    adding or changing, 211–212

    among entities, 134–135

    entities, 2, 12

    E-R (Entity-Relationship) diagrams, 154

    file-oriented system, 2

    identifying, 147

    many-to-many, 134–135, 148, 154

    nonidentifying, 147

    one-to-many, 12, 21, 134, 138, 142, 148, 155, 157

    one-to-one, 135

    between tables, 91